The FLOWERING SHRUB EXPERT

Dr. D.G. Hessayon

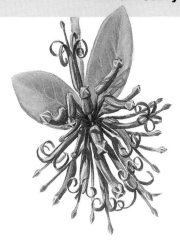

All Editions & Reprints: 427,000 copies

Published 2000
by Expert Books
a division of Transworld Publishers

A catalogue record for this book is available from the British Library

TRANSWORLD PUBLISHERS
61-63 Uxbridge Road, London W5 5SA

a division of the Random House Group Ltd

Distributed in the United States
by Sterling Publishing Co. Inc.,
387 Park Avenue South,
New York,
NY 10016-8810

Distributed in Canada by
Cavendish Books Inc.,
1610, Derwent Way,
Delta, B.C.
Canada.

EXPERT BOOKS

Contents

Reproduction by Spot On Digital Imaging Ltd., Perivale, Middlesex, UB6 7JB
Printed and bound by Mohn Media Mohndruck GmbH

ISBN 0 903505 39 8

CHAPTER 1

INTRODUCTION

One of the important changes in the home garden scene during the last quarter of the 20th century has been the growth in popularity of flowering shrubs. Before World War II the floral part of the average plot was dominated by herbaceous perennials, bedding plants, bulbs and roses — often low-growing and always uninteresting when not in bloom. Nowadays flowering shrubs are used to provide a permanent woody background for the floral display, with a range of types to provide year-round colour. Gone is the old idea that the proper place for shrubs is in a shrub border — the mixed border with shrubs alongside bulbs, border plants, annuals etc has taken over. Many shrubs make fine specimen plants when grown on their own.

Gardening is a thing of fashion, and we are now in an age when conifers and shrubs have become great favourites. But flowering shrubs have been with us since the beginning of gardening in this country. Seventeenth century garden catalogues list many of the plants in this book — Lilac, Honeysuckle, Yucca, Cercis, Hibiscus, Cytisus, Arbutus etc. Rhododendrons and Azaleas were not listed — they only became garden shrubs in Victorian times.

There are many reasons for the recent increase in interest in flowering shrubs, but there are just two basic causes. First, there was the arrival of the container-grown plant and with it the opportunity to plant shrubs at any time of the year. No longer was the gardener restricted to buying a flowerless and often leafless shrub for planting between autumn and spring. Linked with the arrival of the container-grown plant was the arrival of the garden centre — now shrubs could be seen in bloom before purchase, and the range was large and varied. No longer was the gardener restricted to ordering from a mail order catalogue or having to choose from the limited range on offer at the garden shop, department store, market stall or local nursery.

With the increased range on offer at the garden centre and the ability to plant at any time came the realisation that flowering shrubs had many virtues. Much has been written about the labour-saving aspect compared with the cultivation of bedding plants and the herbaceous border. The chore of annual planting or lifting every few years is removed, and so is the need for staking and dead-heading. Slugs are not a threat and the need to water when the weather turns dry is much less pressing.

Apart from these cultural virtues there are environmental ones. Flowering shrubs can be used to create privacy or to produce a wind-break. There are ground covers to control weeds and upright types to soften the stark lines of modern houses.

After all this praise for flowering shrubs it is necessary to sound a note of caution. Plants growing in containers are not cheap, and it is so easy to buy a showy specimen in full flower at the garden centre without checking that it is right for you. Never buy on impulse — check the anticipated height at maturity, soil and site needs, hardiness etc before making your decision. Once you have bought a suitable shrub you must plant it properly — Chapter 3 makes it quite clear that this is not simply a matter of digging a hole and dropping it in, and it also stresses the need to avoid planting shrubs too closely together. It is also necessary to avoid planting vigorous and tall-growing shrubs too close to the house. Once planted and established most flowering shrubs need little regular attention, apart from mulching around the roots in spring. There is, however, one important need for some types — annual pruning. Read the pruning needs of the plant in question and follow the instructions — the commonest fault is to leave a shrub unpruned for years and then to hack it back when it gets out of hand.

A few words of caution, then, but nothing to discourage you from making even more use of this splendid group of plants. Look through the Shrub Selector chapter and you will find that it is possible to have blooms all year round in even a modest garden — blooms to provide colour, fragrance and a wide variety of shapes and sizes. Read on, and meet some old friends you have known for years and some new varieties you may have never seen before.

SOURCES OF SUPPLY

Nowadays the garden centre is the main source of flowering shrubs. It is easy to understand why — neat rows of plants all laid out for you to see and quite often an extensive range from which to choose. But it need not be your only source — where money is short there are cheaper ways to buy the popular sorts and where rarities are wanted it may be necessary to buy from a mail order nursery.

GARDEN CENTRE

The garden centre is the only place to go if you want to choose from a large selection for immediate planting. A visit is one of the joys of gardening, but a few words of advice — go at the start of the planting season, avoid weekends if you can and do not buy on impulse. Always check the suitability of a plant before you buy, and that may mean going home and looking in a gardening book such as this one.

Advantages: You can see exactly what you are buying and you can take it home with you, which means no delays and no transport charges. At larger garden centres there is advice on hand, but do check the advice in the A-Z guide.

Drawbacks: The varieties on offer are usually the more popular sorts and the number of any one variety may be limited — for a massed planting or a hedge you may have to order from a nursery. Garden centres are generally out of town — you will need a car.

If something goes wrong: Take the plant back and explain what happened if you are sure it was not your fault. You will need proof of purchase.

MAIL ORDER NURSERY

Mail order nurseries remain an important source of supply. Try to choose one with a good reputation, one you have used before or one which has been recommended to you. Order early in the season and fill out the form carefully.

Advantages: There is often an excellent catalogue from which you can choose your requirements in the peace and comfort of your own home. Rarities as well as popular ones can be obtained from the larger nurseries and there are establishments which specialise in particular groups such as Heathers and Roses.

Drawbacks: Obviously you cannot see what you are buying and you cannot take your order home with you. This means that the shrubs may arrive when planting is inconvenient. Some of the plants on your order may be out of stock and the delivery charge on container-grown and balled plants may be high.

If something goes wrong: Write to the company and explain what happened if you are sure it was not your fault. Some nurseries will return your money.

MARKET STALL

In many street and indoor markets there is a stall which sells plants — in autumn and spring pre-packaged shrubs are on offer and there may be pots of Heather etc all year round.

Advantages: Plants are inexpensive — the market stall is often the cheapest source of supply. It is also usually conveniently sited and some stallholders are quite knowledgeable.

Drawbacks: The selection is very limited — only fast-moving lines can be stocked and this means the most popular shrubs. In addition the quality of the stock is very variable — a great deal of inferior material is sold on market stalls.

If something goes wrong: You can try complaining, but there is generally very little chance of redress.

HIGH STREET SHOP

In autumn and spring many popular varieties are sold at greengrocers, department stores, supermarkets etc — they are usually available as bare-rooted plants in labelled polythene bags.

Advantages: You can pick up a shrub while doing your everyday shopping — only a virtue if your plot is small and a trip to a garden centre is a chore. A more important advantage is that pre-packaged shrubs are cheaper than container-grown ones.

Drawbacks: The selection is limited as only fast-moving lines can be stocked, and warm conditions in store can lead to drying-out.

If something goes wrong: You can try complaining to the shop, but the response will depend on the policy of the store.

BARGAIN OFFER NURSERY

The 'bargain offers' advertised in newspapers and magazines are sometimes good value, but don't expect too much. However, caution is needed with the 'wonder offers' — phrases such as 'everlasting blooms', 'continuous sheets of colour' etc should not be taken too literally.

Advantage: An inexpensive way to obtain old favourites which are known for their toughness and reliability.

Drawbacks: If the plants are truly cheap, there must be a reason. The shrubs may be only rooted cuttings which will take time to establish or they may be substandard or damaged stock.

If something goes wrong: Write and complain if the plants are dead or diseased, but not if they are smaller than expected.

OWN-GROWN

The idea of raising your own stock from cuttings in a cold frame or propagator may seem like too much work, but there are many varieties which can be propagated from cuttings stuck in the ground in late autumn or by layering, and that involves no aftercare. Get cuttings from your own garden or from a friend — don't steal cuttings from public gardens.

Advantages: The plants are free and there is the satisfaction of having grown your own.

Drawbacks: It takes time for a stem cutting to root and so there is an inevitable delay before the new shrub is ready for planting where it is to grow.

If something goes wrong: If roots fail to develop, try to find out why — learn from your mistakes.

PICTURE DICTIONARY

FLOWER

PETAL
(Petals make up the COROLLA)

STIGMA

STYLE

ANTHER

SEPAL
(Sepals make up the CALYX)

PEDICEL

OVARY
(Stigma, Style and Ovary make up the PISTIL)

FILAMENT
(Anther and Filament make up the STAMEN)

BRACT

PEDUNCLE

FOLIAGE

Simple leaves

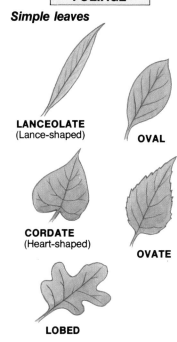

LANCEOLATE
(Lance-shaped)

OVAL

CORDATE
(Heart-shaped)

OVATE

LOBED

FLOWER-HEAD

(Other names: Inflorescence, Truss, Flower cluster)

SPIKE
Stalkless or almost stalkless flowers borne on the stem

RACEME
Like a Spike, but flowers are borne on short stalks

PANICLE
Like a Raceme, but each stalk bears a miniature Raceme

CORYMB
A flattened flower-head — stalks arise from different points and the youngest flowers are at the centre

CYME
A flower-head usually domed or flattened — stalks arise from different points and the oldest flowers are at the centre

CAPITULUM
A flattened flower-head — stalkless flowers tightly packed together on a single disc

UMBEL
A domed or flattened flower-head — stalks arise from a single point and the youngest flowers are at the centre

Compound leaves

TRIFOLIATE

PALMATE

PINNATE

BIPINNATE

Leaf edges

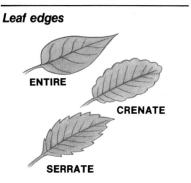

ENTIRE

CRENATE

SERRATE

CHAPTER 2

FLOWERING SHRUBS A~Z

It may seem unnecessary to define the group of plants known as flowering shrubs — everyone knows what they are. A flowering shrub is a perennial which bears several woody stems at ground level and a floral display which lasts for just a few weeks, like Lilac, or for several months, as with Potentilla. Non-flowering shrubs are those grown for their foliage, which may be colourful, but there are no flowers. All very simple.

Not so simple. The ground cover Pachysandra bears flowers in the spring but they are too small to add to the display value of the plant — it is a 'non-flowering' shrub. On the other hand there are shrubs like Fatsia, Fothergilla and Osmanthus which are mainly grown for their attractive foliage, but they do bear small white flowers which are attractive enough for the plants to be classed as flowering shrubs. So we must change our definition a little — a flowering shrub has a floral display which adds to the charm of the plant. Unfortunately the dividing line between a significant and insignificant display is a matter of opinion, and no two experts agree where the line should be.

Another dividing line which is hazy separates shrubs from trees. It should be simple — a tree is a woody plant with just a single woody stem at ground level. But some shrubs such as Cercis and Holly become tree-like when mature. Shrubs or trees? Here they are classed as shrubs.

So gathered here is a large group of bushy shrubs and tree-like shrubs with a floral display which adds to the charm of the plant. Also included here are woody plants with a climbing habit and sub-shrubs (e.g Vinca) where only the base of the stem is woody. Also included are shrubs which bear a significant berry or other fruit display rather than a floral one.

In the following pages you will find pictures and descriptions of hundreds of flowering shrubs, ranging from tiny rockery types to 20 ft giants. Like most gardeners you may just turn to the old favourites — Kerria, Mahonia, Weigela, Forsythia etc. Fine, but there are many unusual ones listed here and it is well worth while to be adventurous and choose a few rarities.

KEY TO THE A-Z GUIDE

Deciduous: Leaves fall in autumn/winter — there may be rich autumn colours before leaf-fall

Semi-evergreen: Some of the leaves fall in autumn/winter — the amount of leaf-fall is influenced by the weather conditions

Evergreen: All or nearly all of the leaves stay on over winter

Latin name (Genus)

Common Name (Popular name, English name)

CARYOPTERIS Blue Spiraea

Small shrub

Deciduous

Colours available

Anticipated height after 10 years under average growing conditions

Large shrub:	Over 10 ft
Medium shrub:	5–10 ft
Small shrub:	2½–5 ft
Dwarf shrub:	1–2½ ft
Prostrate shrub:	Under 1 ft
Climbing shrub:	See text

Flowering period

JANUARY
FEBRUARY
MARCH
APRIL
MAY
JUNE
JULY
AUGUST
SEPTEMBER
OCTOBER
NOVEMBER
DECEMBER

A small bush, growing no more than a few feet high, which is ideal for the front of a sunny border or as a low hedge. It flowers after most other shrubs have finished blooming and the attractive foliage is aromatic. Plant several in group and enjoy the clusters of small, fluffy blue or v¹ blue flowers. It will thrive in all sorts of soils including ones and is reliable in all areas. It is not as sensitive as once thought, and even if some shoots are kil¹ no problem — new stems appear in the spri¹

VARIETIES C. clandonensis is the popula¹ hybrid raised many years a¹ Royal Horticultural Societ¹ grey-green leaves and in 4 in. long terminal clust¹ There are several va¹ after the raiser — it h¹ 'Heavenly Blu¹ rather dark¹ these ar¹ Gold' – ¹ felted ¹

SITE & S

The flower or berry colours which are popularly available. Colours of unlisted rare types may not be included

The main flowering or berrying period in the Midlands. In some regions this period may start earlier or finish later. The flowering period of unusual species may not be included

Description of the basic properties of the genus and its value as a garden plant

Species, varieties and hybrids which are grown in this country. In most cases only a small selection can be shown — this selection features the most widely available types plus a few noteworthy examples which may be listed by only a few suppliers

ABELIA Abelia

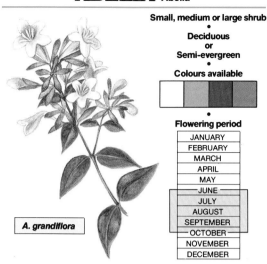

Small, medium or large shrub
•
Deciduous
or
Semi-evergreen
•
Colours available

•
Flowering period

| JANUARY |
| FEBRUARY |
| MARCH |
| APRIL |
| MAY |
| JUNE |
| JULY |
| AUGUST |
| SEPTEMBER |
| OCTOBER |
| NOVEMBER |
| DECEMBER |

A. grandiflora

Abelia should be more popular. This graceful shrub with its clusters of trumpet-shaped blossoms has a reputation for being rather tender, but this does not apply to all species. Its special value is the length of the flowering period — this can stretch from June until September or October. It is not a quick-growing plant — the usual height and spread at maturity are 5–6 ft, and it is happiest when protected by a sunny wall. With some species the reddish pink sepals remain after the petals have fallen.

VARIETIES: The fragrant flowers of **A. chinensis** (6 ft) are white flushed with pink and are freely borne from midsummer to early autumn. The popular type **A. 'Edward Goucher'** has lilac-pink blooms — the greyish-green leaves are semi-evergreen and it is reasonably hardy. Another Abelia which withstands frost is **A. grandiflora** (6 ft) — the arching branches with shiny leaves bear a continuous display of white and pink flowers from July to September. Look for the yellow-leaved variety **'Francis Mason'**. The tallest and hardiest Abelia is the scented **A. triflora** — the rather tender ones are **A. floribunda** (5 ft, cherry red flowers in June) and **A. schumannii** (4 ft, lilac-pink flowers in summer and autumn).

SITE & SOIL: Any free-draining garden soil will do — thrives best in full sun.

PRUNING: Not necessary — cut back any straggly or damaged branches in May.

PROPAGATION: Plant semi-ripe cuttings in a cold frame in summer.

Abelia chinensis

ABELIOPHYLLUM White Forsythia

Small shrub
•
Deciduous
•
Colours available

•
Flowering period

| JANUARY |
| FEBRUARY |
| MARCH |
| APRIL |
| MAY |
| JUNE |
| JULY |
| AUGUST |
| SEPTEMBER |
| OCTOBER |
| NOVEMBER |
| DECEMBER |

A. distichum

You will find this shrub in big garden centres and in larger catalogues, but you won't find it in many gardens. The reason which is often given is that it is an untidy plant which is only sparsely covered with foliage, but it makes an interesting change from the Forsythia bushes which are seen everywhere. The general growth habit and flower form are similar to its popular relative, but there are a number of differences. The flower colour is white or pale pink instead of yellow and there is a strong Almond-like fragrance. It often comes into bloom earlier than Forsythia and it is also slow-growing, reaching a height of 4 or 5 ft and a spread of 3 ft when mature.

VARIETIES: There is a single species — **A. distichum**. It is an undemanding shrub which is not fussy about soil type, but for maximum display plant it against a sunny wall. The winter or early spring flowers appear on the bare purple-tinged stems — each ½ in. star-shaped bloom is pale mauve at first, fading to pink and then white when mature. A few nurseries offer the variety **'Roseum'** with flowers which remain pink. The pale green leaves appear when flowering is over.

SITE & SOIL: Any free-draining garden soil will do — thrives best in full sun.

PRUNING: Cut back damaged branches and shorten some of the most mature ones as soon as flowering has finished.

PROPAGATION: Plant semi-ripe cuttings in a cold frame in summer or hardwood cuttings in the open in late autumn.

Abeliophyllum distichum

ABUTILON Abutilon

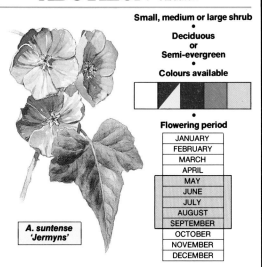

- Small, medium or large shrub
- Deciduous
or
Semi-evergreen
- Colours available

Flowering period

| JANUARY |
| FEBRUARY |
| MARCH |
| APRIL |
| **MAY** |
| **JUNE** |
| **JULY** |
| **AUGUST** |
| **SEPTEMBER** |
| OCTOBER |
| NOVEMBER |
| DECEMBER |

A. suntense 'Jermyns'

If you are looking for a durable and fully hardy shrub then Abutilon is not for you. The shoots may be killed in a cold winter and most types are rather short-lived. For these reasons it has never become a popular shrub, but in the right place it is well worth considering. You need a south- or west-facing wall and some form of support for the thin and flexible stems. The bell-shaped or saucer-like blooms are borne over a long period.

VARIETIES: A. suntense is one of the hardiest types, withstanding temperatures as low as –10°C. It is an upright deciduous bush which will grow about 15 ft high with saucer-shaped flowers between May and July. The most popular variety is **'Jermyns'** (deep mauve). The parent of A. suntense (**A. vitifolium**) is rather similar to its offspring with grey lobed leaves and 2 in. wide flat flowers in summer. Varieties include **'Veronica Tennant'** (mauve) and **'Tennant's White'** (white). **A. megapotamicum** is quite different. It is a somewhat tender plant with colourful bell-like flowers in summer and early autumn — red calyces, yellow petals and dark leaves. A number of colourful types are available — **'Variegatum'** has yellow-splashed leaves.

SITE & SOIL: Any reasonable well-drained soil. Best in full sun, but will tolerate light shade.

PRUNING: Cut back any damaged branches and shorten a few of the most mature ones in spring.

PROPAGATION: Plant semi-ripe cuttings in a cold frame in summer.

Abutilon vitifolium 'Tennant's White'

ACACIA Wattle

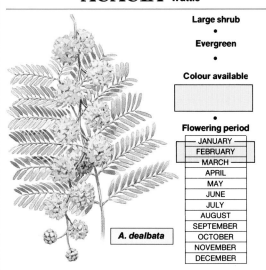

- Large shrub
- Evergreen
- Colour available

Flowering period

| JANUARY |
| **FEBRUARY** |
| MARCH |
| APRIL |
| MAY |
| JUNE |
| JULY |
| AUGUST |
| SEPTEMBER |
| OCTOBER |
| NOVEMBER |
| DECEMBER |

A. dealbata

The best-known Acacia is A. dealbata — the Mimosa sold by florists. It is also quite well-known as a conservatory plant, but it is rarely grown outdoors. The problem is frost — the stems are killed when the temperature stays below –5°C for a prolonged period. You will have to look in some of the larger catalogues to find one of the Acacia species for growing outdoors, but it is worth considering if you have a bare south-facing wall and live in a mild area. The spreading branches bear feathery leaves or spiny false leaves known as phyllodes.

VARIETIES: The flower-heads bear clusters of small powder-puffs in winter or early spring. **A. armata** (Kangaroo Thorn) is a dense bush which produces scented flower-heads above the dark green prickly 'leaves' in early spring. **A. mucronata** is claimed to be the hardiest Acacia, capable of withstanding –10°C for short periods. It bears lance-shaped phyllodes and bright yellow flowers. **A. dealbata** produces strongly-scented flowers in winter and early spring. It is quick-growing, reaching 12 ft or more under favourable conditions. This plant shoots from the base in spring if the stems are killed in winter.

SITE & SOIL: Plant in lime-free soil against a sheltered wall in full sun.

PRUNING: Cut back all frost-damaged branches and shorten a few of the most mature ones in May.

PROPAGATION: Plant semi-ripe cuttings in a cold frame in summer.

Acacia armata

ACTINIDIA Actinidia

- Climbing shrub
- Deciduous

Colours available

Flowering period

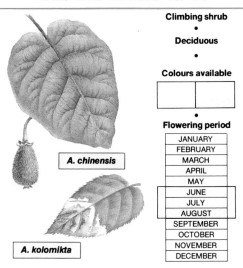

A. chinensis

A. kolomikta

| JANUARY |
| FEBRUARY |
| MARCH |
| APRIL |
| MAY |
| JUNE |
| JULY |
| AUGUST |
| SEPTEMBER |
| OCTOBER |
| NOVEMBER |
| DECEMBER |

The Actinidias are hardy and vigorous climbers which are useful for clothing walls, pergolas and tree stumps with foliage. The most popular garden species is grown for its leaves and not for the small flowers which appear in early summer, but others are planted for their floral display linked with the production of edible fruit. With these fruiting types you should plant both a male and female specimen close together as Actinidias are generally unisexual.

VARIETIES: The only species you are likely to find at an ordinary garden centre is **A. kolomikta**. When planted against a sunny wall the upper parts of the oval leaves on the 15 ft twining stems turn cream and red. Small white flowers appear in June and these are followed by egg-shaped edible fruits. **A. chinensis** (**A. deliciosa**) is quite different — the stems can reach 25 ft or more and the large heart-shaped leaves are covered with reddish hairs. Fragrant, creamy flowers appear in July and August and later on the brown, furry fruits appear on the female plants. These are the well-known Kiwi Fruit (Chinese Gooseberry) — they need a good summer to mature. **A. arguta** is a white-flowered species.

SITE & SOIL: Any reasonable fertile soil will do. Thrives best in full sun.

PRUNING: Not necessary — remove any dead or unwanted stems in winter.

PROPAGATION: Plant semi-ripe cuttings in a propagator in summer.

Actinidia chinensis

AESCULUS Buckeye

- Medium or large shrub
- Deciduous

Colours available

Flowering period

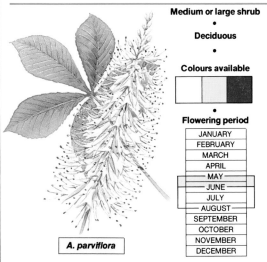

A. parviflora

| JANUARY |
| FEBRUARY |
| MARCH |
| APRIL |
| MAY |
| JUNE |
| JULY |
| AUGUST |
| SEPTEMBER |
| OCTOBER |
| NOVEMBER |
| DECEMBER |

The Buckeyes or Shrubby Horse Chestnuts are dwarf relatives of the 60 ft giants which are such a glorious sight in May. These modest types produce floral candles in late spring or summer in which the flowers may be more loosely arranged than on the Common Horse Chestnut. The leaves have the standard palmate pattern and all are easy to grow in almost any garden soil. A good choice where you want a large reliable shrub but do not have the space for a Horse Chestnut tree.

VARIETIES: The most popular Shrubby Horse Chestnut is **A. parviflora** — a dense rounded bush which grows about 6–8 ft high and 10 ft wide. It is late flowering, the red-anthered white flowers appearing in 10 in. high candles in July or August — the tubular blooms give a 'bottle-brush' effect. The leaves turn an attractive golden colour in autumn. You should also be able to find the rather taller **A. pavia** (Red Buckeye) in the catalogues or larger garden centre. The crimson flowers open in June or July. For the richest red flowers choose the variety **'Sanguinea'**. For May-flowering types you will have to search through the catalogues — there is the colourful **A. neglecta 'Erythroblastos'** (20 ft) with leaves which change from pink to yellow, then green and finally orange as the season progresses. The flowers are yellow.

SITE & SOIL: Any reasonable soil in sun or light shade.

PRUNING: Not necessary — cut out dead and diseased branches in early spring.

PROPAGATION: Layer stems in summer.

Aesculus pavia 'Sanguinea'

AKEBIA Akebia

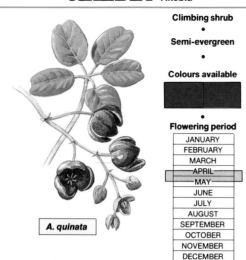

Climbing shrub

•

Semi-evergreen

•

Colours available

Flowering period

JANUARY
FEBRUARY
MARCH
APRIL
MAY
JUNE
JULY
AUGUST
SEPTEMBER
OCTOBER
NOVEMBER
DECEMBER

A. quinata

Akebia is a vigorous twining plant from China and Japan. It is a slow starter, but after a few years it will rapidly cover a bare wall or a large dead tree. A number of stalked leaflets make up each leaf and a group of small and fragrant purplish blooms make up each flower-head. An individual bloom is relatively insignificant, but they often compensate for this lack of size by their abundance. The catalogue may talk about the long sausage-shaped fruits which follow the flowers, but they very rarely appear.

VARIETIES: A. quinata is the popular one. The 20 ft high stems bear leaves composed of five oval leaflets, and the drooping flower-heads which appear in spring have tiny male blooms at the apex and larger female blooms at the base of each cluster. When these claret-coloured flowers have faded, dark purple fruits may develop if the spring and summer weather has been favourable. **A. trifoliata** (**A. lobata**) is an even more vigorous climber, capable of growing 30 ft high. The leaflets are arranged in threes rather than in fives as with A. quinata, and the flowers are dark purple rather than wine-coloured. The violet fruits, when they appear, are about 4 in. long. **A. pentaphylla** is a hybrid of the two species described above.

SITE & SOIL: Any reasonable well-drained soil will do. Thrives in sun or light shade.

PRUNING: Not necessary — remove dead or unwanted stems in May.

PROPAGATION: Layer runners in May.

Akebia quinata

AMELANCHIER Snowy Mespilus

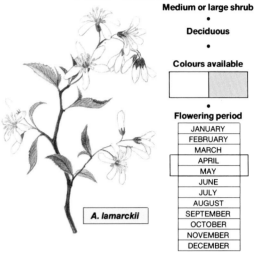

Medium or large shrub

•

Deciduous

•

Colours available

Flowering period

JANUARY
FEBRUARY
MARCH
APRIL
MAY
JUNE
JULY
AUGUST
SEPTEMBER
OCTOBER
NOVEMBER
DECEMBER

A. lamarckii

The Snowy Mespilus is for the larger garden — nearly all species grow to 10 ft or more. If you have the space it is worth considering for its changing colour display — young pink or coppery foliage, white flowers which open just as the leaves begin to appear, red berries which turn black, and green leaves which change to yellow or red in autumn. The small flowers are not particularly long-lasting, but the floral clusters are borne in large numbers in spring — the berries which ripen in June are edible.

VARIETIES: The species you are most likely to find is the Shadbush (**A. canadensis**). It is a large shrub which suckers freely, reaching a height of 10–15 ft in time. The young leaves are pink and the erect flower-heads are present in April or May. **A. lamarckii** is very similar, but the young leaves are coppery rather than pink and the flowers are borne in loose clusters. The variety **'Rubescens'** has pale pink flowers. One of the best Amelanchiers is **A. 'Ballerina'** — a compact hybrid which has larger flowers than the others. Confusion continues to reign over the naming of Snowy Mespilus — you can find identical plants named A. canadensis, A. lamarckii, **A. grandiflora** or **A. laevis**, depending where you shop!

SITE & SOIL: Requires a moist soil which is neutral or acid. Thrives in sun or partial shade.

PRUNING: Not necessary — cut back in late winter if growth has to be kept in check.

PROPAGATION: Remove rooted suckers from the parent shrub and plant in autumn.

Amelanchier canadensis

ANDROMEDA Andromeda

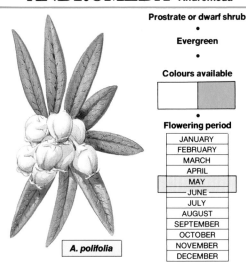

Prostrate or dwarf shrub

•

Evergreen

•

Colours available

•

Flowering period

JANUARY	
FEBRUARY	
MARCH	
APRIL	
MAY	
JUNE	
JULY	
AUGUST	
SEPTEMBER	
OCTOBER	
NOVEMBER	
DECEMBER	

A. polifolia

These slow-growing shrubs make excellent companions for Azaleas, Rhododendrons, Callunas and other acid-loving plants. Most varieties grow about 2 ft high — they have an open habit and the slender stems bear strap-like leaves. In late spring or early summer the flowers appear — ¼ in. bells hanging in clusters from the tips of the branches. The colour range is limited to white and pink and the leaf colour is restricted to green, which means that the Andromedas have none of the wide colour range of the Callunas. Another difference is that Andromeda stems can be killed if the temperature falls to –10°C or below.

VARIETIES: The dominant species is **A. polifolia** or Bog Rosemary — a native of the British Isles. The bluish-green leaves are white below, and the pale pink urn-shaped flowers appear in May and continue into June. There are several varieties — **'Compacta'** has bright pink flowers and grows only 1 ft high. **'Minima'** is even smaller as it is a prostrate mat-forming type. **'Alba'** bears white flowers and **'Major'** is the tallest variety. The only other species is **A. glaucophylla** —pink-flowered and very similar to A. polifolia but with leaves which are hairy below.

SITE & SOIL: Moist, acid soil is necessary — add peat at planting time. Thrives in light shade.

PRUNING: Not necessary — cut back any straggly or damaged branches in late autumn.

PROPAGATION: Plant softwood cuttings in a cold frame in late summer.

Andromeda polifolia

ARALIA Japanese Angelica

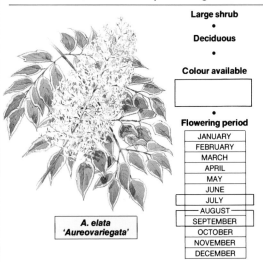

Large shrub

•

Deciduous

•

Colour available

•

Flowering period

JANUARY	
FEBRUARY	
MARCH	
APRIL	
MAY	
JUNE	
JULY	
AUGUST	
SEPTEMBER	
OCTOBER	
NOVEMBER	
DECEMBER	

A. elata 'Aureovariegata'

A shrub which is definitely not for the small garden. It should be grown as a specimen plant with enough room to display its architectural twisted form in winter and its huge foliage during the growing season. Each leaf is 3 or 4 ft long, neatly divided up into a complex pattern of leaflets. The thorny branches grow 10 ft high or more, and the large bush suckers freely. It is a hardy plant, but you should choose a sheltered spot to protect the leaves from the wind.

VARIETIES: A. elata is the only species you are likely to find. It is grown mainly for its foliage display, but in early autumn large branching panicles of tiny white flowers grow up to 2 ft high. These impressive flower-heads can cover the upper part of the shrub under favourable conditions. Two variegated forms are available — both are more compact and a little more tender than the basic species. Suckers should be removed from these coloured-leaf types. In spring the foliage of **'Aureovariegata'** is edged with yellow — **'Variegata'** with creamy-white. Later in the season the variegation of both turns silvery-white. **A. spinosa** is a spiny-stemmed species which blooms in July.

SITE & SOIL: Light and well-drained soil is preferred. Thrives in sun or light shade.

PRUNING: Not necessary — cut back damaged and unwanted branches in spring.

PROPAGATION: Remove rooted suckers from the parent shrub and plant in autumn.

Aralia elata 'Variegata'

ARBUTUS Strawberry Tree

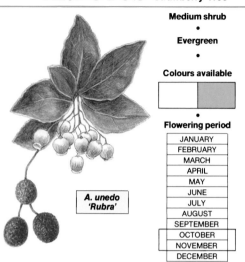

Medium shrub
•
Evergreen
•
Colours available

Flowering period

| JANUARY |
| FEBRUARY |
| MARCH |
| APRIL |
| MAY |
| JUNE |
| JULY |
| AUGUST |
| SEPTEMBER |
| OCTOBER |
| NOVEMBER |
| DECEMBER |

A. unedo 'Rubra'

An interesting plant to grow if you want something out of the ordinary. The only species you are likely to find is A. unedo. The odd feature is that the clusters of pendent urn-shaped flowers appear at the same time in late autumn as the ripening fruits from the previous year's flowers. These fruits are rather like Strawberries in appearance but not in flavour — they are tasteless. Arbutus is slow-growing and the coloured peeling bark is often ornamental. Plant in pairs to ensure cross-fertilisation and choose a sheltered spot in the garden.

VARIETIES: A. unedo keeps its shrubby form for many years, eventually becoming a tree about 8 ft high. The leaves are dark and leathery, and the bark is dark brown. The flowers are white and the fruits are orange or red — these 'Strawberries' may remain on the bush throughout the winter. The variety **'Rubra'** has a more compact growth habit and the flowers are pink. Both the species and the variety make good specimen plants which tolerate salt-laden air. **A. andrachnoides** flowers in winter, but is grown for its red bark rather than its floral display. Somewhat tender spring-flowering species include **A. menziesii** and **A. andrachne**.

SITE & SOIL: Any reasonable garden soil will do — it need not be acid. Thrives in sun or light shade.

PRUNING: Not necessary — cut back weak and straggly branches in early spring.

PROPAGATION: Difficult — sow seed under glass or plant semi-ripe cuttings in a propagator in summer.

Arbutus unedo

ARCTOSTAPHYLOS Bearberry

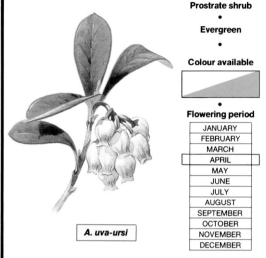

Prostrate shrub
•
Evergreen
•
Colour available

Flowering period

| JANUARY |
| FEBRUARY |
| MARCH |
| APRIL |
| MAY |
| JUNE |
| JULY |
| AUGUST |
| SEPTEMBER |
| OCTOBER |
| NOVEMBER |
| DECEMBER |

A. uva-ursi

A number of lime-hating dwarf Heaths and Heathers are included in this book — Calluna, Andromeda, Daboecia, Vaccinium, Gaultheria etc. Arctostaphylos is another one, with the group characteristics. Leaves are narrow and evergreen, and the pendent flowers are variously described as bell-, urn- or pitcher-shaped. You can grow it as an unusual alternative to one of the other members of the group but it has no special advantages. It is quite fussy about soil type and should only be planted where other lime-haters such as Rhododendrons have succeeded.

VARIETIES: The Red Bearberry (**A. uva-ursi**) appears in some but certainly not all catalogues and garden centres, and other species such as the tiny **A. myritifolia** and the tall **A. manzanita** are even more difficult to find. A. uva-ursi is a native plant — a creeping ground-hugging shrub with slender branches and 1 in. long leathery leaves. It is slow-growing — the maximum height is about 9 in. and it takes many years to reach its mature spread of about 3 ft. The pink-tipped white flowers are borne in drooping clusters in spring, and in autumn there are bright red shiny berries. **A. nevadensis** is similar but less hardy.

SITE & SOIL: Well-drained, acid soil is necessary — full sun is preferred. Add peat at planting time.

PRUNING: Not necessary — cut back in late winter if growth has to be kept in check.

PROPAGATION: Remove rooted runners from the parent shrub and plant in autumn.

Arctostaphylos uva-ursi

ARISTOLOCHIA Dutchman's Pipe

Climbing shrub
•
Deciduous
•
Colour available

•
Flowering period

JANUARY	
FEBRUARY	
MARCH	
APRIL	
MAY	
JUNE	
JULY	
AUGUST	
SEPTEMBER	
OCTOBER	
NOVEMBER	
DECEMBER	

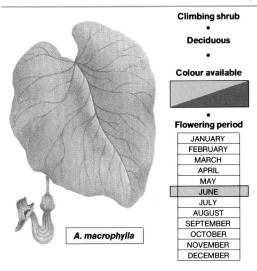

A. macrophylla

Most species in this group of vigorous twiners are too tender to grow outdoors, but there are a few which are hardy enough to withstand our winters. The two key features of the Aristolochias are large, heart-shaped leaves and small curiously-shaped flowers — for showy blooms you will have to grow one of the tender species in a greenhouse or conservatory. Outdoors the hardy species flower only when the plant is grown in a warm spot sheltered from the wind.

VARIETIES: The common species is **A. macrophylla** (other names **A. durior**, **A. sipho**). It will grow about 20 ft high if the conditions are favourable, and can be used to cover all sorts of things — tree stumps, sheds, fences, walls, dead trees etc. The heart- or kidney-shaped leaves are 1 ft or more in length, hiding the pipe-shaped flowers which open in June. Each bloom is about 1 in. long and a thing of interest rather than beauty — yellowish-green with a purplish-brown mouth. You will find A. macrophylla in a number of catalogues but you will have to search to find the other hardy Aristolochias. Examples are **A. heterophylla** (yellow/purple flowers) and the downy-leaved **A. tomentosa**.

SITE & SOIL: A fertile soil is necessary. Thrives in sun or light shade.

PRUNING: Not necessary — remove any dead or unwanted stems in winter.

PROPAGATION: Layer stems in late summer or plant softwood cuttings in a propagator in summer.

Aristolochia macrophylla

AUCUBA Aucuba

Medium shrub
•
Evergreen
•
Colour available

•
Berrying period

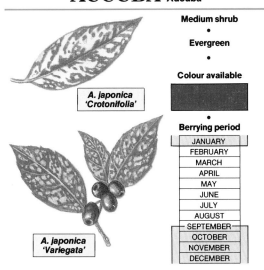

A. japonica
'Crotonifolia'

JANUARY	
FEBRUARY	
MARCH	
APRIL	
MAY	
JUNE	
JULY	
AUGUST	
SEPTEMBER	
OCTOBER	
NOVEMBER	
DECEMBER	

A. japonica
'Variegata'

The variegated types are known as Spotted Laurels, and no other broad-leaved shrub can match them for brightening up an area in deep shade. Aucuba is also unrivalled in its ability to flourish in all soils — the only problem is that new growth may be scorched by cold winds. The leaves are glossy, and toothed along the upper half. With almost all varieties the insignificant flowers are either male or female, which means that berries will only appear on a female variety if a male one is grown nearby.

VARIETIES: The basic species is **A. japonica**, a rounded 7 ft x 7 ft shrub with all-green leaves. This foliage is usually broadly oval — the narrow or lance-leaved varieties include **'Salicifolia'** (female), **'Longifolia'** (female) and **'Lance Leaf'** (male). The popular Aucubas are the varieties speckled or splashed with yellow or gold — examples include **'Crotonifolia'** (male), **'Variegata'** (female), **'Golden King'** (male) and **'Gold Dust'** (female). Rather different is the female **'Picturata'** which produces foliage with a central golden blotch. If you have room for only one plant but wish to ensure that it will berry freely, choose the variety **'Rozannie'** which bears both male and female flowers.

SITE & SOIL: Will succeed in almost any garden soil and situation, including sun and deep shade.

PRUNING: Not necessary, but will withstand drastic pruning in May.

PROPAGATION: Plant semi-ripe cuttings in a cold frame in summer or hardwood cuttings in the open in late autumn.

Aucuba japonica 'Longifolia'

AZALEA Azalea

See RHODODENDRON

AZARA Azara

Large shrub
•
Evergreen
•
Colour available

•
Flowering period

JANUARY	
FEBRUARY	
MARCH	
APRIL	
MAY	
JUNE	
JULY	
AUGUST	
SEPTEMBER	
OCTOBER	
NOVEMBER	
DECEMBER	

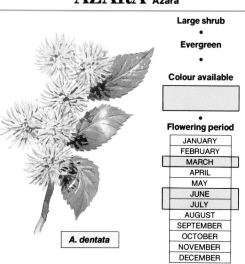

A. dentata

An attractive S. American plant which may be tree-like or distinctly bushy. It is not often seen in gardens as it needs the protection of a sheltered wall. The yellow flowers appear in spring or summer, depending on the species, and each one is tiny and fragrant with showy stamens instead of petals. These flowers are borne in clusters.

VARIETIES: A. microphylla is the most popular species, growing 10–15 ft high and bearing small divided leaves. The flowers appear on the underside of the branches in March — in the variety **'Variegata'** the leaves are edged with cream. For a better floral display choose **A. serrata** (leaves not felted below, flowers in July) or the rather more delicate **A. dentata** (leaves felted below, flowers in June) — the flower clusters are more prominent and the growth habit is bushier.

SITE & SOIL: Any reasonable well-drained soil will do. Thrives in sun or light shade.

PRUNING: Not necessary — cut back in late winter if growth has to be kept in check.

PROPAGATION: Plant semi-ripe cuttings in a cold frame in summer.

Azara serrata

BERBERIDOPSIS Coral Plant

Climbing shrub
•
Evergreen
•
Colour available

•
Flowering period

JANUARY	
FEBRUARY	
MARCH	
APRIL	
MAY	
JUNE	
JULY	
AUGUST	
SEPTEMBER	
OCTOBER	
NOVEMBER	
DECEMBER	

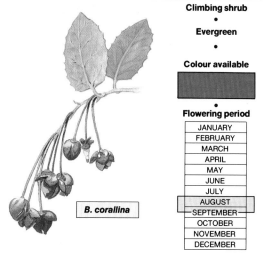

B. corallina

You should not have too much trouble in finding a supplier of this unusual climber by looking through the catalogues of tree and shrub nurseries, but don't even think about growing one unless you have the right conditions. It needs damp, peaty soil without a trace of chalk and it needs a shady, sheltered spot such as a north- or west-facing wall. Finally, it will be cut down by very hard frosts. A fussy plant indeed, but an eye-catching twining or scrambling shrub which will give a fine display of late summer flowers in a mild area of the country.

VARIETY: There is just one species — **B. corallina**. The woody lax stems will grow up to 10 ft high in a suitable locality. The dark green leaves are oval and leathery, with spiny teeth along the edges. In late summer or early autumn the shrub is in flower — long pendent clusters of red blooms at the tips of the stems. Each flower is about ½ in. across and is borne on a long stalk. As stated in the introduction, the combination of the need for shade and mild winter conditions makes this an unsuitable plant for most gardens, but it is a good specimen plant for the conservatory.

SITE & SOIL: Requires acid soil which is moist but well-drained. Thrives in partial shade.

PRUNING: Cut back all dead and frost-damaged stems in May.

PROPAGATION: Layer stems or plant softwood cuttings in a cold frame in summer.

Berberidopsis corallina

BERBERIS Barberry

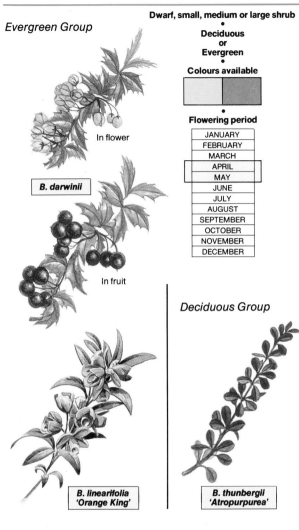

Evergreen Group

In flower

B. darwinii

In fruit

Dwarf, small, medium or large shrub
•
Deciduous or Evergreen
•
Colours available

Flowering period

| JANUARY |
| FEBRUARY |
| MARCH |
| APRIL |
| MAY |
| JUNE |
| JULY |
| AUGUST |
| SEPTEMBER |
| OCTOBER |
| NOVEMBER |
| DECEMBER |

Deciduous Group

B. linearifolia 'Orange King'

B. thunbergii 'Atropurpurea'

All the Berberis species and varieties have a few features in common — they are easy to grow and will thrive in almost any soil, they are all spiny to some degree and the flower colour is yellow or orange. But the genus is a large one, and even a modest garden centre will usually offer a wide choice of Berberis types. There are both dwarfs and giants, and you should be able to find a suitable Berberis for the rock garden as well as the shrub border, for hedging, for covering banks and for screening, and for growing on its own as a specimen bush. Always buy container-grown plants, and little or no pruning is required apart from cutting back to keep the plant in check.

VARIETIES: The *Evergreen Group* are grown for their glossy, deep green leaves and have been used for hedging and screening for hundreds of years. Many produce a bright display of flowers in spring and purple berries in autumn. Perhaps the most popular one is **B. darwinii** (8 ft, shiny foliage like miniature Holly leaves, reddish flower buds and a bright display of drooping clusters of deep yellow flowers in April). Another popular evergreen is **B. stenophylla** (8 ft, narrow foliage, arching thorny stems and golden flowers in April and May). The variety **'Irwinii'** is a 3 ft compact bush and **'Corallina Compacta'** is a 1 ft high dwarf. Other evergreens include **B. linearifolia 'Orange King'** (6 ft, rich orange flowers), **B. verruculosa** (4 ft, small glossy leaves, solitary yellow flowers and black berries), **B. candidula** for ground cover (2 ft, dense mounds bearing yellow flowers in May) and **B. julianae** for screening (11 ft, leaves turning red in autumn). The *Deciduous Group* are grown for their colourful foliage and bright berries. The basic species is the stiff-branched **B. thunbergii** (5 ft x 5 ft) with bright red autumn leaves and berries. There are several interesting varieties. **B. thunbergii 'Atropurpurea'** (6 ft) and its dwarf and almost thornless form **'Nana'** (2 ft) have dark bronzy foliage which turns red in autumn. **B. thunbergii 'Aurea'** (5 ft) has yellow leaves which turn green in late summer. Other colourful varieties include **'Rose Glow'** (pink-mottled purple leaves), **'Harlequin'** (white-speckled deep pink leaves) and **'Red Chief'** (wine red leaves). **B. 'Bagatelle'** is a 1 ft dwarf — **B. wilsonae** (4 ft) bears orange berries in autumn and **B. ottawensis 'Purpurea'** (6 ft) has arching stems and rich purple leaves.

SITE & SOIL: Any reasonable soil will do, in sun or partial shade.

PRUNING: Not necessary — remove unwanted branches from evergreens immediately after flowering and from deciduous varieties in February.

PROPAGATION: Layer branches or plant semi-ripe cuttings in a cold frame in summer.

Berberis darwinii

Berberis stenophylla

Berberis wilsonae

BUDDLEIA Butterfly Bush

Medium or large shrub
•
Deciduous
or
Semi-evergreen
•
Colours available

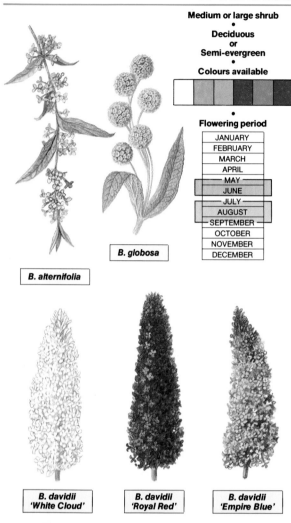

Flowering period

| JANUARY |
| FEBRUARY |
| MARCH |
| APRIL |
| MAY |
| JUNE |
| JULY |
| AUGUST |
| SEPTEMBER |
| OCTOBER |
| NOVEMBER |
| DECEMBER |

B. globosa

B. alternifolia

B. davidii
'White Cloud'

B. davidii
'Royal Red'

B. davidii
'Empire Blue'

Buddleia (sometimes listed as Buddleja) is one of the mainstays of the shrub border, and its popularity is not surprising. It is quick-growing and soon reaches 6 ft or more. It is also not fussy about the growing conditions, succeeding in dry infertile soils and salt-laden air. The Buddleias have tapered leaves which are usually downy below and all bear pretty flower clusters. These blooms appear in late spring or late summer, depending on the species. The plant itself is rarely a thing of beauty, although one (B. alternifolia) can be considered an attractive bush when not in flower. The only problem with Buddleias is that their display is often dimmed by neglect.

VARIETIES: **B. davidii** is by far the most popular species. Left unpruned the bush will grow 8 ft or more — when pruned regularly growth is more compact and the flower-heads are larger but appear later. These flower-heads are cone-shaped spikes and may be up to 18 in. long — a mass of tiny, honey-scented blooms between late July and mid September. They are highly attractive to butterflies — hence the common name. There are scores of named varieties, including **'Black Night'** (dark purple), **'Border Beauty'** (crimson-red, compact growth), **'Empire Blue'** (violet-blue, orange eye), **'Harlequin'** (purple, creamy-white variegated leaves), **'Ile de France'** (violet, strong growth), **'Nanho Blue'** (lilac-blue, compact growth), **'Peace'** (white, orange eye), **'Royal Red'** (purple-red, popular) and **'White Cloud'** (white). **B. alternifolia** is quite different — a Willow-like shrub (10 ft x 10 ft) with arching stems wreathed in clusters of lilac-coloured flowers in June — the variety **'Argentea'** bears silvery leaves. **B. globosa** (Orange Ball Tree) is a straggly semi-evergreen which produces globular 1½ in. heads of small orange flowers in May or June. It lasts well as a cut flower. **B. colvilei** is a 10 ft plant with lax stems and large drooping clusters of flowers in June. The variety **'Kewensis'** has rich red blooms. **B. crispa** is a white-felted and somewhat delicate plant which blooms in late summer — another felted species which needs some shelter and support is **B. fallowiana**. Look for **B. 'Lochinch'** — a compact bush with grey shoots and orange-eyed lavender blooms.

SITE & SOIL: Any well-drained garden soil will do. All Buddleias prefer a sunny position.

PRUNING: With B. davidii, fallowiana and colvilei cut back last year's growth to within 3–4 in. of the old wood in March . With other species cut out one-third of the old wood after flowering.

PROPAGATION: Plant semi-ripe cuttings in a cold frame in summer or hardwood cuttings in the open in late spring.

Buddleia alternifolia

Buddleia davidii 'Harlequin'

Buddleia 'Lochinch'

BUPLEURUM Shrubby Hare's Ear

Medium shrub
•
Evergreen
•
Colour available

Flowering period

JANUARY	
FEBRUARY	
MARCH	
APRIL	
MAY	
JUNE	
JULY	
AUGUST	
SEPTEMBER	
OCTOBER	
NOVEMBER	
DECEMBER	

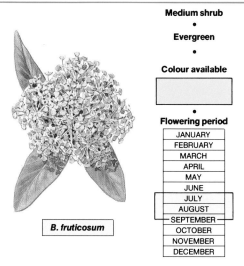

B. fruticosum

There are several species of Bupleurum described in the specialist catalogues, such as the herbaceous B. falcatum which can withstand prolonged heavy frosts. But only one shrubby species (B. fruticosum) is suitable for growing outdoors as a garden plant. You may have to search for this one, and for most gardeners it may not be worth the trouble. The evergreen foliage is attractive, but the flower-heads are not particularly showy. However, this plant thrives in poor, sandy soil and salt-laden air, so it is a good choice for a seaside garden.

VARIETY: There is just one species for garden use — **B. fruticosum**. It is a somewhat lax shrub with slender branches, reaching about 5 ft x 5 ft at maturity. The oval leathery leaves are glossy — greyish-green above and silvery below. The tiny yellow or greenish-yellow flowers are borne in circular heads which measure about 4 in. across — the brown seed-heads remain on the plant over winter. Bupleurum is sometimes described as semi-hardy, but a mature plant should be able to survive winter frosts in most areas. Newly-planted specimens are less hardy and may not survive a cold winter on an exposed site.

SITE & SOIL: Light and well-drained soil is preferred. Thrives in sun or light shade.

PRUNING: Not necessary — cut back any damaged branches in spring.

PROPAGATION: Plant semi-ripe cuttings in a cold frame in summer.

Bupleurum fruticosum

CAESALPINIA Bird of Paradise

Large shrub
•
Deciduous
•
Colour available

Flowering period

JANUARY	
FEBRUARY	
MARCH	
APRIL	
MAY	
JUNE	
JULY	
AUGUST	
SEPTEMBER	
OCTOBER	
NOVEMBER	
DECEMBER	

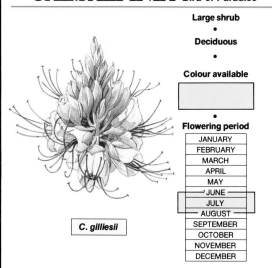

C. gilliesii

This exotic shrub is even more difficult to find in the catalogues than its companion on this page, but its ferny leaves and dramatic showy flowers make it well worth the hunt if you have a sunny and sheltered site — a south-facing wall in a mild area is ideal. It is an untidy tall plant which bears large clusters of flowers in summer. Each of the 20–30 blooms in the terminal cluster has a group of prominent red anthers up to 3 in. long. It is a plant of the semi-tropics, but a good choice for a favoured spot if you like unusual shrubs.

VARIETIES: There are two species — the one you are more likely to find is the rather tender **C. gilliesii**, also known as **Poinciana gilliesii** or the Bird of Paradise. If conditions are suitable the shrub will reach 12 ft x 12 ft — against a sunny wall it may reach 20–25 ft. The leaves are finely divided and in July and August the eye-catching flower-heads appear. The pale yellow blooms with their showy stamens are crowded together in a broad conical spike. **C. japonica** is quite similar, but the stems are spiny and the yellow flowers appear in June. An important difference is that C. japonica can withstand exposure to -10°C.

SITE & SOIL: Requires a fertile, well-drained soil. Thrives best in full sun.

PRUNING: Not necessary — cut back any damaged branches in spring.

PROPAGATION: Plant semi-ripe cuttings in a cold frame in summer.

Caesalpinia gilliesii

CALLICARPA Beauty Berry

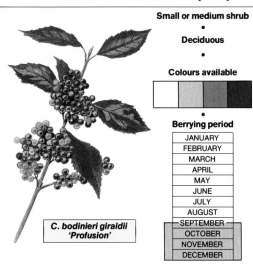

Small or medium shrub
•
Deciduous
•
Colours available

•
Berrying period

| JANUARY |
| FEBRUARY |
| MARCH |
| APRIL |
| MAY |
| JUNE |
| JULY |
| AUGUST |
| SEPTEMBER |
| OCTOBER |
| NOVEMBER |
| DECEMBER |

C. bodinieri giraldii 'Profusion'

The beauty of this shrub is seen in the autumn. The leaves will have turned rose, violet or red and when they fall the polished berries are revealed on the bare stems. The outstanding feature is that these fruits are not the common-or-garden red or black we usually associate with shrub berries — they are lilac, violet or bright purple. The colourful clusters persist until Christmas. Plant the bushes in groups rather than singly to make sure that berries will be plentiful — cut branches are excellent for winter flower arranging.

VARIETIES: The most popular variety is **C. bodinieri giraldii 'Profusion'** — as with all Callicarpas it should be planted in a sheltered spot. The insignificant pale pink flowers appear in August and are followed in late September by masses of purple-blue berries. When mature the bush is about 6 ft x 6 ft. A smaller and more delicate Callicarpa is **C. japonica**, growing 3 ft tall and bearing pink flowers and violet berries. The variety **'Leucocarpa'** bears white berries. Another compact species is the lilac-berried **C. dichotoma**.

SITE & SOIL: Well-drained, reasonably fertile soil is required. Thrives in sun or light shade.

PRUNING: Not essential. Remove unwanted or damaged branches in early spring.

PROPAGATION: Layer shoots in autumn or plant semi-ripe cuttings in a cold frame in summer.

Callicarpa bodinieri giraldii 'Profusion'

CALLISTEMON Bottle Brush

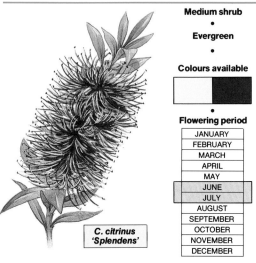

Medium shrub
•
Evergreen
•
Colours available

•
Flowering period

| JANUARY |
| FEBRUARY |
| MARCH |
| APRIL |
| MAY |
| JUNE |
| JULY |
| AUGUST |
| SEPTEMBER |
| OCTOBER |
| NOVEMBER |
| DECEMBER |

C. citrinus 'Splendens'

The Bottle Brush is generally thought of as a conservatory or house plant rather than as an outdoor shrub, but it can be grown against a sunny wall in many areas of the country. The secret is to choose one of the hardier species. The basic features of these Australian plants are long narrow leaves and a flower-head which looks like a bottle-brush. The individual blooms bear prominent stamens (the 'bristles') and are tightly packed along a cylindrical spike which is crowned by a short leafy shoot. Callistemon will grow quickly in a mild and sunny locality.

VARIETIES: The most popular choice is **C. citrinus 'Splendens'** — a 7 ft tall shrub which bears leaves which emit a distinct lemon aroma when crushed, and bright red bottle-brushes in summer. Not one for colder areas, however, as it is damaged when exposed to prolonged temperatures below −5°C. **C. rigidus** is a hardier species, with narrow stiff leaves and red flower-heads. Another reasonably hardy red Callistemon is **C. linearis** which bears long bottle-brushes with a distinct greenish tinge. There are cream-coloured species, including the Willow-like **C. salignus** and the hardiest of all — **C. sieberi**.

SITE & SOIL: Requires lime-free soil which is well-drained. Full sun is essential.

PRUNING: Not necessary — cut back dead and frost-damaged stems in spring.

PROPAGATION: Plant semi-ripe cuttings in a cold frame in summer.

Callistemon rigidus

CALLUNA Scotch Heather, Ling

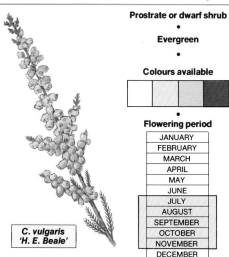

Prostrate or dwarf shrub

•

Evergreen

•

Colours available

•

Flowering period

| JANUARY |
| FEBRUARY |
| MARCH |
| APRIL |
| MAY |
| JUNE |
| JULY |
| AUGUST |
| SEPTEMBER |
| OCTOBER |
| NOVEMBER |
| DECEMBER |

C. vulgaris 'H. E. Beale'

Calluna is a popular choice as a ground cover for acid soil, growing 4 in.-2 ft high, depending on the variety, and blooming in summer or autumn. Many types have coloured foliage — golden, grey, bronze, red or purple, and some of the green-leaved ones change colour in autumn. It is easy to confuse Callunas with low-growing Ericas. There are differences — with most Callunas the showy part of the flower is the calyx and not the petals, no Calluna can tolerate lime and there are no winter- or spring-flowering varieties.

VARIETIES: There is only one species (**C. vulgaris**). A few of the more popular varieties are listed below, together with their height, flowering period and colour. **'Alba Plena'** (1½ ft, August–September, double white), **'Beoley Gold'** (1¼ ft, August–September, white, golden foliage), **'Blazeaway'** (1½ ft, August–September, lilac, red foliage in winter), **'Peter Sparkes'** (1¼ ft, September–October, double pink), **'Tib'** (1 ft, July–August, rose), **'H. E. Beale'** (1½ ft, September–October, double pink), **'Kinlochruel'** (1 ft, September–October, double pink) and **'Sunset'** (9 in., August–September, pink, variegated foliage).

SITE & SOIL: Well-drained, acid soil is necessary — full sun is preferred. Add peat at planting time.

PRUNING: Lightly clip over the plants in March to remove dead flowers — cut back straggly stems.

PROPAGATION: Layer shoots in spring or plant 1 in. cuttings in a cold frame in summer.

Calluna vulgaris 'Beoley Gold'

CALYCANTHUS Allspice

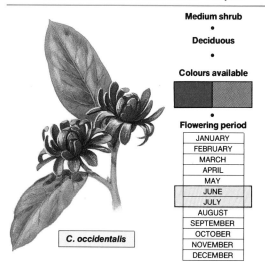

Medium shrub

•

Deciduous

•

Colours available

•

Flowering period

| JANUARY |
| FEBRUARY |
| MARCH |
| APRIL |
| MAY |
| JUNE |
| JULY |
| AUGUST |
| SEPTEMBER |
| OCTOBER |
| NOVEMBER |
| DECEMBER |

C. occidentalis

It is hard to explain why this American plant is a rarity. Allspice is easy to grow, it is hardier than many more popular shrubs and its flowers are eye-catching. Throughout summer the large many-petalled blooms are borne on the mature wood. The colour of the petals and sepals is brown or red, depending on the species. All parts of the plants are aromatic — flowers, leaves, roots and bark. Some dieback of the shoots may occur if the shrub is exposed to strong icy winds in winter.

VARIETIES: There are two basic types, separated by flower colour. The Calycanthus which bears 2 in. wide flowers with a mass of reddish-brown strap-like petals and sepals is the Carolina Allspice and is offered as **C. floridus**, **C. fertilis**, **C. glaucus** or **C. laevigatus**. There are subtle differences between them, but the same plant may be listed under any of these names. The variety **'Purpureus'** has leaves which are purplish below. The second type of Calycanthus is **C. occidentalis** (Californian Allspice) — it grows to about the same size (7 ft x 7 ft) but the leaves are larger and the flowers are deep red rather than reddish-brown. Either of these Allspice species is worth growing, if you can find one.

SITE & SOIL: Any free-draining garden soil will do. Thrives in sun or light shade.

PRUNING: Not necessary — cut back dead or damaged branches in spring.

PROPAGATION: Layer branches or plant semi-ripe cuttings in a cold frame in summer.

Calycanthus floridus

CAMELLIA Camellia

Medium or large shrub
•
Evergreen
•
Colours available

•
Flowering period

| JANUARY |
| FEBRUARY |
| MARCH |
| APRIL |
| MAY |
| JUNE |
| JULY |
| AUGUST |
| SEPTEMBER |
| OCTOBER |
| NOVEMBER |
| DECEMBER |

C. japonica
'Adolphe Audusson'

C. japonica
'Alba Simplex'

C. japonica
'Lady Clare'

C. williamsii
'Donation'

C. 'Leonard Messel'

C. williamsii
'J. C. Williams'

Some experts consider the Camellia to be the queen of flowering shrubs. Unlike the Rose it keeps its leaves all year round and needs no pruning — unlike the Rhododendron its popular varieties are in full flower when little else is in bloom in the garden. The foliage is oval and glossy — the showy blooms are 2–5 in. across, depending on the variety, and may be single, double, Anemone- or Paeony-shaped. Despite these virtues it is not yet a best seller, because it has not quite lived down its reputation for being rather tender. In fact it is as hardy as most shrubs, but the Camellia does have several pet hates. Firstly, it will not succeed in alkaline soil, although unlike the Rhododendron it is quite happy in neutral as well as acid surroundings. It also does not like being exposed to icy winds and early morning sun, as frost and quick thawing can damage early spring flower buds.

VARIETIES: There are hundreds of varieties from which to choose, and some of the more popular and interesting ones are listed below together with flower size, form and colour. The size of the shrub can vary from the 4 ft high **C. sinensis** (Tea Plant) to 15 ft giants, but the usual dimensions are about 6 ft x 6 ft. Most Camellias are varieties of **C. japonica**, blooming between February and early May. Here you will find **'Adolphe Audusson'** (4–5 in., semi-double, red), **'Alba Simplex'** (4–5 in., single, white), **'Apollo'** (3–4 in., semi-double, white-blotched red), **'Elegans'** (5 in. or more, Anemone-shaped, peach-pink), **'Grand Slam'** (5 in. or more, Anemone-shaped, deep red), **'Hawaii'** (3–5 in., Paeony-shaped, pale pink), **'Jupiter'** (3–4 in., semi-double, white-blotched red), **'Lady Clare'** (4–5 in., semi-double, deep pink) and **'Nobilissima'** (3–4 in., Paeony-shaped, yellow-tinged white). Striped and streaked blooms include **'Tricolor'** (3–4 in., semi-double, red-streaked white) and **'Contessa Lavinia Maggi'** (4–5 in., double, rose-striped white). The hybrids of **C. williamsii** are a step forward — the shrubs are hardier, taller, freer flowering from December to May and the dead blooms drop off naturally. Look for **'Donation'** (4–5 in., semi-double, pink), **'Anticipation'** (4–5 in., Paeony-shaped, pale red), **'J. C. Williams'** (3–4 in., single, pale pink) and **'Saint Ewe'** (3–4 in., single, rose pink). Small (2–3 in.) and fragrant blooms are produced in winter and early spring by the rather tender **C. sansaqua** — the variety **'Narumi-gata'** (white, edged pink) is the most reliable. Popular hybrids include **C. 'Leonard Messel'** (4–5 in., semi-double, bright pink) and **C. 'Cornish Snow'** (2–3 in., single, white).

SITE & SOIL: Avoid chalky soil — incorporate peat at planting time. Light shade is best, but will thrive in full sun if a mulch is applied each spring.

PRUNING: Not necessary — cut back weak, damaged and unwanted branches in May.

PROPAGATION: Layer shoots in autumn or plant semi-ripe cuttings in a cold frame in summer.

Camellia japonica 'Jupiter'

Camellia japonica 'Tricolor'

Camellia williamsii 'Anticipation'

CAMPSIS Trumpet Vine

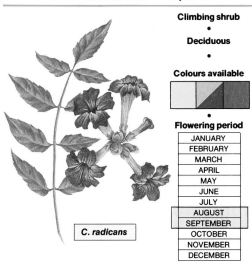

Climbing shrub
•
Deciduous
•
Colours available
•
Flowering period

| JANUARY |
| FEBRUARY |
| MARCH |
| APRIL |
| MAY |
| JUNE |
| JULY |
| AUGUST |
| SEPTEMBER |
| OCTOBER |
| NOVEMBER |
| DECEMBER |

C. radicans

Campsis is a vigorous climbing shrub which is grown for its brightly coloured, trumpet-like flowers which appear in terminal clusters in late summer. It needs shelter, support and as much sun as possible — a south-facing wall is ideal. Despite the eye-catching flowers it remains an unusual plant, as it is considered to be rather tender. However, the most popular variety (C. tagliabuana 'Madame Galen') is hardy — the problem with Campsis is that the floral display is disappointing and may even be absent if the summer is not warm and dry.

VARIETIES: The largest species is **C. grandiflora (C. chinensis).** The thin stems can grow more than 20 ft high, so a firm support is necessary. Each leaf is made up of seven or more leaflets and the red and gold blooms, each one 2–3 in. long, are borne in drooping clusters on current year shoots. The other species which is grown as a garden shrub is **C. radicans** — hardier, smaller and self-clinging with aerial roots like Ivy. Tie the stems to a support until the plant is well-established. The flower colour is red and gold — the variety **'Elava'** is yellow. **C. tagliabuana 'Madame Galen'** is a hybrid of the two species — its blooms are reddish-salmon.

SITE & SOIL: Plant in fertile soil in a sheltered spot. Full sun is essential.

PRUNING: In late winter cut back old stems which have flowered.

PROPAGATION: Layer shoots in early winter or plant semi-ripe cuttings in a cold frame in summer.

Campsis grandiflora

CARAGANA Pea Tree

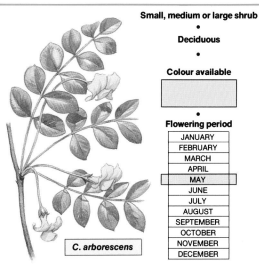

Small, medium or large shrub
•
Deciduous
•
Colour available
•
Flowering period

| JANUARY |
| FEBRUARY |
| MARCH |
| APRIL |
| MAY |
| JUNE |
| JULY |
| AUGUST |
| SEPTEMBER |
| OCTOBER |
| NOVEMBER |
| DECEMBER |

C. arborescens

There is little chance of finding this bushy or weeping plant at your local garden centre. It is classed as a rarity, and there are several reasons why a shrub may lack popular appeal. For some it is because of fussy requirements or lack of hardiness, but not so with Caragana. It comes from the wastes of Siberia and is one of the toughest of plants, growing in starved soil or windswept locations where little else could survive. The problem with Caragana is that the flowers are small and not particularly numerous, but it is a good choice as a specimen bush, tree or hedge for a difficult site.

VARIETIES: C. arborescens is the basic species — a 10–15 ft high fast-growing shrub which produces sweet-smelling small yellow flowers in clusters. The leaves are made up of about 12 leaflets, oval on the species but thread-like on the variety **'Lorbergii'**. This form is a graceful shrub with attractive grey-green foliage which turns bright yellow in autumn. There are two varieties which are top-grafted on to stems of C. arborescens to produce weeping specimens — there is the oval-leaved **'Pendula'** on 5 ft or 8 ft stems and the thread-leaved **'Walker'** on 3 ft stems.

SITE & SOIL: Any soil in sun or light shade.

PRUNING: Cut back one-third of the previous season's growth immediately after flowering.

PROPAGATION: Plant semi-ripe cuttings in a cold frame in summer.

Caragana arborescens

CARPENTERIA Tree Anemone

Medium shrub
•
Evergreen
•
Colour available

•
Flowering period

JANUARY
FEBRUARY
MARCH
APRIL
MAY
JUNE
JULY
AUGUST
SEPTEMBER
OCTOBER
NOVEMBER
DECEMBER

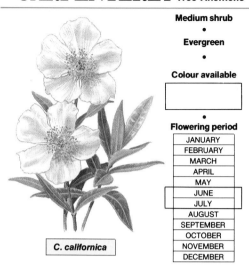

C. californica

You will not find this evergreen shrub in any of the popular collections offered for sale as it is a rather tender plant. It needs to be grown against a south- or west-facing wall for protection, and prolonged temperatures below -5°C will kill some of the shoots. Regrowth occurs, but flowers arise on old wood and that means you will have to wait a couple of years for the display to begin again. Don't let this frighten you off if you have a suitable site — it is a beautiful rounded bush studded with large and fragrant flowers in summer.

VARIETIES: There is only one species — **C. californica**. The bush grows to about 6 ft x 6 ft and is clothed with glossy lance-shaped leaves which are covered with fine white felt below. It is usual for some of these leaves to turn brown and fall in winter. In midsummer the clusters of pure white flowers appear, each one bearing a central boss of showy golden stamens. The variety **'Ladham's Variety'** is freer-flowering and its saucer-shaped blooms can measure 3 in. or more across. It is claimed that the rare variety **'Bodnant'** is hardier than any other Carpenteria. Nursery stock tends to be variable — where possible buy a container-grown Carpenteria when in flower.

SITE & SOIL: Full sun and some shelter are essential. Any reasonable garden soil will do if it drains freely.

PRUNING: Pruning is not necessary — remove unwanted or damaged branches in spring.

PROPAGATION: Layer shoots or plant semi-ripe cuttings in a cold frame in summer.

Carpenteria californica

CARYOPTERIS Blue Spiraea

Small shrub
•
Deciduous
•
Colours available

•
Flowering period

JANUARY
FEBRUARY
MARCH
APRIL
MAY
JUNE
JULY
AUGUST
SEPTEMBER
OCTOBER
NOVEMBER
DECEMBER

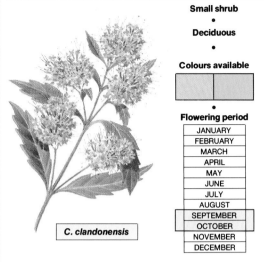

C. clandonensis

A small bush, growing no more than a few feet high, which is ideal for the front of a sunny border or as a low hedge. It flowers after most other shrubs have finished blooming and the attractive foliage is aromatic. Plant several in a group and enjoy the clusters of small, fluffy blue or violet-blue flowers. It will thrive in all sorts of soils including chalky ones and is reliable in all areas. It is not as sensitive to frosts as once thought, and even if some shoots are killed there is no problem — new stems appear in the spring.

VARIETIES: C. clandonensis is the popular Caryopteris — a hybrid raised many years ago by the late Secretary of the Royal Horticultural Society. It is a 3 ft x 3 ft rounded shrub with grey-green leaves and in late summer an attractive display of 4 in. long terminal clusters of pale blue or violet-blue flowers. There are several varieties. **'Arthur Simmonds'** is named after the raiser — it has blue flowers and a neat growth habit. **'Heavenly Blue'** and **'Kew Blue'** have flowers which are a rather darker blue than the basic type. It is not easy to tell these varieties apart, but you can recognise **'Worcester Gold'** — the young foliage is golden. **C. incana** (4 ft) has grey felted leaves.

SITE & SOIL: Any reasonable garden soil will do, provided it is well-drained. Full sun is necessary.

PRUNING: Cut the stems back to about 2 in. above ground level in March.

PROPAGATION: Plant semi-ripe cuttings in a cold frame in summer.

Caryopteris clandonensis 'Kew Blue'

CASSINIA Cassinia

Small shrub
•
Evergreen
•
Colour available

Flowering period

JANUARY
FEBRUARY
MARCH
APRIL
MAY
JUNE
JULY
AUGUST
SEPTEMBER
OCTOBER
NOVEMBER
DECEMBER

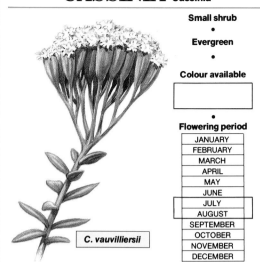

C. vauvilliersii

This Heather-like shrub only just qualifies for inclusion in this book on flowering shrubs. In midsummer large flower-heads of tiny blooms are produced, but it is grown for its foliage rather than for its uninteresting flowers. The leaves may be yellow, green or white depending on the variety, and its size (3–5 ft tall) makes it useful for adding height to a Heather bed. You will find it listed in a large number of catalogues but it is a rarity in gardens. It offers nothing special, but it is worth considering if you have acid soil and are keen on the Heather family.

VARIETIES: The only one which is widely available is **C. fulvida** (**Diplopappus chrysophyllus**). A mass of ½ in. long leaves cover the stems — this foliage is pale yellow in spring and darkens through the growing season to become dull orange in autumn. The plant is sticky at the beginning of the season and in summer the flower-heads appear at the tips of the upright stems. The individual blooms are tiny white Daisies. **C. vauvilliersii** is taller (4–5 ft) and its leaves are dark green. A rather dull plant — it is better to grow the variety **'Albida'** which has a mealy white coating over the stems and leaves.

SITE & SOIL: Well-drained acid soil is necessary and so is full sun. Add peat at planting time.

PRUNING: Cut back all straggly shoots and a few old stems in March.

PROPAGATION: Plant semi-ripe cuttings in a cold frame in summer.

Cassinia fulvida

CASSIOPE Cassiope

Prostrate shrub
•
Evergreen
•
Colour available

Flowering period

JANUARY
FEBRUARY
MARCH
APRIL
MAY
JUNE
JULY
AUGUST
SEPTEMBER
OCTOBER
NOVEMBER
DECEMBER

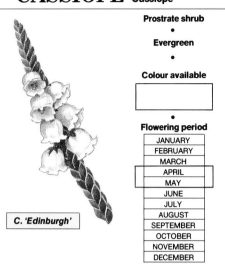

C. 'Edinburgh'

It is easy to see that this plant belongs to the Heather family, and it is easy to spot the difference from ordinary Heaths and Heathers. With Cassiope the leaves are scale-like and clasp the stem, giving a whipcord appearance. A number of different varieties are available from specialist nurseries, but you may find that Cassiope is not stocked by your garden centre. This evergreen is a good choice for a peat bed or rockery, but it demands the right conditions — a cool, moist, acidic and partly shady site. White bell-like blooms appear in late spring on the wiry stems — the buds are damaged by frost so choose a sheltered spot.

VARIETIES: The easiest one to grow is **C. lycopodioides**, a prostrate species which grows only 2–3 in. high but spreads to 1½ ft or more. The cord-like stems are clothed with tiny flowers, each one white with red sepals. Another easy one is the erect hybrid **C. 'Edinburgh'**, a free-flowering plant with dark green leaves and white flowers. **C. 'Muirhead'** has dark green leaves and grows about 9 in. high — **C. tetragona** grows to about the same height and its ¼ in. pendent white bells with their red sepals appear in spring.

SITE & SOIL: Humus-rich acid soil is essential — thrives in light shade.

PRUNING: Not necessary — cut back straggly shoots in early spring.

PROPAGATION: Plant semi-ripe cuttings in a cold frame in summer.

Cassiope tetragona

CEANOTHUS Californian Lilac

Deciduous Group

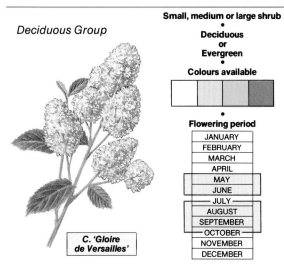

Small, medium or large shrub
•
Deciduous
or
Evergreen
•
Colours available

Flowering period

| JANUARY |
| FEBRUARY |
| MARCH |
| APRIL |
| MAY |
| JUNE |
| JULY |
| AUGUST |
| SEPTEMBER |
| OCTOBER |
| NOVEMBER |
| DECEMBER |

C. 'Gloire de Versailles'

Evergreen Group

C. 'Marie Simon'

C. 'Burkwoodii'

There are many species and varieties of Ceanothus, and together they make up one of the widest ranges of blue in the world of bushy plants. All require a sunny situation and some will fail in a cold, exposed spot, so choose the variety with care. In addition there are no general rules for pruning — as noted below the right method depends on the variety in question. There is a basic division into two groups. Most Ceanothus types belong to the Evergreen Group, and in general they are the less hardy ones which need the shelter of a warm wall. The general features include small, dark green and glossy leaves and tight thimble-like clusters of tiny flowers. Many are upright and may grow to 10 ft or more. The Deciduous Group are hardier and will grow in a sunny border in most areas of the country. The leaves are larger and the flower clusters are bigger and looser. Plant in spring rather than autumn, and choose another shrub if your soil is chalky and shallow.

VARIETIES: You will find a wide choice of *Evergreen Group* varieties in a large garden centre. Nearly all flower in May–June, but there are two exceptions — the popular **C. 'Autumnal Blue'** (soft blue, 8 ft, July–September) and **C. 'Burkwoodii'** (bright blue, 6 ft, July–September). Amongst the late spring-early summer varieties there is a range of sizes from the compact 2–3 ft high mounds of **C. thyrsiflorus 'Repens'** and **C. 'Blue Mound'** to the 15 ft arching stems of **C. 'Cascade'**. One of the hardiest evergreens is the dark blue **C. impressus 'Puget Blue'** — another one noted for its hardiness is the tall-growing **C. thyrsiflorus**. The giant of the group is the rather tender **C. arboreus**, which can reach 20 ft x 20 ft. The flowers are vivid deep blue. For something different you can grow the white-flowered **C. americanus**. The *Deciduous Group* bloom between mid July and mid October, and the average size is 6 ft x 6 ft. By far the most popular one is **C. 'Gloire de Versailles'** which bears large clusters of sky blue flowers. For a more compact growth habit and darker blue flowers choose **C.'Topaz'**. There are one or two pink varieties in the catalogues — look for **C. 'Marie Simon'** and **C. 'Perle Rose'**.

SITE & SOIL: Choose a well-drained site in full sun.

PRUNING: Evergreen Group: Little or no pruning is required. Cut back late-spring bloomers immediately after flowering where trimming is necessary — trim late-summer bloomers if required in April. Deciduous Group: Cut back flowered shoots in March to within 3 in. of the previous year's growth.

PROPAGATION: Plant semi-ripe cuttings in a cold frame in summer.

Ceanothus 'Autumnal Blue'

Ceanothus thyrsiflorus 'Repens'

Ceanothus 'Perle Rose'

CELASTRUS Bittersweet

Climbing shrub

•

Deciduous

•

Colours available

Fruiting period

JANUARY
FEBRUARY
MARCH
APRIL
MAY
JUNE
JULY
AUGUST
SEPTEMBER
OCTOBER
NOVEMBER
DECEMBER

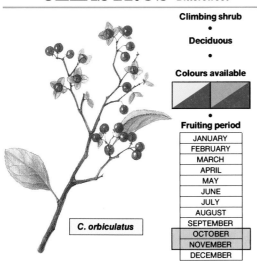

C. orbiculatus

Celastrus is a vigorous twiner which will grow anywhere. The favourite use is to cover old trees and unsightly hedges — it can be used to add colour to a tall conifer. During the spring and summer there is nothing special about this plant — it is an ordinary-looking climber bearing insignificant green flowers in July. In autumn it becomes a colourful shrub. The foliage turns bright yellow and the brownish seed capsules burst open to reveal the bright red seeds within.

VARIETIES: The one to buy is **C. orbiculatus** (**C. articulatus**). It is a strong climber which can grow 30 ft or more. The stems bear short spines and the small, rounded leaves are plentiful enough to provide dense cover. In autumn each seed capsule opens to display the yellow lining and scarlet seed — the capsules are plentiful and the winter display is striking. Grow the Hermaphrodite form to ensure that the female flowers are fertilised. Do not choose **C. scandens** — it is not as vigorous, the red seeds in their orange cases are not produced freely and you need to buy a pair of plants to make sure of fruit development.

SITE & SOIL: Any reasonable garden soil will do. Thrives in sun or partial shade.

PRUNING: Shorten stems in spring to keep the plants in check and to increase fruiting.

PROPAGATION: There are several methods. You can sow seed in autumn or spring, layer stems in early summer or plant semi-ripe cuttings in a cold frame in summer.

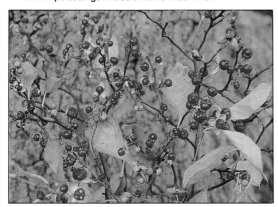

Celastrus orbiculatus

CERATOSTIGMA Hardy Plumbago

Dwarf or small shrub

•

Deciduous

•

Colours available

Flowering period

JANUARY
FEBRUARY
MARCH
APRIL
MAY
JUNE
JULY
AUGUST
SEPTEMBER
OCTOBER
NOVEMBER
DECEMBER

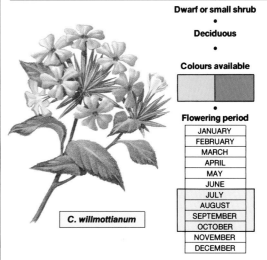

C. willmottianum

The Hardy Plumbagos are a small group of low-growing shrubs. Despite the common name, the three species of Ceratostigma shrubs which are offered for sale are not fully hardy. In a cold winter the stems may be killed by frost, but hard pruning in spring will ensure the appearance of new stems. Flowering begins in midsummer and continues intermittently until the first frosts arrive. These blooms are borne in clusters — each one bright blue and Phlox-like. The seed-heads are brown and the leaves take on attractive autumnal colours.

VARIETIES: The one to choose is **C. willmottianum** — it is the hardiest and the most readily available Ceratostigma. It produces a mass of rich blue flowers when conditions are right — a dry, sheltered and sunny spot is ideal. It grows about 2½ ft high — 3–4 ft when planted against a wall. The foliage turns reddish-orange in autumn. **C. griffithii** is offered by numerous nurseries which specialise in shrubs — it is more compact than C. willmottianum, bears broader foliage and is less hardy. On the credit side the flowers are a deeper blue and the autumn tints are often more conspicuous. The dwarf **C. minus** is rare and tender.

SITE & SOIL: Any soil with good drainage will do. Full sun and some wind protection are necessary.

PRUNING: Once the bush is established cut back the stems almost to ground level each April.

PROPAGATION: Plant semi-ripe cuttings in a cold frame in summer.

Ceratostigma willmottianum

CERCIS Cercis

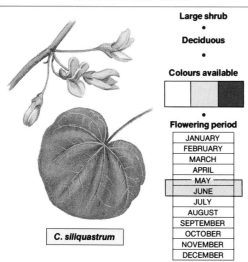

Large shrub

•

Deciduous

•

Colours available

•

Flowering period

| JANUARY |
| FEBRUARY |
| MARCH |
| APRIL |
| MAY |
| JUNE |
| JULY |
| AUGUST |
| SEPTEMBER |
| OCTOBER |
| NOVEMBER |
| DECEMBER |

C. siliquastrum

A tall and spreading shrub which after a number of years reaches tree-like proportions. The leaves are large and rounded with prominent veins — the Pea-like flowers are usually pink and are borne along the branches in late spring or early summer. There are several species but not one of them is truly at home in this country. It is not a plant for cold or clayey soils, but you can grow it with confidence in mild areas.

VARIETIES: The best-known Cercis is **C. siliquastrum**. It is the Judas Tree — legend has it that it is the tree on which Judas hanged himself. The leaves are kidney-shaped and in May the bare branches are wreathed in rosy-lilac blooms. In July the seed pods turn red and in autumn the foliage changes to yellow. Two varieties are available — **'Alba'** with white flowers and **'Bodnant'** with purple ones. The shrub grows to about 10 ft in 10 years. **C. canadensis** is the Redbud of N. America — a smaller shrub (6 ft x 6 ft) than the Judas Tree and not free-flowering in Britain. This lack of flowers is made up for by the reddish-purple foliage on the variety **'Forest Pansy'**. **C. chinensis** is a tender pink-flowering species.

SITE & SOIL: Any reasonable well-drained soil will do. Full sun is required.

PRUNING: Not necessary — unwanted branches on mature shrubs can be trimmed back in early spring.

PROPAGATION: Sow seed under glass in spring or layer shoots in autumn.

Cercis siliquastrum 'Bodnant'

CHAENOMELES Japonica

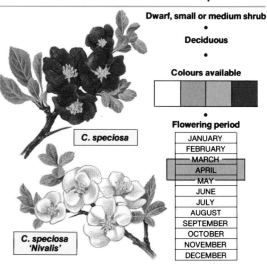

Dwarf, small or medium shrub

•

Deciduous

•

Colours available

•

Flowering period

C. speciosa

| JANUARY |
| FEBRUARY |
| MARCH |
| APRIL |
| MAY |
| JUNE |
| JULY |
| AUGUST |
| SEPTEMBER |
| OCTOBER |
| NOVEMBER |
| DECEMBER |

C. speciosa 'Nivalis'

An old favourite which you can find in gardens everywhere. The latest latin name is Chaenomeles, but it is better known as Japonica, Cydonia or Ornamental Quince. The reasons for its popularity are obvious — it thrives in all soils, it flourishes in both sun and shade and its bright spring flowers are followed by large golden fruits which are edible, but rather tasteless. Grow it as a bush which will reach 3–5 ft or plant it against a wall where it may climb to 8 ft or more.

VARIETIES: There are two main species. **C. speciosa** is branched and sometimes sparsely leaved, and is a good wall plant. Varieties to look for include **'Moerloosei'** (pale pink and white), **'Nivalis'** (large white, vigorous growth) and **'Simonii'** (semi-double red, low-growing). The second main species is **C. superba** with a range of varieties which are dense, rounded bushes for the border. A well-known one is **'Knap Hill Scarlet'** (orange-red flowers) — others include **'Crimson & Gold'** (red petals, golden anthers), **'Nicoline'** (large red, spreading growth habit) and **'Pink Lady'** (red buds, pink flowers). The dwarf is the creeping **C. japonica 'Alpina'** (orange flowers).

SITE & SOIL: Any garden soil will do. Thrives in full sun or shade.

PRUNING: Not necessary for bushes. Cut back some of the old branches of wall-trained plants in summer.

PROPAGATION: Plant semi-ripe cuttings in a cold frame in summer or plant rooted suckers in autumn.

Chaenomeles superba 'Knap Hill Scarlet'

CHIMONANTHUS Winter Sweet

- Medium shrub
- Deciduous

Colours available

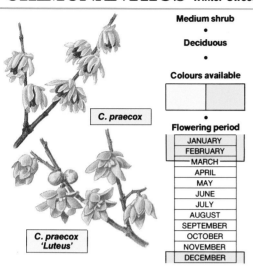

C. praecox

C. praecox 'Luteus'

Flowering period

JANUARY
FEBRUARY
MARCH
APRIL
MAY
JUNE
JULY
AUGUST
SEPTEMBER
OCTOBER
NOVEMBER
DECEMBER

The small flowers borne on the leafless stems of this Willow-like shrub are not particularly eye-catching, but they appear at a most welcome time — from December to March. Even more welcome is the strong spicy aroma, so plant Chimonanthus close to the house or driveway. It will succeed in the open garden provided the site is sheltered, but it is much better to grow it against a south- or west-facing wall. When grown as a free-standing bush it will reach about 6 ft — against a wall it may grow to 9 ft or more. Cut some branches for indoor decoration — that is all the pruning you will need. Be patient after planting — it may take several years before the first blooms appear.

VARIETIES: The best-known type is **C. praecox (C. fragrans)**. The waxy, hanging flowers are ivory or pale yellow, with claw-like petals and a purple stain at the centre. Both leaves and flowers are fragrant. The variety **'Grandiflorus'** is a showier plant as the flowers are deeper yellow and there is a prominent red stain in the throat of each bloom. Like the species it blooms for months, but is less fragrant. **'Luteus'** is different — the clear yellow flowers do not appear until February and do not have a central stain.

SITE & SOIL: Any reasonable soil will do, provided it is well-drained. Choose a sunny spot.

PRUNING: Not essential. Remove damaged or unwanted branches immediately after flowering.

PROPAGATION: Sow seed under glass in spring or layer shoots in summer. Striking cuttings is difficult.

Chimonanthus praecox

CHOISYA Mexican Orange Blossom

- Medium shrub
- Evergreen

Colour available

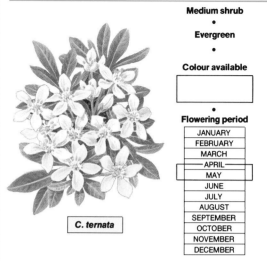

C. ternata

Flowering period

JANUARY
FEBRUARY
MARCH
APRIL
MAY
JUNE
JULY
AUGUST
SEPTEMBER
OCTOBER
NOVEMBER
DECEMBER

A shrub which is warmly recommended by all the experts. When not in flower it is a handsome rounded bush which is densely clothed with bright green and glossy foliage. Each evergreen leaf is made up of three leaflets. The main flush appears in May — flat heads of starry flowers with waxy petals and a strong Orange fragrance. A second smaller flush of flowers usually occurs in autumn, especially if the summer has been warm and dry. It is not a demanding plant — it will grow in acid or alkaline soil and does not mind some shade, but it is mildly sensitive to frost. In northern districts it is best to plant it against a wall.

VARIETIES: C. ternata is the only species you will find in the average garden centre. This shrub will reach 6 ft or more, but it can be kept in check by cutting back in early summer — new shoots are readily produced. Crushed leaves as well as the flowers are fragrant. The golden-leaved variety **'Sundance'** has become popular in recent years — smaller and a little more tender than the species. The species **C. arizonica** is rare and nothing special, but the modern hybrid **C. 'Aztec Pearl'** is definitely worth looking for. The pink-backed blooms are large and profuse.

SITE & SOIL: Any reasonable garden soil will do. Plant in full sun or light shade.

PRUNING: Not essential, but it is helpful to cut back some of the old wood each year immediately after flowering.

PROPAGATION: Plant semi-ripe cuttings in a cold frame in summer.

Choisya 'Aztec Pearl'

CISTUS Rock Rose, Sun Rose

Dwarf, small or medium shrub
•
Evergreen
•
Colours available

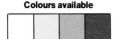

Flowering period

| JANUARY |
| FEBRUARY |
| MARCH |
| APRIL |
| MAY |
| JUNE |
| JULY |
| AUGUST |
| SEPTEMBER |
| OCTOBER |
| NOVEMBER |
| DECEMBER |

C. laurifolius

C. ladanifer

C. cyprius

C. purpureus

C. lusitanicus 'Decumbens'

C. 'Silver Pink'

The Rock Roses are a confusing group. The small ones which grow less than 1 ft high are varieties of Helianthemum — the taller ones which reach 2–6 ft when mature are types of Cistus. Included in this 'Cistus' group are a couple of closely-related Rock Roses, which are now classified as Halimium and its hybrid Halimiocistus. Cistus forms a rounded evergreen bush which is excellent for a mixed border or against a wall. The flowers are short-lived — the papery petals open in the morning and fall before nightfall. But new buds appear regularly during the flowering season, and the shrub is constantly in bloom during the summer months. The flowers measure 1–3 in. across and the base of each petal is often blotched with red or purple. This is not a plant for shade or heavy soil, although it thrives in other problem sites such as chalky soils, sands and seaside gardens. The great enemy is heavy frost — no variety is completely hardy. It is a good idea to take summer cuttings to replace winter casualties.

VARIETIES: The tallest species, which may reach 5–6 ft, tend to be the hardiest. Included here are **C. cyprius** (large white flowers with maroon-blotched centres), **C. laurifolius** (white flowers with yellow anthers) and **C. populifolius** (white flowers with yellow-blotched centres). Compact species with a good reputation for hardiness are **C. corbariensis** (2½ ft, red buds, small white flowers), **C. skanbergii** (2½ ft, pink flowers, grey-green leaves) and the most popular variety — **C. 'Silver Pink'** (2–3 ft, silvery-pink flowers). Another popular Cistus is **C. pulverulentus 'Sunset'** (2½ ft, deep pink flowers) which may continue to bloom until the end of September. **C. aiguilari 'Maculatus'** (3 ft, large white flowers with red-blotched centres) is widely available and so is the upright **C. 'Peggy Sammons'** (4 ft, pink flowers, grey-green leaves). The best low-growing, wide-spreading variety is **C. lusitanicus 'Decumbens'** (2 ft, white flowers with maroon-blotched centres). Unfortunately the most spectacular Rock Roses are often quite tender — examples are **C. purpureus** (4 ft, large rosy-crimson flowers with maroon-blotched centres) and **C. ladanifer** (6 ft, very large white flowers with red-blotched centres). No true Cistus is yellow — the yellow-flowering species are varieties of Halimium, such as **H. lasianthemum**. Its hybrid with Cistus is Halimiocistus — **H. 'Ingwersenii'** and **H. wintonensis** are pure white.

SITE & SOIL: Well-drained soil in full sun is essential. Protect from cold winds.

PRUNING: Not necessary — remove unwanted and frost-damaged stems in spring.

PROPAGATION: Sow seed in spring or plant semi-ripe cuttings in a cold frame in summer.

Cistus pulverulentus 'Sunset'

Cistus purpureus

Cistus ladanifer

CLEMATIS Virgin's Bower

Large-flowered Hybrid Group

C. 'Nelly Moser'

C. 'The President'

C. 'Ville de Lyon'

Climbing shrub
•
Deciduous, Semi-evergreen or Evergreen
•
Colours available

•
Flowering period

| JANUARY |
| FEBRUARY |
| MARCH |
| APRIL |
| MAY |
| JUNE |
| JULY |
| AUGUST |
| SEPTEMBER |
| OCTOBER |
| NOVEMBER |
| DECEMBER |

Species Group

C. montana

C. montana 'Rubens'

C. alpina

C. tangutica

No other climber can match the popularity of Clematis. Its only rival is the Climbing Rose, and as hardiness is not a problem for either of them you will see them both in gardens throughout the country. This does not mean that Clematis is an easy plant — to be successful you will have to learn something about the classification and needs of these beautiful but somewhat demanding climbers. There are two basic types. The Species group bloom in spring, have the smaller flowers and are the easier ones to grow. The Large-flowered Hybrids are showier and, depending on the variety, bloom between May and October. Basic cultural advice always includes the following points. Plant firmly in a spot where the soil around the roots will be shaded but the stems will be in the sun. Set the junction between stem and root about 1 in. below soil level and mulch the plants with compost every spring. Provide adequate support for the twining leaf stalks and water freely in dry weather. Keep watch for clematis wilt which can attack young plants. Affected stems suddenly die — cut out immediately to promote new growth. Follow the pruning instructions on the label. If in doubt, use the technique described below.

VARIETIES: The *Large-flowered Hybrid Group* includes the most popular types. Reaching about 10 ft high, the flat-faced blooms are 4–8 in. across and are followed by silky seed-heads. For the largest flowers choose from **C. 'Nelly Moser'** (pink-tinged white, striped red, May–June and August–September), **'Mrs Cholmondely'** (pale blue, May–August) and **'The President'** (purple, silver reverse, June–September). Other popular ones include **'Comtesse de Bouchard'** (pink, June–August), **'Jackmanii Superba'** (violet-purple, July–September), **'Vyvyan Pennell'** (violet-purple, May–July), **'Ville de Lyon'** (red, darker margin, July–October) and **'Lasurstern'** (deep lavender-blue, May–June and September). The *Species Group* are a large collection of smaller-flowered plants which may grow 30 ft or more. **C. montana** (May) with Almond-scented white flowers is the favourite one — **'Rubens'** is a pink variety with bronzy leaves. **C. macropetala** (May–June) bears semi-double nodding flowers — white, blue and pink varieties are available. **C. alpina** (April–May) is another species with pendent blooms. **C. tangutica** is unusual in every way — the yellow, bell-shaped flowers open in August and it needs hard pruning in March. Another late flowerer which needs hard pruning is the purple **C. viticella 'Etoile Violette'**.

SITE & SOIL: Quite fussy — the soil must be fertile. Sun is essential for stems but shade base with stones or a low-growing shrub.

PRUNING: Complicated. Some require only light pruning — spring-flowering ones immediately after blooming and summer-flowering ones in early spring. Varieties which flower in late summer or autumn need harder pruning — in early spring cut back to within a few inches of previous year's growth.

PROPAGATION: Plant semi-ripe cuttings in a propagator in summer.

Clematis 'Jackmanii Superba'

Clematis 'Ville de Lyon'

Clematis macropetala

CLERODENDRUM Glory Tree

Medium or large shrub

•

Deciduous

•

Colours available

•

Flowering period

JANUARY	
FEBRUARY	
MARCH	
APRIL	
MAY	
JUNE	
JULY	
AUGUST	
SEPTEMBER	
OCTOBER	
NOVEMBER	
DECEMBER	

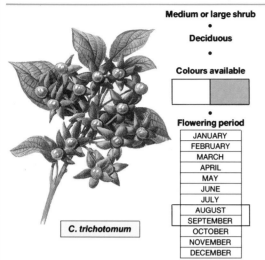

C. trichotomum

'Clerodendrum' or 'Clerodendron' — it depends which book or catalogue you read. Two species are sold for growing outdoors and are occasionally seen in gardens. Both form upright bushes which bear abundant flowers in late summer and early autumn. No other shrub has such a contrast in smells — the flowers have a pleasant fragrance but the leaves when bruised emit a horrible smell.

VARIETIES: C. trichotomum (Glory Tree) is the more popular species and is found in most of the shrub catalogues. It is not difficult to grow and it is hardy down to –10°C, but it is still not often grown despite its spectacular late show. The shrub slowly becomes tree-like and may reach 10 ft or more. The young foliage is purple, and in August the clusters of pinkish buds open into white, starry flowers. When the petals fall the red calyx remains and a turquoise blue berry forms at the centre. Grow the variety **'Fargesii'** which fruits freely. The other species of Clerodendrum is **C. bungei** which looks quite different. The 6 ft high bush suckers freely and can be invasive — in August snowball-like rosy-red flower-heads appear. A tender plant which is cut down by frost, but new shoots appear from the base in spring.

SITE & SOIL: Choose a sunny and sheltered spot. The soil should be well-drained.

PRUNING: Not necessary — cut back unwanted or frost-damaged branches in spring.

PROPAGATION: Sow seed in spring or remove rooted suckers from the parent shrub and plant in spring.

Clerodendrum trichotomum 'Fargesii'

CLETHRA Summersweet

Medium shrub

•

Deciduous

•

Colours available

•

Flowering period

JANUARY	
FEBRUARY	
MARCH	
APRIL	
MAY	
JUNE	
JULY	
AUGUST	
SEPTEMBER	
OCTOBER	
NOVEMBER	
DECEMBER	

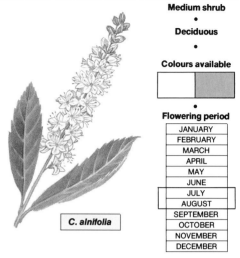

C. alnifolia

Clethra is a summer shrub which has never caught the public fancy. The problem may be that it is not a grow-anywhere plant — it calls for peaty soil without a trace of lime and it needs partial shade. This means that it is a good plant for the woodland garden but it is not for everyone. In July or August the small flowers appear, clustered together in a long terminal spike. These 'bottle-brush' flower-heads have a strong fragrance and the foliage is often attractively coloured in autumn.

VARIETIES: The most popular species is **C. alnifolia** (Sweet Pepper Bush). The white or creamy-white flowers appear in 5 in. long spikes for about a month. **'Paniculata'** is the variety to buy — superior to the species and able to reach a height of 6 ft or more. A pink-tinged variety (**'Rosea'**) with glossy leaves is available — choose **'Pink Spire'** if you want a deeper pink. **C. barbinervis** and **C. fargesii** are species noted for the bright colour of their autumn foliage. For the bigger garden there are two impressive species of Clethra which produce large flower spikes with a Lily-of-the-Valley fragrance, but choose with care — **C. delavayi** is hardy but **C. arborea** is quite tender.

SITE & SOIL: The soil must be acid — a moist situation in light shade is the ideal site.

PRUNING: Not necessary, but old weak branches can be cut back in early spring.

PROPAGATION: Plant semi-ripe cuttings in a cold frame in summer.

Clethra alnifolia 'Rosea'

COLUTEA Bladder Senna

- Medium shrub
- Deciduous

Colours available

Flowering period

| JANUARY |
| FEBRUARY |
| MARCH |
| APRIL |
| MAY |
| JUNE |
| JULY |
| AUGUST |
| SEPTEMBER |
| OCTOBER |
| NOVEMBER |
| DECEMBER |

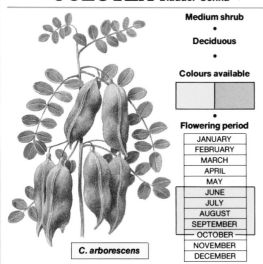

C. arborescens

In Victorian times the Bladder Senna was quite popular in the garden shrubbery and grew wild along railway embankments where it relished the smoky environment. Its time has now passed — this rounded bush is not often seen these days. The leaves are made up of numerous paired leaflets and the Pea-like flowers, though small, appear throughout the summer and autumn. A feature of this plant is the inflated seed pods which pop when pressed, but this is not a good idea as the seeds are poisonous. Stake when grown on an exposed site.

VARIETIES: C. arborescens is the most popular species and the only one you are likely to find at the garden centre. It is a much-branched vigorous shrub, soon reaching 8 ft or more if left unpruned. The flowers are yellow and the 2–3 in. long seed pods are pale brown. The foliage of C. arborescens is an attractive pale green — the other species of Colutea differ in both flower and leaf colour. It is worth searching for **C. media 'Copper Beauty'** — the flowers are pale copper and the foliage is greyish-green. Even harder to find is **C. orientalis** with coppery-red blooms and bluish-green leaves.

SITE & SOIL: Any reasonable garden soil will do. Best in full sun but will tolerate light shade.

PRUNING: Inclined to become leggy — cut back the shoots to half their length in March.

PROPAGATION: Sow seed in spring or plant semi-ripe cuttings in a cold frame in summer.

Colutea arborescens

CONVOLVULUS Shrubby Bindweed

- Dwarf shrub
- Evergreen

Colour available

Flowering period

| JANUARY |
| FEBRUARY |
| MARCH |
| APRIL |
| MAY |
| JUNE |
| JULY |
| AUGUST |
| SEPTEMBER |
| OCTOBER |
| NOVEMBER |
| DECEMBER |

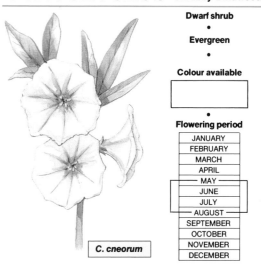

C. cneorum

Convolvulus is well-known to the gardener as a showy annual and a hard-to-kill weed — it is far less known as a low-growing shrub. The single species can be used in a variety of ways — it will provide ground cover at the front of the shrub border or add interest to the sunny part of a rock garden. It can also be grown in a container and the foliage is useful for flower arranging. The big problem is that Shrubby Bindweed is a rather tender plant and must be grown in a dry, sunny and sheltered spot. The best place is against a south-facing wall.

VARIETIES: C. cneorum is widely available although it is not often seen in gardens. The bush grows about 1½ ft high with a spread of 2½ ft and its 1 in. long leaves are covered with silky hairs. These hairs give the shrub a silvery appearance, and in May the pink buds begin to open into trumpet-shaped flowers. These blooms measure about 1½ in. across — white striped with pink on the reverse and with a face which is bluish-white, greenish-white or pure white. Flowering continues at intervals until August. The small (9 in.) blue-flowered **C. mauritanicus** is sometimes listed as a shrub, but it is really an herbaceous perennial.

SITE & SOIL: A well-drained sandy soil is required. Best in full sun.

PRUNING: Not essential — cut back weak and straggly branches in spring.

PROPAGATION: Plant semi-ripe cuttings in a cold frame in summer.

Convolvulus cneorum

CORNUS Flowering Dogwood

Prostrate, medium or large shrub
•
Deciduous
•
Colours available

Flowering period

| JANUARY |
| FEBRUARY |
| MARCH |
| APRIL |
| MAY |
| JUNE |
| JULY |
| AUGUST |
| SEPTEMBER |
| OCTOBER |
| NOVEMBER |
| DECEMBER |

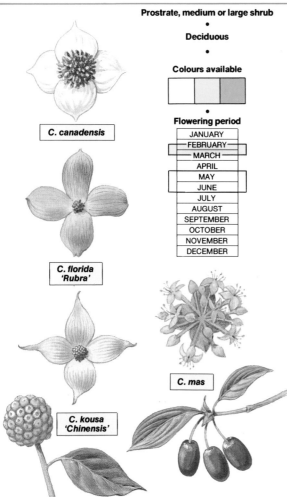

C. canadensis

C. florida 'Rubra'

C. kousa 'Chinensis'

C. mas

Dogwoods are available in a range of shapes and sizes, but they fall into just two basic groups. Firstly there are the Coloured Bark Dogwoods which produce a thicket of erect shoots. They bear small flowers and may have leaves which are variegated but the prime display comes from their coloured stems in winter — the red-stemmed C. alba, the yellow-stemmed C. stolonifera 'Flaviramea' and so on. These are the popular Dogwoods in Britain, but in the U.S it is the second group, the Flowering Dogwoods, which are commonly grown. This group contains a number of attractive shrubs which should be more widely planted. The flowers, often bold, appear in spring or early summer and are followed by fruits which are Strawberry- or Cherry-shaped. Some are tall with strongly architectural tree-like shapes and one is a low-growing ground cover. The leaves often adopt striking colours in autumn.

VARIETIES: The smallest Cornus is the Creeping Dogwood (**C. canadensis**) — a mat-like ground cover which grows about 8 in. high. The white summer flowers are followed by bright red fruits — the leaves turn deep red in autumn. At the other end of the scale from this sub-shrub is the 12 ft tree-like **C. controversa** — the Wedding Cake Tree. The wide-spreading branches are held in horizontal tiers, and above them in June are borne the white flower-heads which form round black fruits in autumn. A more compact type **'Variegata'** with white and green leaves is available. The basic feature of the Flowering Dogwoods is shown by **C. florida**. This species grows to 10 ft or more, and in May or June the flower-heads appear, each one made up of four prominent petal-like bracts. White is the basic colour, but there are variations — pale pink (**'Apple Blossom'**), rose-red (**'Rubra'**) etc. The fruits are Strawberry-like and the autumn leaves richly coloured. **C. kousa** is rather similar, but the bracts are pointed and it is less susceptible to frost damage. **'Chinensis'** is the favourite variety with larger flowers than the species and crimson leaves in autumn. Another tree-like Cornus with the classical four bract flower-head is **C. nuttallii** — the Pacific Dogwood. The white bracts turn pink with age, and it is a more difficult plant to grow than the popular ones. Now for something quite different. The Cornelian Cherry (**C. mas**) produces clusters of small yellow flowers in February, followed by red edible berries and colourful autumn foliage.

SITE & SOIL: Most reasonable soils will do, but C. florida, C. kousa and C. canadensis dislike chalk. Thrives in sun or light shade.

PRUNING: Not necessary — remove unwanted branches in spring.

PROPAGATION: Plant semi-ripe cuttings in a cold frame in summer.

Cornus florida 'Rubra'

Cornus kousa 'Chinensis'

Cornus mas

CORONILLA Coronilla

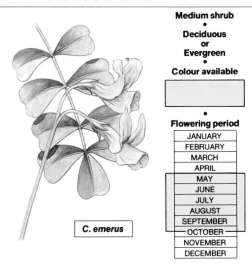

Medium shrub

•

**Deciduous
or
Evergreen**

•

Colour available

•

Flowering period

| JANUARY |
| FEBRUARY |
| MARCH |
| APRIL |
| **MAY** |
| **JUNE** |
| **JULY** |
| **AUGUST** |
| **SEPTEMBER** |
| OCTOBER |
| NOVEMBER |
| DECEMBER |

C. emerus

Coronilla has been grown as a garden plant in this country for over 200 years, but it has never become popular. The problem is that it is a plant of S. Europe and is not fully hardy, but it is reasonably reliable when grown against a sunny wall. If you live in the South or West it is usually worth trying if you like unusual plants. The great merit of Coronilla is that it starts to flower in early May and is in full bloom in late May and June. It then continues to flower at intervals until the frosts of October arrive — a long flowering record matched by very few other plants.

VARIETIES: The hardiest variety is the Scorpion Senna (**C. emerus**). This 8 ft high rounded bush bears dark yellow flowers in small clusters in the leaf axils along the stems. The seed pods are shaped like the end of a scorpion's tail — hence the common name. A less hardy but more widely-available Coronilla is **C. glauca**. This slender bush bears grey-green leaves made up of pairs of leaflets and scented yellow Pea-like flowers from spring to autumn. The variety **'Citrina'** has pale yellow flowers — the tender **'Variegata'** has cream-splashed leaves.

SITE & SOIL: Plant in light well-drained soil. Thrives best in full sun.

PRUNING: Not necessary — cut back damaged or unwanted branches in early spring.

PROPAGATION: Plant semi-ripe cuttings in a cold frame in summer.

Coronilla glauca 'Variegata'

CORYLOPSIS Winter Hazel

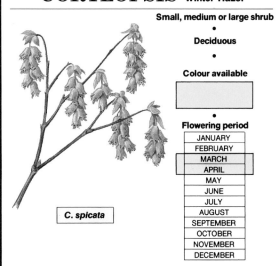

Small, medium or large shrub

•

Deciduous

•

Colour available

•

Flowering period

| JANUARY |
| FEBRUARY |
| **MARCH** |
| **APRIL** |
| MAY |
| JUNE |
| JULY |
| AUGUST |
| SEPTEMBER |
| OCTOBER |
| NOVEMBER |
| DECEMBER |

C. spicata

This shrub bears its yellow flowers in pendent tassels before the leaves appear. These flowers open in March just as the blooming period of Witch Hazel comes to an end, and it is therefore surprising that Corylopsis is so much less popular than its winter-flowering relative. The blooms of Corylopsis are cup-shaped and sweetly scented — the leaves are Hazel-like and often have attractive autumn tints. The problem may be that it is not a robust plant — the flowers may be damaged by frost and so it needs a sheltered site in light shade.

VARIETIES: C. pauciflora is one of the more popular varieties. It forms a small rounded bush about 4 ft high — the leaves are pink when young and the tassels bear only three flowers. **C. spicata** is a larger (6 ft) shrub with 6 in. long tassels of purple-anthered flowers. **C. glabrescens** is even bigger — a wide-spreading shrub which may reach 11 ft or more. The slender tassels are borne very freely. **C. veitchiana** is another large species and can be easily recognised by its red anthers. The best Corylopsis is **C. willmottiae 'Spring Purple'**. This 7 ft shrub bears dense tassels and has purple-coloured young leaves and stems.

SITE & SOIL: Any lime-free garden soil will do — thrives best in light shade. Avoid frost pockets.

PRUNING: Not necessary — remove unwanted or damaged branches after flowering.

PROPAGATION: Layer shoots or plant semi-ripe cuttings in a cold frame in summer.

Corylopsis veitchiana

CORYLUS Hazel

Medium or large shrub

•

Deciduous

•

C. avellana 'Contorta'

Colours available

C. maxima 'Purpurea'

Flowering period

JANUARY
FEBRUARY
MARCH
APRIL
MAY
JUNE
JULY
AUGUST
SEPTEMBER
OCTOBER
NOVEMBER
DECEMBER

The Hazel is usually thought of as a hedging or screening shrub which grows quickly and thrives under all sorts of conditions, but by choosing the right variety you can have a specimen plant which is eye-catching and colourful when in flower and in leaf. The catkins ('lambs' tails') dangle from the bare branches in February — each one made up of numerous tiny male flowers. Yellow is the usual colour, but there is a purple variety. Female flowers are bud-like and insignificant. The nuts are edible, provided the squirrels do not get to them first.

VARIETIES: Our native Hazel is **C. avellana** which grows about 12 ft high and bears large leaves which turn golden in autumn. The variety **'Aurea'** is a compact bush (6 ft x 6 ft) which has yellow leaves — an attractive shrub but the most popular variety of C. avellana is **'Contorta'**, known as the Corkscrew Hazel. The oddly twisted stems carry masses of showy catkins in late winter, but autumn nuts are absent. **C. maxima** (Filbert) is the species to grow for nuts. The catkins, stems and fruits are larger than those of the native Hazel. The variety **'Purpurea'** is a good choice — both leaves and catkins are purple.

SITE & SOIL: Any well-drained soil will do — thrives in sun or partial shade. Excellent for exposed sites.

PRUNING: Cut out old, exhausted branches in March. Can be coppiced (cut to ground level) every 5 years.

PROPAGATION: Layer shoots or remove rooted suckers from the parent bush and plant in autumn.

Corylus avellana 'Contorta'

COTINUS Smoke Bush

Medium or large shrub

•

Deciduous

•

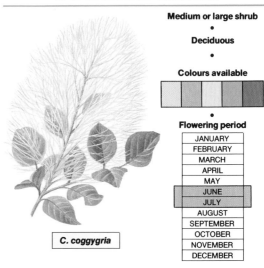

Colours available

C. coggygria

Flowering period

JANUARY
FEBRUARY
MARCH
APRIL
MAY
JUNE
JULY
AUGUST
SEPTEMBER
OCTOBER
NOVEMBER
DECEMBER

Cotinus is unmistakable when in flower. In June the 6 in. long intricately-branched flower-heads appear. When flowering is over the flower stalks remain — it is these feathery stalks which are the main attraction. With the basic species the wispy plumes are fawn at first but turn grey with age. This gives a smoke-like effect — hence the common name. Cotinus is perhaps best grown on its own as a large and showy specimen shrub, although it is frequently seen in mixed borders.

VARIETIES: **C. coggygria** is the modern name for the old favourite **Rhus cotinus**. It grows about 10 ft high if left unpruned, and the autumn leaves turn orange or red. For even brighter autumn tints choose the tree-like variety **'Flame'** for its orange foliage in October. There are a number of varieties with purplish leaves and/or plumes. **'Purpureus'** has purplish-grey plumes and green leaves — types with reddish-purple leaves include **'Velvet Cloak'**, **'Royal Purple'** and **'Foliis Purpureis'**. For purplish-tinted plumes and leaves choose **'Grace'** or **'Notcutt's Variety'**. Where space permits you can grow the pink-plumed **C. obovatus** (20–30 ft) with its red and purple leaves in autumn.

SITE & SOIL: Any reasonable soil will do, but sandy infertile land is best. Full sun is preferred.

PRUNING: Not necessary — cut out unwanted or damaged branches in spring.

PROPAGATION: Remove rooted suckers from the parent bush and plant in autumn.

Cotinus coggygria 'Notcutt's Variety'

COTONEASTER Cotoneaster

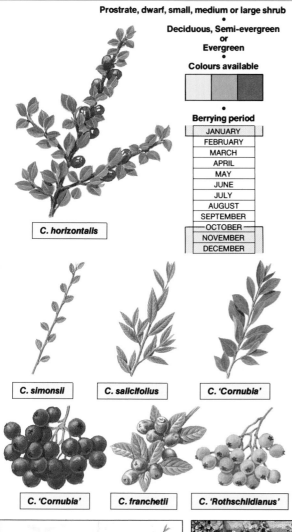

Prostrate, dwarf, small, medium or large shrub
•
Deciduous, Semi-evergreen
or
Evergreen

Colours available

•
Berrying period

| JANUARY |
| FEBRUARY |
| MARCH |
| APRIL |
| MAY |
| JUNE |
| JULY |
| AUGUST |
| SEPTEMBER |
| OCTOBER |
| NOVEMBER |
| DECEMBER |

C. horizontalis

C. simonsii

C. salicifolius

C. 'Cornubia'

C. 'Cornubia'

C. franchetii

C. 'Rothschildianus'

Cotoneaster is one of the most important and useful berrying shrubs in the garden. There is a large range of varieties in all sorts of shapes and sizes, but they all share a number of common features. The oval leaves are smooth-edged and borne on thornless branches, which makes it easy to distinguish this plant from its rival Pyracantha. In May or June pink buds open into small white flowers, which may be plentiful enough to be highly decorative. In autumn there is a display of showy berries which birds do not find particularly attractive and with some varieties there is a bold show of bright autumn colours. The feature which divides the various Cotoneasters is that some keep their leaves throughout the winter and others lose their foliage in autumn.

VARIETIES: In the *Evergreen & Semi-evergreen Group* there are several prostrate types. The popular **C. dammeri** belongs here as does the less widely grown **C. salicifolius 'Repens'**. These plants are used for ground cover or for growing at the front of the border, as are the dwarf spreading varieties such as **C. conspicuous 'Decorus'**, **C. 'Coral Beauty'** and the popular **C. microphyllus** which all grow 1½–3 ft high. There are two other excellent ground covers but they are not free-fruiting — **C. 'Gnom'** and **C. 'Skegholm'**. The favourite rock-garden evergreen Cotoneaster is **C. congestus** (3 in. x 1 ft). At the other end of the scale are the tall evergreens — look for **C. salicifolius** (15 ft, arching), **C. 'Hybridus Pendulus'** (6 ft, weeping), **C. lacteus** (10 ft, excellent for hedging) and the semi-evergreen **C. simonsii** which is widely used for hedging. The favourite amongst the *Deciduous Group* is the Fishbone Cotoneaster (**C. horizontalis**). It is frequently seen in gardens, hugging the bricks of the house or spreading as a low bush, 1–2 ft high, between taller shrubs. The branches have a distinct herring-bone pattern and both berries and autumn leaves are bright red. Another deciduous ground cover, **C. adpressus**, is even more prostrate. Taller types include **C. divaricatus** (6 ft x 6 ft) and **C. bullatus** which grows to a similar height and is recognised by its large, corrugated leaves. Cotoneaster berries are nearly always red and fairly small. For the largest berries choose the tall and semi-evergreen **C. 'Cornubia'**. As a change from red berries there are **C. 'Rothschildianus'** (yellow) and **C. franchetii** (orange).

SITE & SOIL: Any garden soil in full sun or partial shade.

PRUNING: Not necessary — remove unwanted or damaged branches in spring.

PROPAGATION: Plant semi-ripe cuttings in a cold frame in summer.

Cotoneaster 'Hybridus Pendulus'

Cotoneaster horizontalis

Cotoneaster 'Cornubia'

CRATAEGUS Hawthorn

Medium or large shrub
•
Deciduous
•
Colours available

C. monogyna

C. orientalis

Flowering period

| JANUARY |
| FEBRUARY |
| MARCH |
| APRIL |
| MAY |
| JUNE |
| JULY |
| AUGUST |
| SEPTEMBER |
| OCTOBER |
| NOVEMBER |
| DECEMBER |

Crataegus is a familiar sight in the garden as a small tree, large shrub or a hedge. Over the years it has acquired many common names — May, Quickthorn, Hawthorn etc. The general growth pattern needs little description. The thorny branches bear clusters of white, pink or red flowers in May or June and these are followed by red or orange berries in autumn. The leaves may turn orange or red at the end of the season. The great virtue of Crataegus is that once established it will grow almost anywhere — in dry or poorly-drained soil, in clean or polluted air and in coastal areas.

VARIETIES: Our native Crataegus is **C. monogyna** — the Quick or Common Hawthorn. Left unpruned it will develop into a 15 ft tree, bearing fragrant white flowers and red berries ('haws'). The only variety you are likely to find is the column-shaped **'Stricta'**. **C. oxyacantha** (**C. laevigata**) differs from the native species by having less deeply lobed leaves, fewer spines and a less vigorous growth habit. Most of the Hawthorns grown in our gardens are hybrids of this species. Popular examples include **'Paul's Scarlet'** (double red), **'Rosea Flore Pleno'** (double pink) and **'Plena'** (double white). For glossy leaves, long-lasting showy fruit and bright autumn foliage colour, choose **C. prunifolia**. **C. orientalis** bears yellow-tinged red fruit.

SITE & SOIL: Any garden soil will do in sun or partial shade.

PRUNING: Not necessary — trim hedges in summer.

PROPAGATION: Buy named variety from a garden centre.

Crataegus oxyacantha 'Rosea Flore Pleno'

CRINODENDRON Lantern Tree

Medium shrub
•
Evergreen
•
Colours available

C. hookerianum

Flowering period

| JANUARY |
| FEBRUARY |
| MARCH |
| APRIL |
| MAY |
| JUNE |
| JULY |
| AUGUST |
| SEPTEMBER |
| OCTOBER |
| NOVEMBER |
| DECEMBER |

This Chilean plant is available from many tree and shrub suppliers, and the description in the catalogue may prompt you to rush out and order one. The lantern-like blooms dangle on long stalks from the branches — like baubles from a Christmas Tree according to one lyrical nurseryman. These flowers are unusual in more ways than one. The buds form in autumn and swell when the growing season starts. They develop colour in early or late summer, depending on the species. Despite the novelty value of this charming plant, take care before you buy. It needs a mild and sheltered spot, and the soil must be acid, well-drained and moist.

VARIETIES: There are just two species. The more popular and somewhat hardier one is **C. hookerianum** (**Tricuspidaria lanceolata**). In good conditions the stiff and upright branches can grow 8 ft or more, and in late spring or early summer the flowers hang down like coral red lanterns. The 2 in. long leaves are dark green and lance-shaped. **C. patagua** (**Tricuspidaria dependens**) bears smaller flowers and these are bell-shaped. Unlike C. hookerianum the blooms do not open until late in the summer.

SITE & SOIL: Moist, lime-free soil is necessary — add peat at planting time. Thrives in light shade.

PRUNING: Not necessary — remove any dead or unwanted branches in spring.

PROPAGATION: Plant semi-ripe cuttings in a cold frame in summer.

Crinodendron hookerianum

CYTISUS Broom

Prostrate, dwarf, small, medium or large shrub
•
Deciduous
•
Colours available
•
Flowering period

JANUARY	
FEBRUARY	
MARCH	
APRIL	
MAY	
JUNE	
JULY	
AUGUST	
SEPTEMBER	
OCTOBER	
NOVEMBER	
DECEMBER	

Bushy Group

C. scoparius

C. 'Andreanus'

Dwarf Group

C. purpureus

C. kewensis

Tall Group

C. battandieri

C. albus

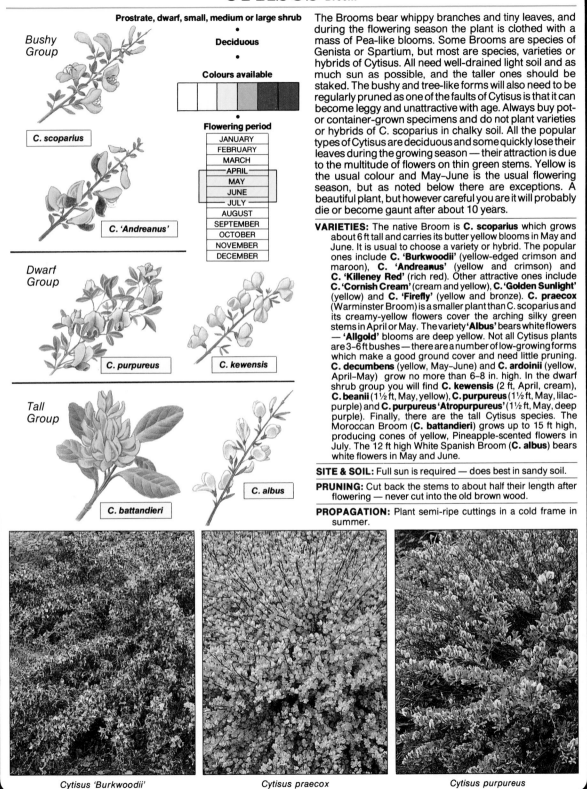

The Brooms bear whippy branches and tiny leaves, and during the flowering season the plant is clothed with a mass of Pea-like blooms. Some Brooms are species of Genista or Spartium, but most are species, varieties or hybrids of Cytisus. All need well-drained light soil and as much sun as possible, and the taller ones should be staked. The bushy and tree-like forms will also need to be regularly pruned as one of the faults of Cytisus is that it can become leggy and unattractive with age. Always buy pot- or container-grown specimens and do not plant varieties or hybrids of C. scoparius in chalky soil. All the popular types of Cytisus are deciduous and some quickly lose their leaves during the growing season — their attraction is due to the multitude of flowers on thin green stems. Yellow is the usual colour and May–June is the usual flowering season, but as noted below there are exceptions. A beautiful plant, but however careful you are it will probably die or become gaunt after about 10 years.

VARIETIES: The native Broom is **C. scoparius** which grows about 6 ft tall and carries its butter yellow blooms in May and June. It is usual to choose a variety or hybrid. The popular ones include **C. 'Burkwoodii'** (yellow-edged crimson and maroon), **C. 'Andreanus'** (yellow and crimson) and **C. 'Killeney Red'** (rich red). Other attractive ones include **C. 'Cornish Cream'** (cream and yellow), **C. 'Golden Sunlight'** (yellow) and **C. 'Firefly'** (yellow and bronze). **C. praecox** (Warminster Broom) is a smaller plant than C. scoparius and its creamy-yellow flowers cover the arching silky green stems in April or May. The variety **'Albus'** bears white flowers — **'Allgold'** blooms are deep yellow. Not all Cytisus plants are 3–6 ft bushes — there are a number of low-growing forms which make a good ground cover and need little pruning. **C. decumbens** (yellow, May–June) and **C. ardoinii** (yellow, April–May) grow no more than 6–8 in. high. In the dwarf shrub group you will find **C. kewensis** (2 ft, April, cream), **C. beanii** (1½ ft, May, yellow), **C. purpureus** (1½ ft, May, lilac-purple) and **C. purpureus 'Atropurpureus'** (1½ ft, May, deep purple). Finally, there are the tall Cytisus species. The Moroccan Broom (**C. battandieri**) grows up to 15 ft high, producing cones of yellow, Pineapple-scented flowers in July. The 12 ft high White Spanish Broom (**C. albus**) bears white flowers in May and June.

SITE & SOIL: Full sun is required — does best in sandy soil.

PRUNING: Cut back the stems to about half their length after flowering — never cut into the old brown wood.

PROPAGATION: Plant semi-ripe cuttings in a cold frame in summer.

Cytisus 'Burkwoodii'

Cytisus praecox

Cytisus purpureus

DABOECIA Irish Heath

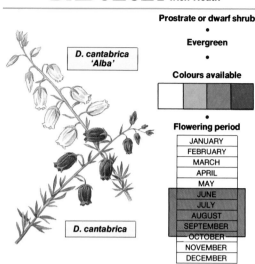

Prostrate or dwarf shrub
•
Evergreen
•
Colours available

•
Flowering period

JANUARY
FEBRUARY
MARCH
APRIL
MAY
JUNE
JULY
AUGUST
SEPTEMBER
OCTOBER
NOVEMBER
DECEMBER

D. cantabrica 'Alba'

D. cantabrica

Daboecia is another bushy plant in the Heath and Heather group which is dominated by the varieties of Calluna and Erica. It is hard to say why the Irish Heath has never become popular like its rivals — it is no more difficult to grow than Calluna and requires just the same conditions. D. cantabrica is certainly more eye-catching — the wiry stems bearing narrow ½ in. long leaves grow up to 1½ ft and are topped by numerous pendent bell-like flowers. These blooms are larger than ordinary Heather flowers, and the flowering period is remarkably extended. Perhaps the problem is that the blooms are not densely clustered and are not borne all round the flower stalks.

VARIETIES: The only species you are likely to find at your garden centre is **D. cantabrica**. The leaves are purplish-green (silvery below) and the flowers are pale purple. Varieties with other flower colours are available — there are many suppliers of **'Alba'** (white flowers), **'Atropurpurea'** (deep purple), **'Bicolor'** (white and purple) and **'Praegerae'** (deep pink). **D. scotica** is the only other species in the catalogues — look for the varieties **'Jack Drake'** (9 in., deep red) and **'William Buchanan'** (1½ ft, deep purple).

SITE & SOIL: Well-drained, acid soil is necessary — add peat at planting time. Grow in sun or light shade.

PRUNING: Trim plant lightly to remove faded flower-heads as soon as blooming has finished. Cut back straggly growths.

PROPAGATION: Plant 1–2 in. cuttings in a cold frame in summer.

Daboecia cantabrica 'Bicolor'

DAPHNE Daphne

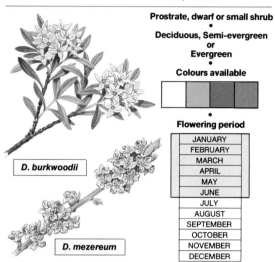

Prostrate, dwarf or small shrub
•
Deciduous, Semi-evergreen or Evergreen
•
Colours available

•
Flowering period

JANUARY
FEBRUARY
MARCH
APRIL
MAY
JUNE
JULY
AUGUST
SEPTEMBER
OCTOBER
NOVEMBER
DECEMBER

D. burkwoodii

D. mezereum

One of the most popular February-flowering shrubs is Daphne mezereum, but it is not typical of the whole genus. Some species are prostrate ground covers — others do not flower until May or June. The features that all the popular ones share are an abundance of fragrant starry flowers which are followed by poisonous berries.

VARIETIES: The deciduous **D. mezereum** (Mezereon) is sold everywhere — stiff, upright 3 ft stems are clothed with purplish-red flowers in February-March. **'Alba'** is a white variety. Another winter-flowering Daphne is **D. bholua** (5 ft x 3 ft) which bears purplish-rose flowers in January–February and black berries later in the year. **D. odora 'Aureomarginata'** (4 ft x 5 ft) is a colourful evergreen bush with cream-edged leaves and purplish-rose blooms in February–March. The popular May–June flowering Daphne for the shrub border is **D. burkwoodii** (3 ft, pale pink blooms in clusters, semi-evergreen). For the rock garden there are the popular **D. cneorum** (6 in., pink blooms in April–May, evergreen) and **D. retusa** (1½ ft, purplish-rose blooms in May, evergreen). **D. tangutica** is another evergreen, growing 2 ft high with March–April flowers.

SITE & SOIL: Well-drained, humus-rich soil is required. Thrives in sun or light shade.

PRUNING: Not required — hard pruning should be avoided. Remove damaged wood immediately after flowering.

PROPAGATION: Difficult. Plant semi-ripe cuttings in a cold frame in summer.

Daphne retusa

DECAISNEA Blue Bean

Large shrub
•
Deciduous
•
Colour available

D. fargesii

Fruiting period

JANUARY
FEBRUARY
MARCH
APRIL
MAY
JUNE
JULY
AUGUST
SEPTEMBER
OCTOBER
NOVEMBER
DECEMBER

This is a tall shrub which is interesting rather than attractive. It earns its place in many catalogues because of a single unique feature — in late autumn, metallic blue pods hang from the branches, and these sausage-shaped fruits may be 1 ft or even longer if the summer has been hot and dry. Obviously Decaisnea is a shrub for the collector of the unusual rather than for the gardener who wants popular and pretty plants. It is hardy, but it is best grown against a wall as the stems may be damaged by late spring frosts.

VARIETY: D. fargesii is the only species which is available — it has been cultivated for over 100 years but has never become widely grown. The stems are stout and upright, slightly arching and covered with a bluish bloom. The plant grows 10–12 ft high and the 2 ft long leaves are made up of a series of paired leaflets which have a bluish tinge in spring. In May the 1½ ft long flowering clusters hang down from the branches. Each of the yellowish-green bell-shaped flowers produces a sausage-like pod, and these grow to 4–15 in. long depending on the conditions. You will need patience — new plants take several years to reach the bean-bearing stage.

SITE & SOIL: Moist and well-drained soil is required. Thrives best in light shade.

PRUNING: Remove old and damaged stems in spring after the danger of frost has passed.

PROPAGATION: Sow seed under glass in late summer.

Decaisnea fargesii

DESFONTAINIA Desfontainia

Medium shrub
•
Evergreen
•
Colours available

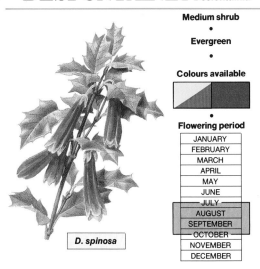

D. spinosa

Flowering period

JANUARY
FEBRUARY
MARCH
APRIL
MAY
JUNE
JULY
AUGUST
SEPTEMBER
OCTOBER
NOVEMBER
DECEMBER

Desfontainia is not often seen in gardens as it is a difficult shrub to grow unless the conditions are right. It certainly is not a grow-anywhere plant and has none of the robust constitution of Holly which it resembles. The ideal home for this shrub from China is a reasonably mild region of the country with a partially shaded wall to protect it from icy winds. The soil must be neutral or acid and it should be fertile. The reward is a splendid display of bright flowers and attractive leaves.

VARIETIES: There is just one species — **D. spinosa**. It is a dense bush which is covered with small, glossy Holly-like leaves. Desfontainia is slow-growing, and it takes many years to reach its mature height of 6–10 ft. In summer the flowers appear — showy 1½ in. long red trumpets with yellow mouths. This floral display will continue until October provided the soil is kept moist — this calls for applying a mulch in late spring and water during dry weather in summer. Several specialist tree and shrub suppliers offer the variety **'Harold Comber'**. The flowers are rather larger than the species and are all-red.

SITE & SOIL: Requires well-drained, lime-free soil which is rich in humus. Thrives best in partial shade.

PRUNING: Not necessary — remove dead and unwanted branches in spring.

PROPAGATION: Plant semi-ripe cuttings in a cold frame in summer or sow seed in a warm greenhouse in spring.

Desfontainia spinosa

DEUTZIA Deutzia

Small or medium shrub

•

Deciduous

•

Colours available

Flowering period

| JANUARY |
| FEBRUARY |
| MARCH |
| APRIL |
| MAY |
| JUNE |
| JULY |
| AUGUST |
| SEPTEMBER |
| OCTOBER |
| NOVEMBER |
| DECEMBER |

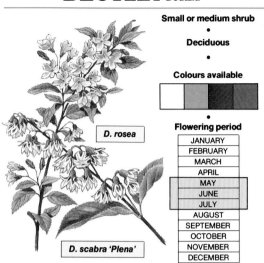

D. rosea

D. scabra 'Plena'

Deutzia is a good plant for the smaller garden as the usual height is 3–5 ft. Unfortunately it is often crowded in with other shrubs, but if given sufficient room the whole plant will be covered with small blooms in summer. These flowers are open bells in white, pink, red or pale purple and may be single or double. It is an easy plant which will grow in any reasonable soil as long as the roots are not allowed to become dry in summer. The only problem is that late frosts can damage the buds of May-flowering varieties.

VARIETIES: The earliest Deutzia is **D. rosea** (3 ft) which produces clusters of pink blooms on arching branches in May. The variety **'Carminea'** bears carmine-red blooms. The popular species **D. scabra** is taller (6 ft) and bears its large clusters of white blooms later (June–July). Varieties with double blooms include **'Plena'** and **'Candidissima'**. Another tall Deutzia is **D. magnifica** which bears masses of double white flowers. For a small rounded bush 3 ft high grow the deep pink **D. elegantissima 'Rosalind'** — for the largest flowers grow one of the 6 ft hybrids, such as **D. 'Magicien'** (white-edged pink) or **D. 'Mont Rose'** (carmine-blotched pink).

SITE & SOIL: Not fussy — any well-drained soil will do. Thrives best in light shade.

PRUNING: After flowering, cut back shoots which have bloomed. Remove old, unproductive wood.

PROPAGATION: Plant hardwood cuttings in the open in late autumn.

Deutzia scabra

DIPELTA Dipelta

Medium or large shrub

•

Deciduous

•

Colours available

Flowering period

| JANUARY |
| FEBRUARY |
| MARCH |
| APRIL |
| MAY |
| JUNE |
| JULY |
| AUGUST |
| SEPTEMBER |
| OCTOBER |
| NOVEMBER |
| DECEMBER |

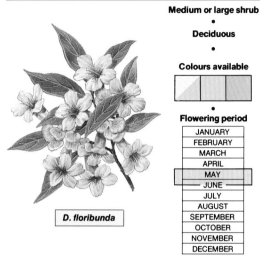

D. floribunda

This attractive spring- or early summer-flowering plant can easily be mistaken for a large Weigela. Both bear long, pointed leaves and the trumpet-shaped blooms are borne in small clusters which cover the whole bush. It is hardy and just as easy to grow as Weigela, but there are millions of gardens with the ever-popular relative and yet hardly a catalogue or garden centre which contains Dipelta. The reason is that Dipelta is notoriously difficult to propagate and is therefore generally avoided by nurserymen.

VARIETIES: All species are rarities, but you will find **D. floribunda** in a few of the specialist catalogues. It is an upright shrub which grows to about 10 ft in time, and has no fussy requirements. The yellow-throated blooms appear in great profusion, either singly or in small clusters. The fruits are pinkish-green flat discs — a feature which separates this plant from Weigela. The leaves turn an attractive golden colour in autumn. There are two other species. **D. yunnanensis** (7 ft) has arching stems and creamy-pink flowers with orange throats. Like D. floribunda it has attractive peeling bark. **D. ventricosa** bears lilac-pink flowers with orange throats.

SITE & SOIL: Any reasonably fertile soil will do — thrives best in light shade.

PRUNING: Prune back the shoots which have flowered and cut back unwanted branches in late June.

PROPAGATION: Difficult. Plant hardwood cuttings in a sheltered spot in the open in autumn.

Dipelta floribunda

DORYCNIUM Canary Clover

- Dwarf shrub
- Semi-evergreen
- Colour available
- Flowering period

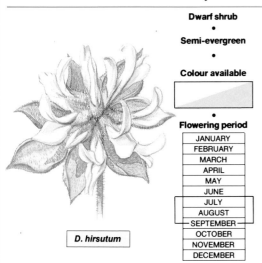

D. hirsutum

| JANUARY |
| FEBRUARY |
| MARCH |
| APRIL |
| MAY |
| JUNE |
| JULY |
| AUGUST |
| SEPTEMBER |
| OCTOBER |
| NOVEMBER |
| DECEMBER |

A low-growing silvery shrub from the Canary Islands — hence the common name. It is widely available, and is worth considering if you have light land and a site in full sun. It is a plant which is not often seen, but it makes an excellent contribution to a grey or white garden. Dorycnium is a semi-evergreen with leaves which over-winter on the spreading stems in mild districts, but it is best treated as a sub-shrub. This calls for cutting back the previous year's stems to the woody base each spring. The crop of new stems which arise will bear Clover-like flowers in summer and early autumn.

VARIETY: There is just one garden species — **D. hirsutum**, which is sometimes listed as **Lotus hirsutum**. It grows about 2 ft high and spreads 3 ft or more. The foliage is attractive — the closely-packed leaflets are greyish-green and covered with silvery hairs. At the top of the erect stems the flower clusters appear from late June or early July. Each bloom is white with a distinct pink tinge — it is a plant of quiet charm rather than eye-catching beauty. As each flower fades it is replaced by a reddish-brown seed pod. Never feed Dorycnium — it blooms best under starvation conditions.

SITE & SOIL: Requires well-drained soil which is not heavy. Full sun is essential.

PRUNING: Cut back all old shoots to the base of the plant in early spring.

PROPAGATION: Sow seed in autumn or plant semi-ripe cuttings in a cold frame in summer.

Dorycnium hirsutum

ELSHOLTZIA Mint Bush

- Small or medium shrub
- Deciduous
- Colours available
- Flowering period

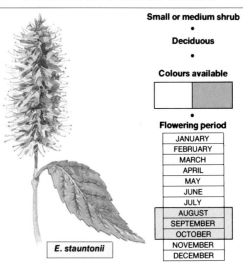

E. stauntonii

| JANUARY |
| FEBRUARY |
| MARCH |
| APRIL |
| MAY |
| JUNE |
| JULY |
| AUGUST |
| SEPTEMBER |
| OCTOBER |
| NOVEMBER |
| DECEMBER |

Crush one of the lance-shaped leaves of this shrub and the strong minty aroma reveals the origin of its common name. Although it is quite different in flower form and foliage shape from its partner on this page, these two genera have several features in common. Both are rarely seen in gardens, both bloom late in the year, and both are pruned down to ground level in late winter or early spring. The similarities stop there. Elsholtzia needs fertile soil and its flower-heads are large and showy.

VARIETIES: E. stauntonii is the only one you are likely to find in the catalogues. It is an upright bush, growing about 4 or 5 ft high with a spread of about 2 ft. The 6 in. long leaves are dark green and toothed — in autumn this foliage turns yellow, orange or red. In August the 8 in. high flower-heads (panicles) appear — upright and colourful. Each one bears numerous pink or purplish flowers and the display lasts until autumn — a valuable long-lasting splash of colour for the shrub border at the end of the growing season. The white variety **'Alba'** is a rarity — so is the white-flowered species **E. fruticosa** which grows about 6 ft high.

SITE & SOIL: Well-drained and fertile soil is necessary — full sun is essential.

PRUNING: Cut back all old shoots to ground level in late winter or early spring.

PROPAGATION: Plant softwood or semi-ripe cuttings in a cold frame in summer.

Elsholtzia stauntonii

EMBOTHRIUM Chilean Fire Bush

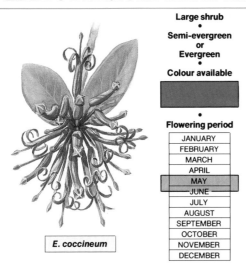

Large shrub
•
Semi-evergreen
or
Evergreen
•
Colour available

•
Flowering period

| JANUARY |
| FEBRUARY |
| MARCH |
| APRIL |
| MAY |
| JUNE |
| JULY |
| AUGUST |
| SEPTEMBER |
| OCTOBER |
| NOVEMBER |
| DECEMBER |

E. coccineum

You may never have heard of this tall-growing shrub, but if you like plants with bright and exotic-looking blooms then it is certainly worth getting to know. In late spring or early summer the unusual flowers appear in 4 in. clusters which may be so numerous that the bush appears to be on fire. Each bloom is a very narrow tube from which the style protrudes. Don't rush out and buy one unless you can give it the conditions it needs — Embothrium is a very fussy plant. The soil must be deep, moist, humus-rich and lime-free. As with Clematis the roots need to be shaded and the protection of a wall is helpful if the site is exposed. It is happiest in a woodland garden.

VARIETIES: The basic species is **E. coccineum** — an upright slender shrub which may reach 15 ft or more when mature. The leaves are oblong and glossy — the flowers are bright orange-scarlet. Under good growing conditions this plant suckers freely, and these suckers can be used for propagation — see below. There are two varieties — **'Longifolium'** with strap-shaped leaves is an evergreen and is hardier than the species, and **'Lanceolata'** with bright scarlet flowers.

SITE & SOIL: Requires well-drained, acid soil — thrives best in light shade.

PRUNING: Not necessary. Avoid removing branches unless cutting back is essential.

PROPAGATION: Layer shoots or remove rooted suckers from the parent bush and plant in autumn.

Embothrium coccineum 'Lanceolata'

ENKIANTHUS Pagoda Bush

Autumn leaves

Spring flowers

E. campanulatus

Medium or large shrub
•
Deciduous
•
Colours available

•
Flowering period

| JANUARY |
| FEBRUARY |
| MARCH |
| APRIL |
| MAY |
| JUNE |
| JULY |
| AUGUST |
| SEPTEMBER |
| OCTOBER |
| NOVEMBER |
| DECEMBER |

It is a pity that many gardeners blessed with an area of acid soil turn straight away to Rhododendrons, Azaleas and Heathers, and forget this beauty. It will grow anywhere that produces a satisfactory Rhododendron display, and the brilliant yellows and flaming reds of the autumn foliage are not outshone by any other shrub. In late spring an impressive display of long-lasting pendent flowers appears — bell-shaped or urn-like depending on the species. An easy plant, but do mulch every spring.

VARIETIES: The usual Enkianthus is **E. campanulatus**. It grows about 6 ft high with the upper branches arranged in tiers. The drooping bell-shaped flowers are sulphur yellow with red veins and edges. **'Albiflorus'** is a creamy-white variety. **E. cernuus 'Rubens'** is another colourful Enkianthus — the flowers are deep red and the leaves turn reddish-purple in autumn. The giant of the group is **E. chinensis** — a handsome bush or small tree which can reach 15 ft or more. It bears red-stalked leaves and bell-shaped dark-veined flowers in red and yellow. Much more compact is **E. perulatus** (5 ft) — a neat shrub noted for its white urn-shaped flowers and brilliant foliage colours in autumn.

SITE & SOIL: Lime-free, moist soil is essential. Thrives best in light shade.

PRUNING: Not required — remove dead or unwanted branches immediately after flowering.

PROPAGATION: Plant semi-ripe cuttings in a cold frame in summer.

Enkianthus perulatus

ERICA Heath, Heather

Prostrate, dwarf, small or medium shrub

•

Evergreen

•

Colours available

•

Flowering period

JANUARY
FEBRUARY
MARCH
APRIL
MAY
JUNE
JULY
AUGUST
SEPTEMBER
OCTOBER
NOVEMBER
DECEMBER

Lime-hating Group

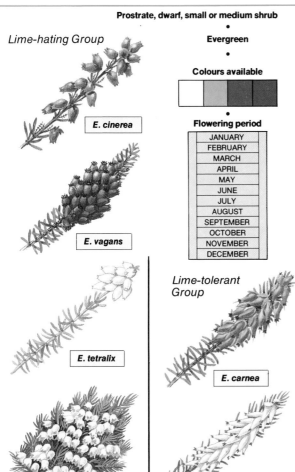

E. cinerea

E. vagans

E. tetralix

E. arborea

Lime-tolerant Group

E. carnea

E. darleyensis

Erica has the typical Heather form — wiry stems, narrow leaves and bell-like flowers, but there is a surprisingly wide range of shapes, sizes, colours and cultural needs. The typical Erica is a compact plant which grows about 9 in. high and is widely used for ground cover, but there are tiny ones for the rockery as well as a 6 ft giant for the shrub border. Flower colours range from pure white to near black, and there are both lime-hating and lime-tolerant species. There is no standard flowering period — by choosing carefully you can have a Heather bed in bloom all year round. The basic rules are to plant firmly and each year to mulch around the plants with peat in late spring.

VARIETIES: Be guided by the soil type and the final expected height of the plant. If your land is not acid, then you must choose from one of the four species listed below. **E. carnea** (Winter Heather) is by far the most important one. It is a spreading plant about 9 in. high, and is in flower between January and April. The variety list is enormous — favourite ones include **'Aurea'** (golden leaves, pink flowers), **'Foxhollow'** (golden leaves, pale pink flowers), **'King George'** (rose-pink flowers), **'Pink Spangles'** (rose-red flowers), **'Springwood White'** (white flowers) and **'Vivellii'** (bronze leaves, deep red flowers). **E. darleyensis** (November-April) is a 2 ft high lime-tolerant species — popular varieties include **'Arthur Johnson'** (rose-pink), **'Darley Dale'** (pink) and **'Molten Silver'** (white). The two tall lime-tolerant ones are **E. mediterranea** (Irish Heath — 3 ft, white or pink, March-May) and **E. terminalis** (Corsican Heath — 4 ft, pink, July-September). The most popular lime-hating Erica is **E. cinerea** (Bell Heather) and its host of varieties. It grows 9 in.–1 ft high and is in flower between July and September. Favourite ones include **'Alba Minor'** (6 in. dwarf, white flowers), **'C. D. Eason'** (deep pink flowers), **'Golden Drop'** (golden leaves, occasional pink flowers), **'P. S. Patrick'** (purple flowers) and **'Velvet Knight'** (blackish-purple flowers). **E. tetralix** is the Cross-leaved Heath, growing about 9 in. high with silvery-grey foliage and white or pink flowers in June-October. **E. ciliaris** (Dorset Heath, July-October) grows about 1 ft high, **E. vagans** (Cornish Heath, July-October) reaches 2 ft and the lime-hating 6 ft giant is **E. arborea** (Tree Heath, April).

SITE & SOIL: Well-drained soil is necessary — thrives best in full sun. Add peat at planting time.

PRUNING: Trim plants lightly as soon as the blooms have faded. Prune back straggly shoots but do not cut into old wood.

PROPAGATION: Layer shoots or plant 1–2 in. cuttings in a cold frame in summer.

Erica carnea 'Springwood White'

Erica tetralix 'Pink Star'

Erica vagans 'Holden Pink'

ESCALLONIA Escallonia

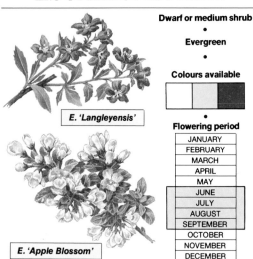

E. 'Langleyensis'

Dwarf or medium shrub
•
Evergreen
•
Colours available
•
Flowering period

| JANUARY |
| FEBRUARY |
| MARCH |
| APRIL |
| MAY |
| JUNE |
| JULY |
| AUGUST |
| SEPTEMBER |
| OCTOBER |
| NOVEMBER |
| DECEMBER |

E. 'Apple Blossom'

Escallonia is a popular shrub — a common sight in coastal areas. Upright at first and then arching downwards, the stems are clothed with small, shiny leaves. The small, bell-shaped flowers cover the bush in June and then appear intermittently until early autumn. The average height is 6–8 ft and it is not fussy about soil type — Escallonia tolerates chalky soil, dry conditions and salt-laden air.

VARIETIES: E. macrantha is the large and vigorous Escallonia widely used for seaside hedging — it has aromatic leaves and deep rose flowers. Another excellent hedging variety is **E. rubra 'Crimson Spire'** (red flowers). The usual choice is a named hybrid and there are many to choose from. The most popular one is **E. 'Apple Blossom'** — a slow-growing bush with white and pink flowers. Other favourites include **E. 'C. F. Ball'** (red flowers, vigorous), **'Donard Radiance'** (large rose-red flowers, vigorous), **'Donard Seedling'** (pink buds, white flowers), **'Iveyi'** (white flowers in large clusters, autumn-blooming) and **E. 'Langleyensis'** (rose-pink flowers). There is a dwarf variety — **E. rubra 'Woodside'** (red flowers) grows only 1½ ft high.

SITE & SOIL: Any reasonable garden soil in sun or partial shade. In the North plant against a wall.

PRUNING: In autumn cut back about a third of the wood from shoots which have flowered. Trim hedges at the same time.

PROPAGATION: Plant semi-ripe cuttings in a cold frame in summer.

Escallonia 'Donard Seedling'

EUCRYPHIA Brush Bush

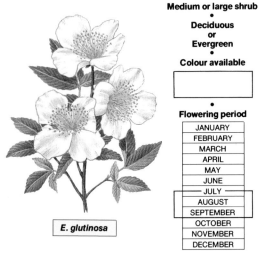

E. glutinosa

Medium or large shrub
•
**Deciduous
or
Evergreen**
•
Colour available
•
Flowering period

| JANUARY |
| FEBRUARY |
| MARCH |
| APRIL |
| MAY |
| JUNE |
| JULY |
| AUGUST |
| SEPTEMBER |
| OCTOBER |
| NOVEMBER |
| DECEMBER |

One of the showiest specimen shrubs available, but not often seen in gardens. There are a couple of problems. The most popular ones are large shrubs which become tree-like in time, and so shortage of space rules it out for many gardeners. The other problem is that it is not easy to grow, requiring shelter and a fertile, well-drained site. Begin with a container-grown specimen and plant it close to a wall to protect it from strong winds. Grow ground cover plants around the base of the newly-planted shrub. Your reward will be a stunning display of large white blooms.

VARIETIES: The most popular Eucryphia is **E. nymansensis 'Nymansay'**. This plant was raised at Nymans Gardens, Sussex, and it is a beauty — a dense 10 ft high conical shrub clothed with leathery evergreen leaves and in late summer a mass of 2½ in. wide pure white flowers. **E. milliganii** is a widely-available evergreen species which bears small cup-shaped blooms in July. Another early bloomer is **E. lucida** with pendent fragrant flowers. The slender **E. intermedia 'Rostrevor'** (8 ft) is smaller than most varieties and **E. glutinosa** is a 15 ft deciduous shrub with abundant flowers in August and orange-red leaves in autumn.

SITE & SOIL: Requires deep, lime-free soil in light shade. Not suitable for exposed northern sites.

PRUNING: Not necessary — remove dead and damaged shoots in April.

PROPAGATION: Plant semi-ripe cuttings in a cold frame in summer. Layer shoots of E. glutinosa.

Eucryphia nymansensis 'Nymansay'

EUONYMUS Spindleberry

Large shrub
•
Deciduous
•
Colours available

•
Fruiting period

| JANUARY |
| FEBRUARY |
| MARCH |
| APRIL |
| MAY |
| JUNE |
| JULY |
| AUGUST |
| SEPTEMBER |
| OCTOBER |
| NOVEMBER |
| DECEMBER |

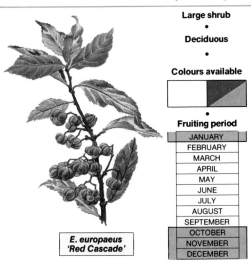

E. europaeus 'Red Cascade'

The popular Euonymus is the variegated evergreen shrub which is so widely used for ground cover — E. fortunei radicans 'Silver Queen', 'Emerald 'n' Gold' etc. They are colourful but flowerless and so outside the scope of this book. We are concerned here with the tall-growing deciduous Spindleberries which bear colourful autumn foliage and fruits which split to reveal the seeds within. The yellow-green flowers in spring are insignificant. Grow several if possible to ensure cross-pollination.

VARIETIES: The Common Spindle (**E. europaeus**) will grow to a height and spread of 12 ft, its oval leaves turning pink or red in autumn. The ¾ in. lobed fruits split open to reveal the orange seeds within. For even brighter colours choose the variety **'Red Cascade'** — a more compact plant with branches weighed down by the fruit. Much more difficult to find is the white variety **'Albus'**. E. europaeus and its varieties may be colourful but they are troublesome — the fruits are poisonous and the branches are hosts to both aphids and caterpillars. For a relatively pest-free Spindleberry grow **E. planipes (E. sachalinensis)**.

SITE & SOIL: Any reasonable garden soil will do — thrives best in light shade.

PRUNING: Little or no pruning is required, but you can cut the stems back in late spring.

PROPAGATION: Layer shoots or plant semi-ripe cuttings in a cold frame in summer.

Euonymus europaeus

EXOCHORDA Pearl Bush

Small, medium or large shrub
•
Deciduous
•
Colour available

•
Flowering period

| JANUARY |
| FEBRUARY |
| MARCH |
| APRIL |
| MAY |
| JUNE |
| JULY |
| AUGUST |
| SEPTEMBER |
| OCTOBER |
| NOVEMBER |
| DECEMBER |

E. racemosa

Exochorda illustrates that there may be other factors than floral beauty to consider when choosing a shrub for the garden. This plant is a beautiful bush when in bloom — its long arched branches are clothed with spikes of papery white flowers, each one 1–2 in. across and looking like an oversized Pear blossom. But there is a drawback — the flowering period lasts for only 7–10 days. Exochorda generally needs plenty of space and dislikes shallow chalky soils.

VARIETIES: For the largest flowers choose **E. giraldii 'Wilsonii'**. This is a large, arching bush which grows about 9 ft high. It is free-flowering and an impressive sight when in full bloom in late spring. **E. racemosa** is a spreading rather than an arching shrub and may reach 12 ft or more. It is easier to find than E. giraldii 'Wilsonii', but the most widely available Exochorda is now the compact **E. macrantha 'The Bride'**. This shrub forms a weeping mound 3–6 ft high and is the freest-flowering of all. It is a good choice — the display may be short-lived but the mass of white flowers covering the dark green leaves makes it stand out in any shrub border. The largest Exochorda is the rare **E. korolkowii** (15 ft).

SITE & SOIL: Any free-draining garden soil will do — thrives best in full sun.

PRUNING: Immediately after flowering cut back shoots bearing faded blooms. Remove weak branches.

PROPAGATION: Plant softwood cuttings in a propagator in summer or dig up and plant rooted suckers.

Exochorda macrantha 'The Bride'

FABIANA Fabiana

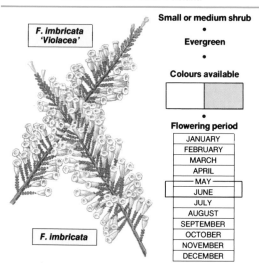

F. imbricata 'Violacea'

F. imbricata

- Small or medium shrub
- Evergreen

Colours available

- **Flowering period**

JANUARY
FEBRUARY
MARCH
APRIL
MAY
JUNE
JULY
AUGUST
SEPTEMBER
OCTOBER
NOVEMBER
DECEMBER

This unusual shrub looks very like one of the taller Ericas known as Tree Heaths. The thin branches bear small needle-like leaves and the plant dislikes chalky soil. In late May or June the stems are clothed with small blooms, but the similarity between Fabiana and Erica ends there. On close inspection the Fabiana petals are fused to form an open-mouthed tube and not a bell, and this plant belongs to the Potato and not to the large Heather family. A good choice if you like rarities.

VARIETIES: There is just one species — **F. imbricata**. It is a slow-growing spreading bush which after about 10 years reaches 6 ft if conditions are suitable. The white flowers in late spring or early summer give the branches a plume-like look, and are numerous enough to make each branch look like a flower-head. For the small garden or large rockery the variety **'Prostrata'** is a better choice. It forms a 3 ft high mound and is rather hardier than the species. The white blooms are tinged with mauve. There is just one other variety — **'Violacea'** which grows to about 6 ft and bears lavender-coloured flowers. You won't find Fabiana in the average garden centre but it is in numerous catalogues.

SITE & SOIL: Well-drained neutral or acid soil is required — choose a sheltered spot. Full sun is necessary.

PRUNING: Not necessary — cut back unwanted branches in July after flowering.

PROPAGATION: Plant softwood cuttings in a propagator in summer.

Fabiana imbricata

FATSIA Fatsia

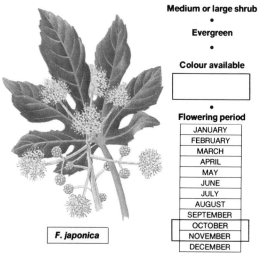

F. japonica

- Medium or large shrub
- Evergreen

Colour available

- **Flowering period**

JANUARY
FEBRUARY
MARCH
APRIL
MAY
JUNE
JULY
AUGUST
SEPTEMBER
OCTOBER
NOVEMBER
DECEMBER

Fatsia is a plant for shady sites — the north-facing wall, the enclosed town garden etc. It is also recommended for seaside situations — its great advantage is that it will quickly clothe a sunless spot with large and glossy leaves all year round and bear candelabra-like flower-heads of globular groups of tiny flowers in autumn. It is a plant you will find in all the indoor gardening books and the house plant sections of garden centres, but it is not in all the shrub guides. So a word of caution — buy a plant which is being sold as an outdoor shrub and not as a house plant. Specimens grown under glass need a lengthy hardening-off period before being able to withstand winter conditions.

VARIETIES: There is just one species — **F. japonica**. Aralia, Fig-leaf Palm and the Castor Oil Plant are some of its common names, and it is quite unmistakable. The huge leaves (1 ft or more across) have 7–9 finger-like lobes and the plant can reach 10 ft x 10 ft when mature. Against a wall it can grow even higher. The flowers are silvery-green in bud and creamy-white when open — these tiny blooms are followed by black berries. The variety **'Variegata'** has white-edged leaf lobes — it is not frost-hardy.

SITE & SOIL: Any reasonable garden soil will do — thrives best in a partially shaded and sheltered site.

PRUNING: Not necessary — cut back in spring only if the plant is getting too large.

PROPAGATION: Plant semi-ripe cuttings in a cold frame in summer. Alternatively sow seed in spring.

Fatsia japonica 'Variegata'

FORSYTHIA Golden Bell Bush

Small, medium or large shrub

•

Deciduous

•

Colours available

•

Flowering period

JANUARY
FEBRUARY
MARCH
APRIL
MAY
JUNE
JULY
AUGUST
SEPTEMBER
OCTOBER
NOVEMBER
DECEMBER

F. suspensa

F. intermedia 'Spectabilis'

F. 'Beatrix Farrand'

F. intermedia 'Lynwood'

F. ovata 'Tetragold'

Forsythia is one of the heralds of spring. In March and April masses of yellow flowers on leafless branches appear in gardens throughout the country. A few purists find the brightness of the colour too much, but for the rest of us this shrub is a great favourite. It will grow almost anywhere and is fully hardy. The leaves are oval and toothed — the blooms are widely-flared shallow bells in colours ranging from palest yellow to amber. There are Forsythias to clothe walls, to cover bare ground, to serve as screens or hedges and to stand alone as specimen bushes. This shrub has just two enemies. There are the birds which strip off the flower buds (thread black cotton between branches if necessary) and there are the gardeners who shorten all the branches each summer 'to keep the bush tidy'. The result is lots of growth and very few flowers next year.

VARIETIES: F. intermedia (Border Forsythia) is a vigorous bushy species which grows 8–10 ft high. It is very popular, but it is one of the varieties and not the basic species which is generally chosen. **'Spectabilis'** is the old favourite with narrow and twisted golden-yellow petals, but **'Lynwood'** with broad petals is regarded as a better choice. **'Spring Glory'** is noted for its free-flowering habit, **'Karl Sax'** for its strong growth habit, deep canary yellow flowers and purple leaves in autumn, and **'Arnold Giant'** for the large size of its pendent blooms. **F. giraldiana** is one of the first to bloom — pale yellow flowers on arching branches in late February. Not all species grow as upright or spreading bushes — some are rambling weak-stemmed plants. **F. suspensa** has stems which in time reach 12 ft or more in length, and can be left to trail over the ground or may be trained against a vertical support. The variety **'Nymans'** has reddish-purple stems — the branches of **'Atrocaulis'** are almost black. There are several Forsythias which deserve to be better known. **F. ovata 'Tetragold'** bears its amber flowers in late February and **F. viridissima 'Bronxensis'** will still be in bloom in May. **F. 'Robusta'** is a vigorous 10 ft shrub with early blooms and **F. 'Tremonia'** is easily recognised by its Parsley-like foliage. **F. 'Beatrix Farrand'** has large 2 in. wide flowers and the dwarf **F. 'Arnold Dwarf'** (3 ft) spreads widely but is not free-flowering.

SITE & SOIL: Any reasonable garden soil will do. Best in full sun, but will grow in partial shade.

PRUNING: Avoid excessive pruning. Cut out about one-third of the oldest branches which have flowered. Do this as soon as the blooms have faded.

PROPAGATION: Layer shoots or plant hardwood cuttings in the open in autumn.

Forsythia intermedia 'Spectabilis'

Forsythia suspensa

Forsythia 'Beatrix Farrand'

FOTHERGILLA Witch Alder

F. gardenii

Small or medium shrub
•
Deciduous
•
Colour available

•
Flowering period

Flowering period
JANUARY
FEBRUARY
MARCH
APRIL
MAY
JUNE
JULY
AUGUST
SEPTEMBER
OCTOBER
NOVEMBER
DECEMBER

F. major

Fothergilla is classed as a flowering shrub because it produces bottle-brush flower-heads in spring before the leaves appear. All blossom is welcome in April, but these fluffy white balls are interesting rather than beautiful. Each blossom is made up of a cluster of white stamens — there are no petals. Its need for peaty, moist soil makes this slow-growing shrub a good choice for a woodland setting, although the shape of the shrub and the large Hazel-like foliage are nothing special. Fothergilla comes into its own in autumn when the leaves provide a brilliant display of yellow, orange and red.

VARIETIES: The small one is **F. gardenii** (Dwarf Fothergilla). It is an upright bush, reaching 3 ft x 3 ft when fully grown. The autumn foliage colours are bright but the flower-heads are small and growth is not robust. **F. major** (Large Fothergilla) is a better choice — the floral bottle brushes are larger and the shrub grows about 6 ft high. In autumn there is a brilliant display of yellow, gold and deep orange. Nurserymen differ over how to treat the Alabama Fothergilla (**F. monticola**). It is virtually identical to F. major, but the autumn foliage is predominantly red. Some suppliers believe there is no difference between the two.

SITE & SOIL: Acid, moist soil is necessary — thrives in sun or partial shade.

PRUNING: Not necessary — cut back dead or unwanted stems in winter.

PROPAGATION: Layer stems in autumn.

Fothergilla monticola

FREMONTODENDRON Flannel Flower

F. californicum

Large shrub
•
Semi-evergreen
or
Evergreen
•
Colour available

•
Flowering period

Flowering period
JANUARY
FEBRUARY
MARCH
APRIL
MAY
JUNE
JULY
AUGUST
SEPTEMBER
OCTOBER
NOVEMBER
DECEMBER

The experts cannot agree whether this American shrub is hardy or not. A few say that it is sensitive to frost and that it will only withstand a milder-than-average winter, but others say that once established it can withstand a severe frost. It does seem to be hardy, but needs the protection from wind which a south-facing wall provides. Nobody argues about its charm — it is a showy shrub which bears large yellow flowers from late spring to mid autumn. It grows quickly, bearing leathery lobed leaves on its down-covered stems — hence the common name. A word of warning — this down can be extremely irritating.

VARIETIES: F. californicum (sometimes listed as **Fremontia californicum**) is the most popular species — the leaves bear three lobes and the yellow flowers appear freely. These blooms have no petals — there is a large saucer-like calyx. It will reach 12 ft or more in time. Even more popular is the hybrid **F. 'California Glory'** — an upright shrub which grows 15 ft high and bears a mass of yellow flowers which measure more than 2 in. across. The rare **F. mexicanum** is different — the leaves have five lobes and the flowers are star-shaped rather than saucer-like.

SITE & SOIL: Any well-drained soil will do, including chalk. Thrives best in full sun.

PRUNING: Not necessary — cut back dead or unwanted stems in spring.

PROPAGATION: Plant softwood cuttings in a propagator in spring.

Fremontodendron 'California Glory'

FUCHSIA Fuchsia

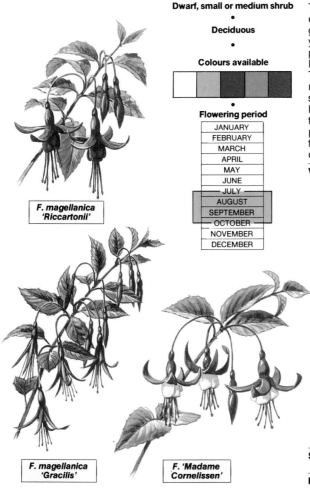

Dwarf, small or medium shrub

•

Deciduous

•

Colours available

•

Flowering period

| JANUARY |
| FEBRUARY |
| MARCH |
| APRIL |
| MAY |
| JUNE |
| JULY |
| AUGUST |
| SEPTEMBER |
| OCTOBER |
| NOVEMBER |
| DECEMBER |

*F. magellanica
'Riccartonii'*

*F. magellanica
'Gracilis'*

*F. 'Madame
Cornelissen'*

There are a number of varieties and hybrids which are classed as 'hardy' as they can be relied upon to produce graceful arching branches and pendent bell-like flowers year after year. In the mildest areas the woody stems are permanent and may grow 6 ft high. A Fuchsia hedge is a lovely thing, but in many areas the stems are killed by frost. This is not a serious problem — if you have chosen a type recommended for outdoor use then new shoots will sprout from the base in the following spring. The stem and leaf colours range from pale green to purplish-green and the general flower pattern is a skirt of four sepals with the petals and stamens hanging below. Add organic matter to the soil and plant rather deeply. Cover the crown with sand or peat in winter.

VARIETIES: **F. magellanica** is the most popular species. The flowers are slender with red sepals and purple petals. It is usual to grow a variety rather than the species, and there are several from which to choose. **'Riccartonii'** is an old favourite with a good reputation for hardiness, **'Gracilis'** has small and narrow blooms, **'Alba'** has mauve-tinged white flowers, **'Variegata'** has leaves with creamy-yellow edges and there is the colourful **'Versicolor'** (**'Tricolor'**) with scarlet-violet flowers and grey-green leaves which are tinted pink at first and then splashed creamy-white later. Apart from F. magellanica and its varieties there is a host of hybrids. Some of them are offered outdoors in the spring at the garden centre or are listed in the catalogues in the 'Shrub' section — choose one of the following. **F. 'Alice Hoffman'** (scarlet sepals, white petals, purple-tinged leaves, compact and widely available), **F. 'Blue Gown'** (double flower — scarlet sepals, purple petals, compact), **F. 'Chillerton Beauty'** (rose-tinted white sepals, mauve petals), **F. 'Doctor Foster'** (very large flower — scarlet sepals, violet petals), **F. 'Lady Thumb'** (semi-double flower — pink sepals, white petals, 1½ ft high dwarf), **F. 'Madame Cornelissen'** (large flower — red sepals, white petals), **F. 'Margaret'** (semi-double flower — crimson sepals, purple petals, free-flowering), **F. 'Mrs Popple'** (large flower — scarlet sepals, violet petals, one of the hardiest and widely available), **F. 'Prosperity'** (double flower — pink sepals, pink veined white petals) and finally **F. 'Tom Thumb'** (pale red sepals, violet petals, 1½ ft high dwarf).

SITE & SOIL: Any ordinary well-drained soil, provided it is water-retentive and well-fed. Full sun or light shade.

PRUNING: Cut back stems to 1 in. above the ground in April.

PROPAGATION: Plant softwood cuttings in a cold frame in early summer.

Fuchsia magellanica 'Alba'

Fuchsia 'Alice Hoffman'

Fuchsia 'Mrs Popple'

GARRYA Silk Tassel Bush

Medium or large shrub
•
Evergreen
•
Colour available

Flowering period

JANUARY	
FEBRUARY	
MARCH	
APRIL	
MAY	
JUNE	
JULY	
AUGUST	
SEPTEMBER	
OCTOBER	
NOVEMBER	
DECEMBER	

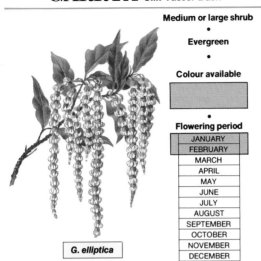

G. elliptica

Garrya is grown for winter interest. It is a rounded evergreen bush with oval leathery leaves which are glossy green above and woolly grey below. Male plants are the ones which are grown, and in January and February long and slender catkins appear. Female plants are generally not offered as their shorter fruit catkins are much less eyecatching. Garrya is a tough shrub in several respects — it will grow quite happily in industrial areas and close to the coast, it doesn't mind chalky or poor, sandy soil and is quite happy in sun or shade. It does suffer, however, when exposed to cold winter winds which may cause the leaves to fall — the answer is to choose a sheltered spot.

VARIETIES: You are likely to find only one species on offer — **G. elliptica**. It grows 8–12 ft high and in winter the male plant is festooned with 6–10 in. long tassels — grey-green at first and then dull cream. Don't buy the species — buy the variety **'James Roof'** with thicker catkins which may grow 14 in. long. For the collector of rarities there is **G. issaquahensis 'Pat Ballard'** with purplish catkins and **G. fremontii** with twisted leaves and small catkins.

SITE & SOIL: Any free-draining garden soil will do — thrives in sun or partial shade. Plant against a wall in cold gardens.

PRUNING: Not necessary — trim back dead or unwanted branches in spring.

PROPAGATION: Plant semi-ripe cuttings in a cold frame in summer.

Garrya elliptica 'James Roof'

GAULTHERIA Wintergreen

Prostrate, dwarf or small shrub
•
Evergreen
•
Colours available

Flowering period

JANUARY	
FEBRUARY	
MARCH	
APRIL	
MAY	
JUNE	
JULY	
AUGUST	
SEPTEMBER	
OCTOBER	
NOVEMBER	
DECEMBER	

G. shallon

Gaultheria is an excellent carpeter for planting under lime-hating plants such as Rhododendrons and Camellias. Urn-shaped flowers looking like Lily-of-the-Valley blooms open in late spring or summer and these are followed by showy berries in autumn and winter — a bright display in white, pink, red, blue or purple. The usual height is 1½ ft or less but there are one or two species which are bushy and taller. The one drawback is that it can be invasive.

VARIETIES: The best-known Gaultheria is the Checkerberry (**G. procumbens**). The spreading branches bear shiny, dark green leaves and this neat mat grows about 6 in. high. White flowers appear in July and there are bright red berries and reddish foliage in autumn. **G. cuneata** has narrow leaves, white flowers and white fruits — **G. miqueliana** also has white flowers in June with fruits which may be white or pink. Both of these white-berrying Gaultherias grow 1–1½ ft high — **G. shallon** is quite different, growing 5 ft high and bearing clusters of dark purple berries in winter. Less easy to find is the Gaultheria x Pernettya hybrid **Gaulnettya**. Look for the variety **'Wisley Pearl'** — a small shrub with large red berries.

SITE & SOIL: Requires moist and lime-free soil. Thrives best in partial shade.

PRUNING: Not necessary — cut back straggly or damaged shoots in early spring.

PROPAGATION: Layer shoots in spring or lift and plant rooted suckers.

Gaultheria procumbens

GENISTA Broom

Prostrate, dwarf, small, medium or large shrub

•

Deciduous

•

Colours available

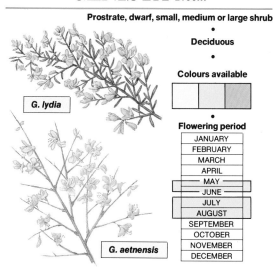

G. lydia

G. aetnensis

•

Flowering period

| JANUARY |
| FEBRUARY |
| MARCH |
| APRIL |
| MAY |
| JUNE |
| JULY |
| AUGUST |
| SEPTEMBER |
| OCTOBER |
| NOVEMBER |
| DECEMBER |

This group of Brooms have wiry stems, tiny leaves and a mass of yellow or golden flowers. All are sun-lovers and do best in light land, but the generalisations end there. There are spiny and thornless species, and heights range from 2 in. to 12 ft depending on the variety. The most popular types are the low-growing ones which can be used for covering dry banks or low walls. A key feature is the abundance of blooms — in the right conditions both leaves and stems are covered by the flowers. Do not feed — fertile soil reduces flowering.

VARIETIES: G. lydia is the most popular one — a spreading ground cover with arching branches growing about 2 ft high. In May and June the plant is covered with golden flowers. **G. hispanica** (Spanish Gorse) blooms at about the same time, the yellow flowers covering the 1 ft high cushion of spiny branches. **G. pilosa** and its variety **'Vancouver Gold'** are thornless carpeters blooming in May — the most unusual of the prostrate types is **G. sagitallis** with flattened, winged stems and flowers in terminal spikes. The taller Genistas generally bloom in July–August — included here are **G. aetnensis** (12 ft) and **G. tenera 'Golden Shower'** (6 ft).

SITE & SOIL: Any reasonable well-drained soil will do, but sandy ground is best. Full sun is required.

PRUNING: Not necessary — prune back over-long branches after flowering but do not cut into old wood.

PROPAGATION: Plant semi-ripe cuttings (plus heel) in a cold frame in summer.

Genista hispanica

GREVILLEA Spider Flower

Small or medium shrub

•

Evergreen

•

Colours available

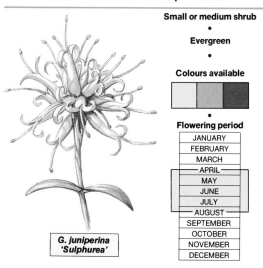

G. juniperina 'Sulphurea'

•

Flowering period

| JANUARY |
| FEBRUARY |
| MARCH |
| APRIL |
| MAY |
| JUNE |
| JULY |
| AUGUST |
| SEPTEMBER |
| OCTOBER |
| NOVEMBER |
| DECEMBER |

According to some experts this unusual plant from Australia has no place in this book. It is referred to in most textbooks as a shrub to be set out in its pot during the summer months and then brought back into the greenhouse or conservatory during the winter. It certainly cannot stand up to heavy frosts but it may not be as delicate as is generally assumed. If you live in a mild area of the country and if you can provide the protection of a sunny wall, it may be worth taking the risk. The curious shape of the flowers would certainly attract attention.

VARIETIES: The variety which is most likely to survive the winter is **G. juniperina 'Sulphurea'**. The bush grows about 6 ft high and bears narrow bright green leaves. Between May and June the flower-heads of pale yellow blooms appear. These are often described as Honeysuckle-like, but they are much more similar to Embothrium (page 42), to which it is related. Each bloom is a narrow tube from which the showy style protrudes. **G. rosmarinifolia** grows to the same height or even taller, and the pink and cream-edged crimson blooms appear in June–August. **G. alpina** is shorter — this 4 ft bush produces red and cream flowers in April and May.

SITE & SOIL: Requires well-drained neutral or acid soil. Full sun and shelter from cold winds are essential.

PRUNING: Not necessary — trim away unwanted or damaged branches after flowering.

PROPAGATION: Plant semi-ripe cuttings (plus heel) in a cold frame in summer.

Grevillea rosmarinifolia

HALESIA Silverbell

Medium or large shrub
•
Deciduous
•
Colours available
•
Flowering period

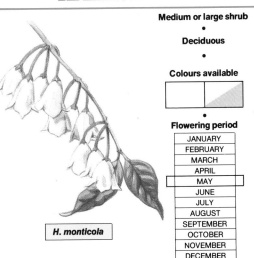

JANUARY
FEBRUARY
MARCH
APRIL
MAY
JUNE
JULY
AUGUST
SEPTEMBER
OCTOBER
NOVEMBER
DECEMBER

H. monticola

It is hard to understand why this spring-flowering shrub remains a rarity. The Snowdrop-like blooms appear before the leaves, hanging like small bells in clusters beneath the branches. It is hardy and will succeed in any soil which supports Rhododendrons or Azaleas. After flowering the winged green fruits appear and in the autumn the foliage turns an attractive shade of yellow. It is quite a big shrub, growing 8–12 ft high with a spreading habit. Halesia takes a few years before it becomes established and free-flowering, but this cannot really explain its lack of popularity.

VARIETIES: You will find just three types listed in the catalogues. **H. carolina (H. tetraptera)** is the Carolina Silverbell — a medium-sized shrub (8 ft) which may become a small tree with age. The pendent white bells are borne in clusters of three to five in May just as the oval leaves are beginning to appear. The fruits are small and Pear-shaped. The other Halesia is **H. monticola** — the Mountain Silverbell. It is a bigger plant with 1 in. wide flowers and 2 in. long fruits — the white blooms of the variety **'Vestita'** are often tinged with pink.

SITE & SOIL: Requires well-drained acid soil — thrives in sun or light shade.

PRUNING: Not necessary — cut back dead or unwanted branches after flowering.

PROPAGATION: Plant semi-ripe cuttings in a cold frame in summer.

Halesia carolina

HAMAMELIS Witch Hazel

Medium shrub
•
Deciduous
•
Colours available
•
Flowering period

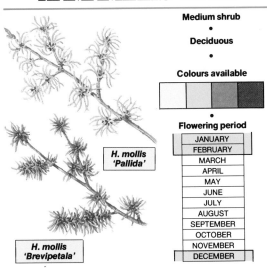

H. mollis 'Pallida'

JANUARY
FEBRUARY
MARCH
APRIL
MAY
JUNE
JULY
AUGUST
SEPTEMBER
OCTOBER
NOVEMBER
DECEMBER

H. mollis 'Brevipetala'

Unlike its partner on this page, Hamamelis is a popular shrub. The showy, spidery flowers appear on the leafless branches for many weeks in winter, and sweet fragrance is a bonus — you can cut a branch or two for indoor decoration. The base of the twisted, strap-like petals is usually tinged with red and the blooms are unaffected by frost. After the flowers have opened the large Hazel-like leaves appear and in autumn these take on attractive tints. An undemanding hardy shrub which needs space, reaching a height and spread of 8–10 ft.

VARIETIES: The most popular species is **H. mollis** — the Chinese Witch Hazel. The large golden flowers are fragrant and plentiful — the leaves turn yellow in autumn. There are several varieties, including **'Pallida'** (sulphur yellow flowers) and **'Brevipetala'** (bronzy-yellow flowers). Also popular are a few varieties of **H. intermedia** — look for **'Diane'** (coppery-red flowers, red autumn leaves) and **'Jelena'** (coppery-orange flowers, red autumn leaves). The Japanese Witch Hazel (**H. japonica**) has less fragrance, fewer flowers and blooms later. **H. virginiana** is a poor choice — the blooms are hidden by the old leaves.

SITE & SOIL: Requires well-drained neutral or acid soil. Thrives best in full sun.

PRUNING: Not necessary. Remove unwanted or damaged branches after flowering — pull out suckers.

PROPAGATION: Nursery-raised plants are grafted — buy container-grown specimens.

Hamamelis intermedia 'Jelena'

HEBE Shrubby Veronica

Prostrate, dwarf, small or medium shrub

•

Evergreen

•

Colours available

Flowering period

JANUARY
FEBRUARY
MARCH
APRIL
MAY
JUNE
JULY
AUGUST
SEPTEMBER
OCTOBER
NOVEMBER
DECEMBER

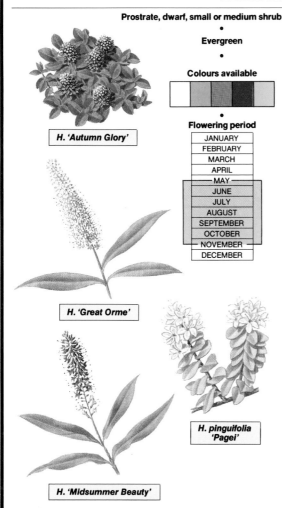

H. 'Autumn Glory'

H. 'Great Orme'

H. 'Midsummer Beauty'

H. pinguifolia 'Pagei'

This large genus of evergreen shrubs from New Zealand was once grouped with Veronica and this still remains the common name. You will find several types on offer at a modest garden centre, and there can be an extensive array at a large nursery. Some have scale-like leaves which hug the stem and give a whipcord-like effect — these have limited or no appeal as flowering plants and are not dealt with here. The rest are bushes with dense oval leaves and small flowers borne in compact or bottle-brush spikes. The Hebes are not as tender as once thought and some of the popular ones are quite hardy. But all are relatively short-lived, and some of the showier ones are killed by severe frosts. As a general rule, the larger the leaf the more tender the plant is likely to be. Tenderness apart, Hebe is easy to grow even in smoky or salt-laden air.

VARIETIES: First of all, the low-growing ones (6 in.–1½ ft high) for ground cover or the rockery. One of the best is **H. pinguifolia 'Pagei'** (1 ft x 3 ft) with branches clothed with greyish-green leaves and white flowers in May–August. Another popular one is **H. 'Carl Teschner'** (9 in. x 3 ft) which bears white-throated violet flowers in June–July. Others include **H. albicans** (white flowers) and **H. pimeleoides 'Quicksilver'** (white flowers). The 'typical' Hebe is a rounded bush 1½–4 ft high — this mid-sized group is dominated by the ever-popular **H. 'Autumn Glory'** (violet-blue flowers, June–November). Many others are widely available, including **H. rakaiensis** (white flowers, June–July) and **H. 'Great Orme'** (bright pink flowers, July–October). Some are hardier than average — look for **H. franciscana 'Blue Gem'** (violet-blue flowers, July–October), **H. 'Marjorie'** (violet and white flowers, July–September), **H. 'Midsummer Beauty'** (lavender flowers, July–October), **H. 'Bowles Hybrid'** (pale lavender flowers, June–September) and the purple-leaved **H. 'Mrs Winder'** (blue flowers, June–September). There are also a number of mid-sized Hebes which are rather tender — **H. macrantha** (white flowers, June–July), **H. 'Purple Queen'** (purple leaves and flowers, June–July) and **H. hulkeana** noted for the large size of its lilac flower-heads in May–June. Finally there are the tall-growing Hebes which can be used for hedging in mild areas. **H. salicifolia** (6–10 ft) has green leaves and spikes of lilac-tinted white flowers in June–September. There is also **H. andersonii 'Variegata'** (6 ft) which has cream-splashed green leaves and pale mauve flowers in August–September.

SITE & SOIL: Any reasonable well-drained garden soil will do — thrives best in full sun.

PRUNING: Not necessary — prune back straggly shoots in May but do not cut into old wood.

PROPAGATION: Plant semi-ripe cuttings in a cold frame in summer.

Hebe 'Carl Teschner'

Hebe 'Autumn Glory'

Hebe salicifolia

HEDYSARUM Hedysarum

Small or medium shrub

•

Deciduous

•

Colours available

•

Flowering period

| JANUARY |
| FEBRUARY |
| MARCH |
| APRIL |
| MAY |
| JUNE |
| JULY |
| AUGUST |
| SEPTEMBER |
| OCTOBER |
| NOVEMBER |
| DECEMBER |

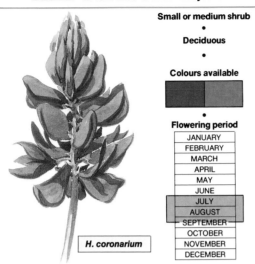

H. coronarium

Hedysarum is another of those rarities which are easier to grow than find at the garden centre. All you need is a sunny site and soil which is on the light side — it doesn't matter whether it is acid or alkaline. The stems arch with age to produce a lax, open bush. The leaves are made up of oval leaflets and the flowers appear during the summer months. These Pea-like blooms are borne in long spikes which can be up to 1 ft long. The flower-heads can be used as cut flowers for indoor decoration. Hedysarum is worth looking for if you have a hot and dry bank to cover or a sunny wall to clothe. Its only drawback is that it may take several years for the shrub to become fully established.

VARIETIES: The best-known species is the Mongolian Sweet Vetch (**H. multijugum**). It grows about 6 ft high as a free-standing bush but may reach 10 ft when grown against a wall. The flowers are rosy-purple and appear intermittently from midsummer to early autumn. The leaves are about 6 in. long. You may find another species on offer — **H. coronarium** or French Honeysuckle. The flowers are bright red and the bush grows about 4 ft high.

SITE & SOIL: Any reasonable well-drained garden soil will do — sandy ground is preferred. Full sun is necessary.

PRUNING: Not essential, but some of the oldest branches can be shortened in early spring if growth has become leggy.

PROPAGATION: Plant softwood cuttings in a cold frame in summer.

Hedysarum coronarium

HELIANTHEMUM Sun Rose, Rock Rose

Prostrate shrub

•

Evergreen

•

Colours available

•

Flowering period

| JANUARY |
| FEBRUARY |
| MARCH |
| APRIL |
| MAY |
| JUNE |
| JULY |
| AUGUST |
| SEPTEMBER |
| OCTOBER |
| NOVEMBER |
| DECEMBER |

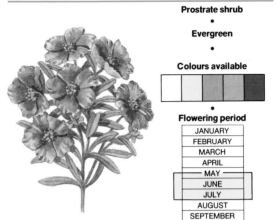

H. nummularium
'Fire Dragon'

You may find this lowly shrub in the Rockery, Border Perennial or Shrub section of your garden centre or catalogue. If your land is sandy and in full sun then few other plants can match Helianthemum for providing a sheet of colour throughout the summer months. Each papery bloom only lasts for a day or two but new ones appear in profusion. This shrub can become straggly and bare when wrongly treated — follow the rules for site selection and pruning to ensure success.

VARIETIES: Choose one of the many named varieties of **H. nummularium**. The average dimensions are height 6–9 in., spread 2 ft and flowers 1 in. across. There are many colours from which to make your choice — the following list includes the favourite ones. **'Amy Baring'** (yellow, single), **'Cerise Queen'** (rose-red, double), **'Fire Dragon'** (orange-red, single), **'Henfield Brilliant'** (deep orange, single), **'Jubilee'** (yellow, double), **'Mrs C. W. Earle'** (deep orange, double), **'Raspberry Ripple'** (white-tipped pink, single), **'The Bride'** (white, single) and the single **'Wisley White'**, **'Wisley Primrose'** and **'Wisley Pink'**. The 'Ben' series is claimed to be the hardiest (**'Ben Hope'**, **'Ben Ledi'** etc.).

SITE & SOIL: Requires light, well-drained and infertile soil — full sun is necessary.

PRUNING: Important. Remove dead flowers and cut back all straggly stems in late July.

PROPAGATION: Plant semi-ripe cuttings in a cold frame in summer.

Helianthemum nummularium 'Raspberry Ripple'

HELICHRYSUM Shrubby Helichrysum

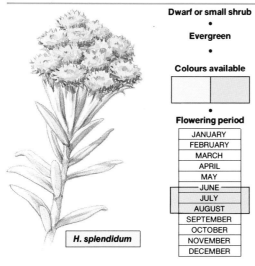

Dwarf or small shrub

•

Evergreen

•

Colours available

•

Flowering period

| JANUARY |
| FEBRUARY |
| MARCH |
| APRIL |
| MAY |
| JUNE |
| JULY |
| AUGUST |
| SEPTEMBER |
| OCTOBER |
| NOVEMBER |
| DECEMBER |

H. splendidum

The best-known Helichrysums are H. bracteatum grown for its 'everlasting' flowers and H. petiolatum grown for its woolly leaves and used very widely these days as a bedding plant. These plants have a number of shrubby relatives and a few of them are hardy enough to be grown outdoors in this country. They have narrow grey-green or silvery leaves and the decorative value of this foliage is equal to or even more important than the clusters of yellow button-like flowers. It tends to get leggy with age — cut it down to an inch or two in spring.

VARIETIES: There are only two Shrubby Helichrysums you are likely to find at the garden centre. The Curry Plant will be labelled **H. serotinum**, **H. italicum serotinum** or **H. angustifolium**. The 1½ ft high bush has sage-green leaves which smell of curry when crushed. Yellow flower-heads appear in June–August. **H. splendidum** is a larger shrub, reaching 3 ft x 3 ft and bearing heads of yellow flowers in summer above the silvery-grey leaves. These flowers dry on the plant and remain during the winter — hence the common name of Everlasting Immortelle. Specialist catalogues may offer **H. italicum**, **H. lanatum** and **H. plicatum**.

SITE & SOIL: Requires light, well-drained and infertile soil — full sun is necessary.

PRUNING: Trim back the stems in April.

PROPAGATION: Plant semi-ripe cuttings in a cold frame in summer.

Helichrysum angustifolium

HIBISCUS Shrubby Mallow

H. syriacus 'Blue Bird'

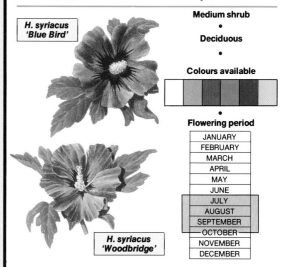

Medium shrub

•

Deciduous

•

Colours available

•

Flowering period

| JANUARY |
| FEBRUARY |
| MARCH |
| APRIL |
| MAY |
| JUNE |
| JULY |
| AUGUST |
| SEPTEMBER |
| OCTOBER |
| NOVEMBER |
| DECEMBER |

H. syriacus 'Woodbridge'

The stiff and upright branches are clothed with large, saucer-shaped blooms which are often dark-centred and are available in a range of beautiful colours. The experts agree that Hibiscus is one of the most attractive of all late-flowering bushes, but it has a number of fussy needs and one or two drawbacks. The soil must be free-draining and both full sun and protection from cold winds are essential. Do have patience — it takes some time to establish.

VARIETIES: Nearly all the types on offer are varieties of **H. syriacus** (8 ft x 8 ft). The single-flowered ones are available in several colours — the most popular one is **'Blue Bird'** (violet-blue with dark eye, 3 in. across). Other widely available varieties include **'Diana'** (pure white, pale foliage), **'Hamabo'** (white with crimson eye), **'Woodbridge'** (rose-pink with dark eye), **'Russian Violet'** (dark violet), **'Pink Giant'** (large, pink) and **'Red Heart'** (white with crimson eye). There are some double-flowering forms (e.g **'Lady Stanley'** with white petals and red centre) but they can be disappointing in a wet summer. **H. sinosyriacus** is a more spreading plant than H. syriacus.

SITE & SOIL: Any free-draining reasonable soil will do — full sun and some shelter are necessary.

PRUNING: Not essential, but keep plants in check by cutting back stems in February.

PROPAGATION: Named varieties are grafted — buy container-grown plants.

Hibiscus syriacus 'Red Heart'

HIPPOPHAE Sea Buckthorn

Large shrub
•
Deciduous
•
Colour available
•
Berrying period

JANUARY	
FEBRUARY	
MARCH	
APRIL	
MAY	
JUNE	
JULY	
AUGUST	
SEPTEMBER	
OCTOBER	
NOVEMBER	
DECEMBER	

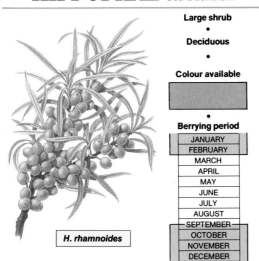

H. rhamnoides

A quick-growing plant which will form a hedge or screen and be colourful throughout the autumn and winter. It has a number of advantages compared with many of the more popular hedging plants. First, it flourishes in any well-drained soil, and is unaffected by salt-laden air, strong winds, starved ground or periods of drought. Next, the sour yellow juice within the berries makes them unattractive to birds, so the fruit display remains untouched. The branches are spiny and growth can be kept in check by regular pruning. The major drawback is that the bushes sometimes sucker freely and so can be invasive.

VARIETY: The only species you will find is **H. rhamnoides**. Left unpruned it will form a round bush reaching 12 ft high, but it can be pruned or trimmed to form a hedge or a tree. The silvery leaves are Willow-like — in shade the attractive colouring is lost and the surface becomes plain green. In March or April the inconspicuous yellow flowers appear and these are followed by masses of orange berries. The plants are unisexed so do not grow a bush on its own — you will need both male and female plants set close together to ensure berry production.

SITE & SOIL: Any well-drained garden soil will do — thrives in sun or light shade.

PRUNING: Not essential — unwanted branches can be cut back in summer.

PROPAGATION: Sow seed from berries in autumn. Alternatively, layer shoots or plant rooted suckers.

Hippophae rhamnoides

HOHERIA Lacebark

Large shrub
•
Deciduous
or
Semi-evergreen
•
Colour available
•
Flowering period

JANUARY	
FEBRUARY	
MARCH	
APRIL	
MAY	
JUNE	
JULY	
AUGUST	
SEPTEMBER	
OCTOBER	
NOVEMBER	
DECEMBER	

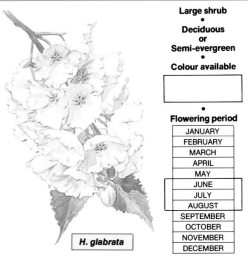

H. glabrata

These imposing shrubs from New Zealand are a rare sight in our gardens. This is not surprising as they need a lot of space and the branches can be seriously damaged by just a few degrees of frost in winter. But they do succeed in mild and sheltered areas, and for the lovers of the unusual it is a risk worth taking — plant against a south or south-west facing wall. 'Free-flowering' or 'floriferous' is the description you will read in the catalogues — the large heads of saucer-shaped white blooms are borne in large numbers in midsummer. The petals are translucent — a fine sight with the sun shining through. The fragrance is distinctly honey-like.

VARIETIES: H. glabrata is claimed to be one of the hardiest species. It is an upright bush, growing about 12 ft tall and bearing large clusters of flowers in June and July which weigh down the branches. It is deciduous, but its variety **'Glory of Amlwch'** is semi-evergreen. **H. lyallii** differs in having leaves which are silvery-grey rather than pale green and with flowers which first appear in July rather than June. Another July-flowering species is **H. sexstylosa** — **H. populnea** has Poplar-like leaves and blooms in August.

SITE & SOIL: Requires well-drained fertile soil — thrives in full sun or light shade.

PRUNING: Not necessary — cut back any unwanted or damaged branches in spring.

PROPAGATION: Plant semi-ripe cuttings in a cold frame in summer or layer shoots in autumn.

Hoheria lyallii

HYDRANGEA Hydrangea

Small, medium, large or climbing shrub

•

Deciduous

•

Colours available

•

Flowering period

JANUARY
FEBRUARY
MARCH
APRIL
MAY
JUNE
JULY
AUGUST
SEPTEMBER
OCTOBER
NOVEMBER
DECEMBER

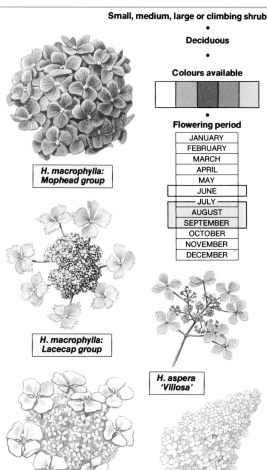

H. macrophylla:
Mophead group

H. macrophylla:
Lacecap group

H. aspera
'Villosa'

H. petiolaris

H. paniculata
'Grandiflora'

Hydrangea is the queen of the late-flowering shrubs. The reason is that large flower-heads are borne in August and September when the shrub border is often rather dull. The most popular ones are the Mopheads or Hortensias with large globular heads of sterile florets. The Lacecap group is quite different — each flat flower-head is made up of a central cluster of small fertile blooms surrounded by sterile florets. As noted below there are other types of Hydrangea — climbers as well as bushy types, cone-shaped flower-headed types as well as the familiar Mopheads and Lacecaps. The feature they all have in common is that they are somewhat demanding plants. Basic needs include good soil, plenty of water during dry spells in summer, regular feeding and some protection against heavy frosts.

VARIETIES: Most garden forms are derived from **H. macrophylla** with flowers from late July to September on bushes about 5 ft x 5 ft. Stem tips can be killed by severe frosts and growth can become untidy and floppy after a number of years. Blue-flowering varieties form pink blooms on alkaline soil — it is difficult to "blue" Hydrangeas on non-acid soil, but you can try applying a blueing powder every 7–14 days. White flowers are unaffected by soil pH, but they take on a reddish tinge in full sun conditions. Popular Mophead varieties include **'Altona'** (pink or blue, depending on soil pH), **'Hamburg'** (pink or blue), **'Pia'** (red or violet) and **'Madame Emile Mouilliere'** (white). The Lacecaps are more graceful than the Mopheads — popular varieties include **'Blue Wave'** (pink or blue), **'Mariesii'** (pink or blue) and **'Geoffrey Chadbund'** (red). Not all garden Hydrangeas are varieties of H. macrophylla. There are **H. arborescens 'Annabelle'** (4 ft, white flowers), **H. aspera 'Villosa'** (10 ft, Lacecap flowers with blue florets) and **H. paniculata 'Grandiflora'** (8 ft with arching branches and large, white cone-shaped flower-heads in August and September) — all are recommended as beautiful plants. Other colourful types include **H. serrata 'Bluebird'** (4 ft, purple or blue), **'Preziosa'** (4 ft, pink turning red with age, leaves purple-tinged when young), and **H. quercifolia** (4 ft, white turning purplish with age, leaves red in autumn). The Climbing Hydrangea is **H. petiolaris** — a self-clinging species which in time can cover an area of 70 ft x 70 ft. Large white Lacecap flowers appear in June.

SITE & SOIL: Requires well-drained fertile soil — add peat at planting time. Light shade is preferred to full sun.

PRUNING: Remove dead flower-heads from Lacecaps once blooming has finished — dead-head Mopheads in March and remove weak branches at the same time. Cut back H. paniculata 'Grandiflora' hard in spring. H. petiolaris does not need pruning.

PROPAGATION: Plant semi-ripe cuttings in a cold frame in summer.

Hydrangea macrophylla 'Hamburg'

Hydrangea macrophylla 'Blue Wave'

Hydrangea paniculata 'Grandiflora'

HYPERICUM St. John's Wort

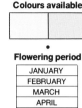

H. inodorum 'Elstead'

Prostrate, dwarf, small or medium shrub
•
Semi-evergreen
or
Evergreen
•
Colours available

•
Flowering period

JANUARY
FEBRUARY
MARCH
APRIL
MAY
JUNE
JULY
AUGUST
SEPTEMBER
OCTOBER
NOVEMBER
DECEMBER

H. polyphyllum

H. calcyinum

H. moserianum 'Tricolor'

H. 'Hidcote'

Hypericum is a very popular choice where we need an undemanding plant which will enliven a dull spot with bright yellow flowers from midsummer until the first frosts arrive. The blooms are flat discs with a central boss of stamens and with some varieties these flowers are followed by showy black or red fruits. Most or all of the leaves are retained in winter. The usual selection is H. calycinum — a completely reliable and undemanding low-growing shrub which will thrive almost anywhere, including under trees or on dry banks. It spreads rapidly, suppressing weeds and producing a mass of Buttercup-like flowers. The main problem is that this species is invasive, so it is worth looking at the other Hypericums which are available. All the flowers are quite similar, but heights vary widely from an inch or two to 6 ft or more. Some of the choice varieties are less hardy than the common-or-garden H. calycinum, but are well worth growing.

VARIETIES: H. calycinum (Rose of Sharon) grows about 1½ ft high and spreads widely — very useful but it can become a weed if left unchecked. If you want a 2–3 ft high Hypericum which is less common and less invasive than Rose of Sharon there are several from which you can take your pick. The flowers of **H. moserianum 'Tricolor'** are small, but the leaves are an eye-catching blend of green, cream and pink. **H. androsaemum** (Tutsan) is a colourful 3 ft x 2 ft shrub — yellow flowers, black berries and red leaves in autumn. **H. prolificum** is an upright shrub noted for its free-flowering habit. In the 3–4 ft high range there are **H. forrestii** (**H. patulum 'Henryi'**) which bears large flowers and bronzy fruits, and the popular **H. inodorum 'Elstead'** with its small starry flowers and attractive red fruits. **H. kouytchense** is another red-berrying form — so is **H. 'Gold Penny'**. The tall Hypericums are perhaps the best of all. **H. 'Hidcote'** is a fine 6 ft shrub bearing an abundance of large golden flowers from July to October. Even finer is **H. 'Rowallane'**, but it is a rather tender plant and needs a sheltered spot. At the other end of the scale are the Rockery Hypericums, dominated by the 6 in. high **H. polyphyllum** (**H. olympicum**). The variety **'Citrinum'** is smaller and bears lemon yellow flowers. **H. coris** (1 ft) is a Heather-like plant with starry flowers and the mat-forming **H. reptans** bears red buds which open into golden yellow flowers.

SITE & SOIL: Any non-waterlogged garden soil will do — thrives in sun or partial shade.

PRUNING: Cut back H. calycinum almost to ground level in March. Taller varieties need less drastic treatment — remove the top third of the branches each spring.

PROPAGATION: Plant semi-ripe cuttings in a cold frame in summer.

Hypericum moserianum 'Tricolor'

Hypericum inodorum 'Elstead'

Hypericum 'Hidcote'

ILEX Holly

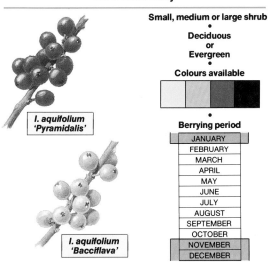

I. aquifolium 'Pyramidalis'

I. aquifolium 'Bacciflava'

Small, medium or large shrub

•

Deciduous
or
Evergreen

•

Colours available

•

Berrying period

| JANUARY |
| FEBRUARY |
| MARCH |
| APRIL |
| MAY |
| JUNE |
| JULY |
| AUGUST |
| SEPTEMBER |
| OCTOBER |
| NOVEMBER |
| DECEMBER |

We all know a Holly when we see one — dark green spiny leaves all year round and red berries in autumn and winter. But there are varieties which differ from this generalisation — smooth-leaved types, golden- and black-berried ones and even one or two rarities which lose their leaves in winter. Holly is slow-growing and very useful for hedging. Here we are concerned with the varieties noted for their berry production, and it is vital to remember that nearly all varieties are either male or female, which means that a group must be planted to ensure berry production.

VARIETIES: If you want just one plant which will produce berries, you must pick a self-fertile one. There are **I. aquifolium 'Pyramidalis'** (12 ft, free-fruiting), **'J. C. van Tol'** (15 ft, almost spineless leaves, red berries) or **'Golden van Tol'** (golden-edged leaves). For the other female varieties listed below you will need to plant nearby a variety labelled 'male'. For large berries there are **I. altaclerensis 'Camelliifolia'** and **'Golden King'** (the best of the variegated forms). For non-red berries pick **I. aquifolium 'Bacciflava'** and **I. aquifolium 'Pyramidalis Fructuluteo'** (yellow) or **I. crenata** (black, 2½ ft, Box-like leaves).

SITE & SOIL: Any reasonable garden soil will do — thrives in full sun or partial shade.

PRUNING: Trim hedges in spring, specimen shrubs in summer. Can be cut back drastically without harm.

PROPAGATION: Slow rooting. Layer branches or plant semi-ripe cuttings in a cold frame in autumn.

Ilex altaclerensis 'Golden King'

INDIGOFERA Indigo Bush

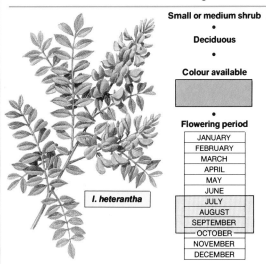

I. heterantha

Small or medium shrub

•

Deciduous

•

Colour available

•

Flowering period

| JANUARY |
| FEBRUARY |
| MARCH |
| APRIL |
| MAY |
| JUNE |
| JULY |
| AUGUST |
| SEPTEMBER |
| OCTOBER |
| NOVEMBER |
| DECEMBER |

At a large garden centre you might find I. heterantha — it will almost certainly appear in the catalogue of a nursery specialising in trees and shrubs. It is worth growing if you like unusual plants as it starts to bloom in late June or July and continues until autumn. You will need to satisfy its basic needs — a sheltered sunny spot and free-draining soil. The main disadvantage is that the leaves do not appear until late May or June. The stems may be damaged or killed in a hard winter but this is not a problem — cut them down to near ground level in spring and new shoots will grow up from the base.

VARIETIES: The only widely available Indigofera is **I. heterantha (I. gerardiana)** — an open bush with long, arching stems which reaches a height of 4 or 5 ft. Graceful upright flower-heads of rosy-purple Pea-like flowers appear in midsummer — these floral spikes arise in the leaf axils. Each leaf is made up of a number of oval leaflets. If the garden is exposed this shrub should be trained against a sunny wall where it will reach a height and spread of about 6 ft. A rarity well worth looking for is **I. potaninii** which has larger flower-heads and blooms which are pure pink. It is virtually identical to **I. amblyantha**.

SITE & SOIL: Well-drained soil is essential — thrives in full sun. Do not feed.

PRUNING: Trim in April — old plants should be cut back close to the base.

PROPAGATION: Plant semi-ripe cuttings in a cold frame in summer.

Indigofera heterantha

ITEA Sweetspire

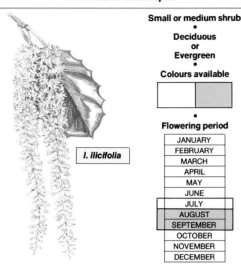

I. ilicifolia

Small or medium shrub
•
Deciduous
or
Evergreen
•
Colours available
•

Flowering period

JANUARY
FEBRUARY
MARCH
APRIL
MAY
JUNE
JULY
AUGUST
SEPTEMBER
OCTOBER
NOVEMBER
DECEMBER

There are two Sweetspires which are available, but neither is common and you may have to search for a supplier. Both species are summer-flowering and both bear floral spikes made up of numerous small blooms. Both are fragrant and their favourite conditions are light shade and moisture-retentive soil. The two species are slow to establish and are best grown against a wall in exposed areas. As described below, one of the most interesting things about Itea is that the similarities end there — the two types look quite different in leaf and in flower.

VARIETIES: I. ilicifolia (Holly-leaf Sweetspire) is the more usual one. It grows into an open bush about 8 ft high, clothed with evergreen Holly-like leaves which are dark green above and silvery below. In August and September drooping racemes of tiny greenish flowers appear — these catkin-like tassels may be 1 ft or more in length. **I. virginica** (Virginia Sweetspire) is quite different. It grows only 3–4 ft high and the oval leaves are not Holly-like. The small flowers are white and are borne in upright cylindrical flower-heads and not in pendent catkins — the flowering season is July. The leaves turn red in autumn and they are deciduous.

SITE & SOIL: Any well-drained reasonably fertile soil will do — thrives in sun or light shade.

PRUNING: Not necessary — cut back dead or unwanted branches in winter.

PROPAGATION: Plant semi-ripe cuttings in a cold frame in summer.

Itea ilicifolia

JASMINUM Jasmine

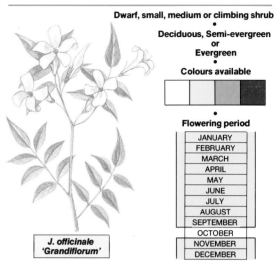

J. officinale 'Grandiflorum'

Dwarf, small, medium or climbing shrub
•
Deciduous, Semi-evergreen
or
Evergreen
•
Colours available
•

Flowering period

JANUARY
FEBRUARY
MARCH
APRIL
MAY
JUNE
JULY
AUGUST
SEPTEMBER
OCTOBER
NOVEMBER
DECEMBER

The key feature of Jasminum is the flower form — a short tube which bears a white, pink, yellow or red star-like face. There are two basic groups — the Bushy Jasmines with green stems, small leaves and yellow flowers, and the Climbing Jasmines with a twining growth habit.

VARIETIES: Winter Jasmine (**J. nudiflorum**) is by far the most popular Bushy variety. The bright yellow flowers open on the leafless and lax stems from November to late February. It is an undemanding plant, and will grow 10 ft or more against a wall. **J. humile 'Revolutum'** (6 ft) bears slightly scented yellow flowers in June. The baby of the group is **J. parkeri** (1 ft) — a low mound covered with small leaves and tiny yellow flowers all summer long. The Climbing Jasmines consist of several lovely plants, but they are all rather tender and will not survive in a cold, exposed site. The best one is **J. officinale 'Grandiflorum'** — between July and September the pink buds open into highly fragrant white flowers. The stems can grow up to 25 ft and will quickly cover a pergola or an old tree. Other climbers include **J. beesianum** (red flowers, summer, black fruits in autumn), **J. primulinus** (semi-double yellow flowers, March–May, tender) and **J. stephanense** (pale pink flowers).

SITE & SOIL: Any reasonable soil will do — Climbing Jasmines need a warm and sunny site.

PRUNING: Bushy Jasmines: Remove one-third of old flowering shoots in March. Climbing Jasmines: Not necessary.

PROPAGATION: Layer shoots or plant semi-ripe cuttings in a cold frame in summer.

Jasminum nudiflorum

KALMIA Kalmia

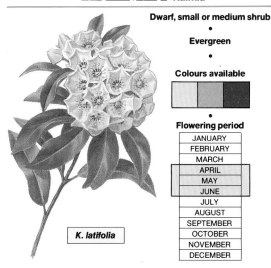

K. latifolia

Dwarf, small or medium shrub
•
Evergreen
•

Colours available

•

Flowering period

JANUARY
FEBRUARY
MARCH
APRIL
MAY
JUNE
JULY
AUGUST
SEPTEMBER
OCTOBER
NOVEMBER
DECEMBER

The largest and most popular species is K. latifolia, and when not in flower it can be easily mistaken for a Rhododendron. In bloom, however, it is quite different. The buds look like miniature chinese lanterns which then open into shallow bowl-shaped flowers which have crimped edges. It requires the same sort of conditions as the Rhododendron and Camellia, and makes an excellent companion for them. Kalmia has the unfortunate habit of waiting several years before flowering freely.

VARIETIES: The usual species is **K. latifolia** (Calico Bush or Mountain Laurel). It grows about 6–8 ft high, and in June the oval glossy leaves are covered by 6 in. wide clusters of pink flowers. It is fully hardy, but it cannot tolerate dry soil. Apply a mulch around the stems in late spring and remove dead blooms after flowering. Look for the varieties **'Ostbo Red'** (deep pink flowers) and **'Olympic Fire'** (red flowers). **K. angustifolia 'Rubra'** (Sheep Laurel) is a 3 ft shrub which looks like an Azalea rather than a Rhododendron. Its rosy-red flowers appear over a long period in May and June. For April flowers there is the dwarf **K. polifolia** (1½ ft) which thrives in boggy soil.

SITE & SOIL: Moist, acid soil is essential — add peat at planting time. Thrives in light shade.

PRUNING: Not required — do not remove branches unless it is really necessary.

PROPAGATION: Layer shoots or plant semi-ripe cuttings in a cold frame in summer.

Kalmia latifolia

KERRIA Jew's Mallow

K. japonica

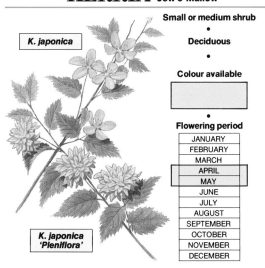

K. japonica 'Pleniflora'

Small or medium shrub
•
Deciduous
•

Colour available

•

Flowering period

JANUARY
FEBRUARY
MARCH
APRIL
MAY
JUNE
JULY
AUGUST
SEPTEMBER
OCTOBER
NOVEMBER
DECEMBER

Cheap and cheerful, Kerria is to be found in many bargain collections. Do not let this popularity discourage you if there is a difficult spot which needs planting. Kerria will grow almost anywhere, in sand or clay and in sun or shade. It is completely reliable but it is not completely trouble-free — you will have to prune the plant after flowering or the shrub will become leggy and unattractive. It also suckers quite freely, and so can become invasive. The flowering period is mid to late spring, when the branches are clothed with bright yellow flowers. Occasional blooms may appear in summer or autumn.

VARIETIES: Most people choose the double form **K. japonica 'Pleniflora'** and train the 8 ft long green stems against a wall or trellis. The blooms look like golden pompons and are generally borne in profusion. As a free-standing bush the basic species **K. japonica** is more graceful with its arching stems growing about 6 ft long and single Buttercup-like flowers. The large-flowering variety **'Golden Guinea'** is becoming increasingly popular — its single blooms are more than 2 in. across. **'Variegata' ('Picta')** is another single-flowered variety — 3 ft high with cream-edged foliage.

SITE & SOIL: Any garden soil will do — thrives in full sun or partial shade.

PRUNING: In June cut back shoots which have flowered and remove a few of the oldest branches to ground level.

PROPAGATION: Use rooted suckers or plant semi-ripe cuttings in a cold frame in summer.

Kerria japonica 'Pleniflora'

KOLKWITZIA Beauty Bush

Medium shrub
•
Deciduous
•
Colour available
•
Flowering period

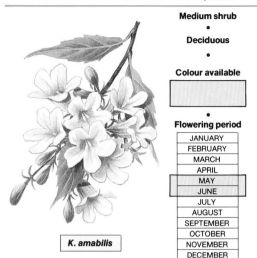

JANUARY	
FEBRUARY	
MARCH	
APRIL	
MAY	
JUNE	
JULY	
AUGUST	
SEPTEMBER	
OCTOBER	
NOVEMBER	
DECEMBER	

K. amabilis

Kolkwitzia has a number of features which should make it a popular plant. In late spring the arching branches are festooned with a mass of attractive, bell-shaped flowers. In addition it will grow in almost any garden soil — light or heavy, acid or chalky. There are no problems about winter hardiness and it establishes readily, so the bush is free-flowering in the season after planting. Despite all these benefits it has never become popular like the rather similar Weigela. The reason remains a mystery — one of the factors against the Beauty Bush may be that it grows rapidly and can reach 8–10 ft if left unpruned, whereas Weigela grows to only 5–6 ft under such conditions.

VARIETIES: There is a single species — **K. amabilis**. It is an attractive plant with a mass of drooping stems — when regularly pruned it grows about 5–6 ft high. The flowers are often described as Foxglove-like but they are much more Weigela-like. Pale pink is the basic colour of the petals with a throat which is yellow. The bush produces suckers so it can be invasive under good growing conditions, and in winter the peeling bark habit can be clearly seen. Many catalogues offer the species — even more sell the variety **'Pink Cloud'.**

SITE & SOIL: Any reasonable garden soil will do — thrives best in full sun.

PRUNING: After flowering cut back stems which bear faded blooms. Remove dead and weak stems.

PROPAGATION: Plant hardwood cuttings in the open in late autumn or use rooted suckers.

Kolkwitzia amabilis 'Pink Cloud'

LAVANDULA Lavender

Dwarf or small shrub
•
Evergreen
•
Colours available
•
Flowering period

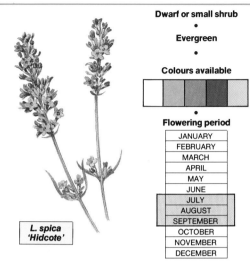

JANUARY	
FEBRUARY	
MARCH	
APRIL	
MAY	
JUNE	
JULY	
AUGUST	
SEPTEMBER	
OCTOBER	
NOVEMBER	
DECEMBER	

L. spica 'Hidcote'

Lavender is a low-growing bush with greyish-green leaves which is extremely useful for growing in clumps at the front of the border. It is often used for dwarf hedging along paths, where it provides a more informal look than neatly-trimmed Box or Yew. The aromatic flowers and stalks have been used for making pot-pourri for centuries — these blooms which appear between July and September are generally but not always blue or lavender in colour.

VARIETIES: The most popular species is Old English Lavender which you will find labelled as **L. angustifolia**, **L. spica** or **L. officinalis**. The pale blue flowers are borne in dense spikes on tall stems — the bush grows about 2½ ft high. There are a number of popular varieties, including **'Hidcote'** (1½ ft, violet flowers), **'Hidcote Pink'** (1½ ft, pink flowers), **'Munstead'** (1½ ft, lavender-blue flowers, green leaves), **'Nana Alba'** (1 ft, white flowers), **'Rosea'** (1½ ft, pink flowers, green leaves) and the robust Dutch Lavender **'Vera'** which grows 3–4 ft high and bears pale blue flowers. For something different you can try **L. lanata** with stems covered in white wool or the rather tender **L. stoechas** (French Lavender) with dark purple flowers.

SITE & SOIL: Any well-drained garden soil will do — thrives in full sun.

PRUNING: Remove flower stalks when blooms fade, then trim back plants in April. Do not cut into old wood.

PROPAGATION: Plant semi-ripe cuttings in a cold frame in summer.

Lavandula spica 'Munstead'

LAVATERA Tree Mallow

Medium shrub
•
Semi-evergreen
•
Colours available

•
Flowering period

JANUARY
FEBRUARY
MARCH
APRIL
MAY
JUNE
JULY
AUGUST
SEPTEMBER
OCTOBER
NOVEMBER
DECEMBER

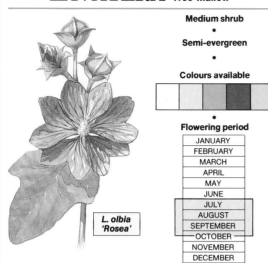

L. olbia 'Rosea'

Lavatera trimestris is a well-known annual, and its woody relatives are now often grown as garden shrubs. In a large garden centre you should find several varieties on offer, and as long as the site is not cold and exposed this grey-green shrub is a good choice. Its main virtue is that the large Hollyhock-like flowers begin to appear in clusters on the stems in June and blooming continues until the onset of frost. Individual blooms are short-lived, but there are always more buds ready to open during the flowering season. A few drawbacks — the plant may need staking and it will need hard pruning each year.

VARIETIES: L. olbia (sometimes more correctly listed as **L. thuringiaca**) is the most popular species. The leaves of this semi-evergreen are lobed and the saucer-shaped flowers are pink. It is a quick-growing shrub, soon reaching 7 ft or more. The species is not often listed — you are much more likely to find one of the varieties such as **'Barnsley'** (pinkish-white with a red eye), **'Ice Cool'** (white), **'Rosea'** (pale pink) and **'Burgundy Wine'** (purplish-red). **L. maritima** is a rather smaller plant, somewhat tender and growing 5 ft high. Flowers are lilac with purple veins.

SITE & SOIL: Any well-drained fertile soil will do — thrives best in full sun against a wall.

PRUNING: Cut back all previous season's growth in April.

PROPAGATION: Plant semi-ripe cuttings in a cold frame in summer or hardwood cuttings in the open in late autumn.

Lavatera olbia 'Barnsley'

LEPTOSPERMUM New Zealand Tea Tree

Dwarf, small or medium shrub
•
Evergreen
•
Colours available

•
Flowering period

JANUARY
FEBRUARY
MARCH
APRIL
MAY
JUNE
JULY
AUGUST
SEPTEMBER
OCTOBER
NOVEMBER
DECEMBER

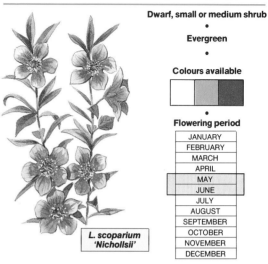

L. scoparium 'Nichollsii'

An attractive shrub when in flower, but it is not surprising that Leptospermum has never become popular. It demands lime-free soil and unless you live in a mild area it needs the shelter of a wall. If the soil and climate are right then you will be rewarded with a mass of long-lasting disc- or rosette-like flowers in early summer. These small blooms are borne along the purplish stems and between the narrow leaves.

VARIETIES: Most of the varieties on offer belong to **L. scoparium**. This species grows as an upright bush, reaching about 8 ft when mature. The flowers are single and white, but there are variations. **'Red Damask'** is a widely available variety with double red flowers and purple-tinged foliage — others include **'Snow Flurry'** (double, white flowers), **'Chapmanii'** (single, bright pink flowers), **'Nichollsii'** (single, red flowers and bronzy-purple leaves) and the 1 ft high **'Nanum'** and **'Kiwi'**. The most colourful variety is **'Spectrocolor'** with red-centred white flowers. **L. lanigerum** (**L. cunninghamii**) is hardier and more compact than L. scoparium. The flowers are white — choose the variety **'Silver Sheen'**.

SITE & SOIL: Requires well-drained loamy or sandy soil — thrives in full sun.

PRUNING: Not necessary — cut back damaged and unwanted branches in early spring.

PROPAGATION: Plant semi-ripe cuttings in a cold frame in summer.

Leptospermum scoparium 'Red Damask'

LESPEDEZA Bush Clover

Medium or large shrub
•
Deciduous
•
Colours available

Flowering period

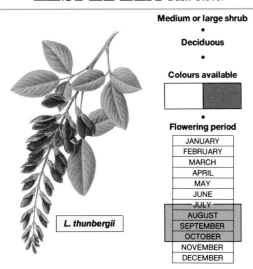

JANUARY	
FEBRUARY	
MARCH	
APRIL	
MAY	
JUNE	
JULY	
AUGUST	
SEPTEMBER	
OCTOBER	
NOVEMBER	
DECEMBER	

L. thunbergii

The weeping species of Lespedeza is sometimes recommended as a specimen bush for the gardener who wants a wide-spreading plant which blooms late in the season. It is certainly wide-spreading, growing up to 8 ft across, and the arching stems are borne down by long flowering trusses in September and October. There are, however, a number of problems. It is hard to find at garden centres and it is not suitable for heavy soil. It comes late into leaf (the foliage not appearing until early summer) and growth is often loose and untidy.

VARIETIES: The weeping species is **L. thunbergii (L. sieboldii)**, growing 4–6 ft high. Each leaf is made up of three leaflets and the autumn flower-heads are spectacularly large. These hanging clusters are made up of rosy-purple Pea-like flowers. The long branches may die down in winter but this is not a problem. Cut away all dead stems in March and new ones will shoot up in late spring. If you search you may find the rare white variety **'Albiflora'**. In a few catalogues you will find **L. bicolor** but this is not as good as L. thunbergii. Growth is semi-erect (10 ft) and the flower-heads are shorter. It blooms in July–September.

SITE & SOIL: Requires well-drained loamy or sandy soil — thrives in full sun.

PRUNING: Cut back in March all stems which have borne flowers.

PROPAGATION: Plant semi-ripe cuttings in a cold frame in summer.

Lespedeza thunbergii

LEUCOTHOE Leucothoe

Small shrub
•
Semi-evergreen
or
Evergreen
•
Colour available

Flowering period

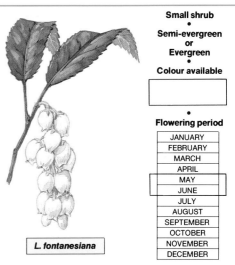

JANUARY	
FEBRUARY	
MARCH	
APRIL	
MAY	
JUNE	
JULY	
AUGUST	
SEPTEMBER	
OCTOBER	
NOVEMBER	
DECEMBER	

L. fontanesiana

Plant this one if you want an unusual and attractive ground cover for acid soil. With the most popular species and its varieties the leaves are attractively coloured in winter, and the stems bear white flowers in late spring or early summer. The flower clusters may be erect or pendent, depending on the type chosen, and all types do well in shady conditions. The Leucothoe species and varieties listed below are either evergreen or semi-evergreen, but one or two deciduous species do exist.

VARIETIES: The basic species is **L. fontanesiana**, sometimes sold as **L. catabaei**. This arching bush with zigzag stems grows about 3 ft high and 5 ft wide with leathery, lance-shaped leaves. It is a colourful plant, with stems which are bright red when young and leaves which are red- or purple-tinged in autumn and winter. In May and June the 1–3 in. long drooping heads of white urn-shaped flowers appear. The variety **'Rainbow'** is even more colourful with leaves which are green splashed with yellow, pink and cream. **L. 'Scarletta'** is another bright Leucothoe with leaves which are red, copper or green depending on the season, but it rarely flowers. **L. davisiae** (3 ft) has erect flower-heads.

SITE & SOIL: Requires fertile acid or neutral soil — thrives in light shade.

PRUNING: Remove about one-third of the oldest stems in spring.

PROPAGATION: Layer stems or plant semi-ripe cuttings in a cold frame in summer.

Leucothoe fontanesiana

LEYCESTERIA Pheasant Berry

Medium shrub
•
Deciduous
•
Colours available

•
Flowering period

JANUARY
FEBRUARY
MARCH
APRIL
MAY
JUNE
JULY
AUGUST
SEPTEMBER
OCTOBER
NOVEMBER
DECEMBER

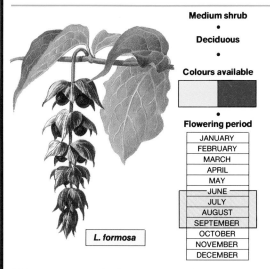

L. formosa

This easy-to-grow shrub is not a thing of beauty in winter — all you can see is a thicket of tall and leafless Bamboo-like stems which are covered with a waxy bloom. These hollow shoots may be killed by severe frosts, but new ones readily grow up from the base when spring arrives. The leaves are large and oval, and from midsummer to autumn the plant puts on its finery of attractive flower-heads. Leycesteria illustrates how plants can go out of fashion. It was a favourite shrubbery specimen in Victorian times but is rarely seen nowadays.

VARIETIES: L. formosa has a number of common names, such as Pheasant Berry, Flowering Nutmeg and Himalayan Honeysuckle. It is quick-growing — stems can reach 6 ft in a single season. In summer the unusual flower-heads appear — these 4 in. long tassels are made up of claret-red bracts within which are white flowers. After the blooms have faded the purple berries appear. These berries are much loved by birds and this plant has long been a favourite for pheasant covets — hence its most popular common name. A rare relative is **L. crocothyrsos** which has flower clusters made up of yellow tubular blooms.

SITE & SOIL: Any reasonable garden soil will do — thrives in sun or light shade.

PRUNING: Cut back old and damaged shoots in March to a few inches above ground level.

PROPAGATION: Sow seed in spring or plant semi-ripe cuttings in a cold frame in summer.

Leycesteria formosa

LIGUSTRUM Privet

Medium or large shrub
•
Deciduous, Semi-evergreen
or
Evergreen
•
Colours available

•
Flowering period

JANUARY
FEBRUARY
MARCH
APRIL
MAY
JUNE
JULY
AUGUST
SEPTEMBER
OCTOBER
NOVEMBER
DECEMBER

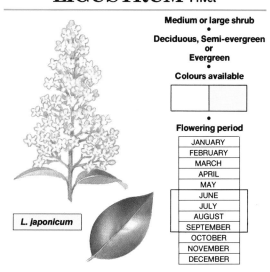

L. japonicum

It will seem strange to many gardeners that Privet should appear in a book on Flowering Shrubs. For generations countless urban plots have been hedged in by them — resistant to both smoky air and dense shade. Regular pruning kept flowering to a minimum, and when unpruned hedges of the Common Privet (L. vulgare) were left to bloom, the small heads of pungent-smelling white flowers appeared in June or July. There are, however, a number of choice types with large flower-heads which can be grown as specimen shrubs in the border.

VARIETIES: The queen of the flowering Privets is **L. quihoui**. This deciduous shrub grows about 8 ft high and in August and September the large flower-heads appear, snowy white cones up to 1 ft long. Another fine species is the semi-evergreen **L. chenaultii** with narrow leaves up to 6 in. long and large flower-heads in August. It is a big plant, reaching more than 10 ft when mature — for a more compact bush choose the Japanese Privet (**L. japonicum**). Camellia-like leaves cover the 6 ft shrub and large sprays of white flowers appear from July onwards. **L. sinense** is a tall, free-flowering species.

SITE & SOIL: Any reasonable garden soil will do — thrives in sun or partial shade.

PRUNING: Not necessary — cut away damaged or unwanted branches in spring.

PROPAGATION: Plant semi-ripe cuttings in a cold frame in summer or hardwood cuttings in the open in late autumn.

Ligustrum sinense

LONICERA Honeysuckle

Climbing Group

Small, medium, large or climbing shrub

•

Deciduous, Semi-evergreen
or
Evergreen

•

Colours available

•

Flowering period

| JANUARY |
| FEBRUARY |
| MARCH |
| APRIL |
| MAY |
| JUNE |
| JULY |
| AUGUST |
| SEPTEMBER |
| OCTOBER |
| NOVEMBER |
| DECEMBER |

L. periclymenum

L. tellmanniana

L. americana

L. brownii
'Dropmore Scarlet'

Shrubby Group

L. tatarica

L. pileata

Honeysuckles are usually thought of as climbing plants with sweetly scented flowers, but there are numerous shrubby species and varieties. The most popular one is used for hedging, but there are low-growing types used for ground cover and fine tall-growing ones to use as specimen bushes. There are winter-, spring- and summer-flowering shrubby Honeysuckles — the flowers are borne in pairs and are followed by berries. Choose with care — some varieties are free-flowering but there are others which produce few blooms. The climbing Honeysuckles have many virtues — they produce masses of colourful, tubular flowers and often bloom over a long period. They are easy to raise from cuttings and will grow quite happily in the shade. Many but not all have a spicy fragrance but there is one fault — Lonicera is a rather untidy plant and looks better if left to scramble over fences rather than being tied against a house wall.

VARIETIES: The commonest species in the *Shrubby Group* is the evergreen **L. nitida** (6 ft) which is often grown as a hedge. The leaves may be colourful (**'Baggesen's Gold'** has yellow foliage) but the yellow flowers in May are insignificant. Another sparse bloomer is **L. syringantha** (3 ft) — the small lilac flowers in early summer are very fragrant. **L. tatarica** (10 ft) produces abundant pink flowers in May–June and these are followed by red berries — for scented creamy-white flowers throughout winter grow **L. fragrantissima** (7 ft). The favourite ground-cover type is **L. pileata** (3 ft x 3 ft, shiny berries). The *Climbing Group* offers a larger choice. **L. periclymenum** is our native Honeysuckle or Woodbine. In July–August the fragrant flowers appear on the 20 ft stems — red outside and cream within. The variety **'Belgica'** blooms earlier than the species and **'Serotina'** continues until October. **'Graham Thomas'** blooms over a long period — white in bud and yellow in flower. Woodbine is deciduous and so are the summer-flowering and fragrant **L. americana** and the yellow-flowered **L. tellmanniana** which produces its scentless blooms in June-July. Another popular scentless Honeysuckle which loses its leaves in the winter is the vigorous climber **L. brownii 'Dropmore Scarlet'** which bears clusters of bright red flowers from June until September or October. The most popular evergreen species is the tall-growing **L. japonica**, which keeps its leaves in an average winter but often hides its summer yellow flowers in the foliage. **'Aureoreticulata'** has yellow netted leaves. The bright yellow **L. tragophylla** (June–July) is reputed to have the largest of all Honeysuckle blooms.

SITE & SOIL: Requires moist soil — thrives in sun or light shade.

PRUNING: Shrubby varieties: Cut back shoots which bear faded blooms. Climbing varieties: Remove unwanted growth and a few old stems after flowering.

PROPAGATION: Layer shoots or plant semi-ripe cuttings in a cold frame in summer.

Lonicera tatarica

Lonicera periclymenum 'Serotina'

Lonicera tragophylla

LUPINUS Tree Lupin

Medium shrub
•
Evergreen
•

Colours available

Flowering period

JANUARY	
FEBRUARY	
MARCH	
APRIL	
MAY	
JUNE	✓
JULY	✓
AUGUST	✓
SEPTEMBER	
OCTOBER	
NOVEMBER	
DECEMBER	

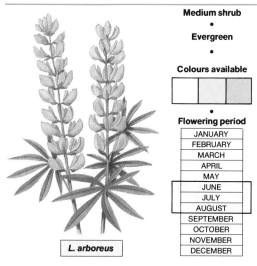

L. arboreus

One of the most popular plants in the flower border is the herbaceous Lupin, but the shrubby form known as the Tree Lupin is a rarity in the shrub border. This evergreen is a soft-stemmed bush which grows 5–6 ft high and in summer bears colourful flowering spikes of the typical Lupin form. These heads, however, are shorter than the impressive spikes produced by the modern herbaceous hybrids. The Tree Lupin is a quick-growing plant but it does not live for more than a few years. It is worth searching for if you have an unfriendly situation such as a windy spot near the sea or poor, sandy soil.

VARIETIES: There is a single species — **L. arboreus**. The upright spikes bear numerous pale yellow flowers which are sweet smelling. This floral display lasts throughout the summer, and it is easy to raise new stock from seed. The progeny is not always yellow like its parent — occasional pale blue-flowering plants may be produced. If you want to be sure of a variant to the basic pale yellow colour of the species then grow one of the three varieties — **'Snow Queen'** (white), **'Golden Spire'** (deep yellow) or **'Mauve Queen'** (pale purple).

SITE & SOIL: Requires a free-draining site — do not grow in heavy or rich soil. Thrives in full sun.

PRUNING: Shorten the stems in March or April to keep growth in check.

PROPAGATION: Raise L. arboreus from seed — plant cuttings of named varieties in a cold frame in summer.

Lupinus arboreus

LYCIUM Duke of Argyll's Tea Tree

Medium shrub
•
Deciduous
•

Colour available

Flowering period

JANUARY	
FEBRUARY	
MARCH	
APRIL	
MAY	
JUNE	✓
JULY	✓
AUGUST	✓
SEPTEMBER	✓
OCTOBER	
NOVEMBER	
DECEMBER	

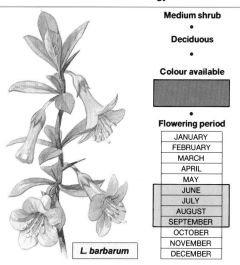

L. barbarum

Like its partner on this page this scrambling untidy shrub will not be found at the average garden centre, but despite its rarity in gardens (although it was introduced into this country before 1800) it flourishes in dry, sandy soil near the sea. Lycium is invasive and is not recommended as a specimen plant for the shrub border — it should be grown as a windbreak, hedge or as cover for a sandy bank in coastal areas where the salt-laden air would be a problem for more choice plants. It has become naturalised in a number of areas around the coast and you may well have seen it as an informal hedge at seaside resorts.

VARIETY: There is just one species sold for garden planting — **L. barbarum** (**L. chinense**). It is a spreading, arching plant growing about 6 ft high and 10–12 ft wide. The spiny branches bear short, strap-like leaves and funnel-shaped flowers between June and September. It is a fast-growing and fully hardy shrub with a hatred for wet soil. When the clusters of flowers fade the egg-shaped fruits appear, orange or red and often more showy than the flowers which are sometimes half-hidden by the foliage. These berries are about 1 in. long.

SITE & SOIL: Requires free-draining sandy soil — full sun is essential.

PRUNING: Cut out one-third of the old wood to ground level in March.

PROPAGATION: Plant semi-ripe cuttings in a cold frame in summer.

Lycium barbarum

MAGNOLIA Magnolia

M. soulangiana

M. soulangiana 'Rustica Rubra'

Small, medium or large shrub
•
Deciduous
or
Evergreen
•
Colours available

•
Flowering period

JANUARY
FEBRUARY
MARCH
APRIL
MAY
JUNE
JULY
AUGUST
SEPTEMBER
OCTOBER
NOVEMBER
DECEMBER

M. grandiflora

M. stellata

Many gardeners consider the Magnolia to be the most beautiful of flowering shrubs. Others may choose the Rhododendron or Rose, but all agree that a choice Magnolia in full bloom is a splendid sight. All of this beauty comes at a price — you will have to learn a few rules if you are not to be disappointed when planting one in your garden. First of all, make sure you have room for the specimen you have chosen — some can grow 25 ft high in time. Nearly all need to be grown away from touching shrubs so they can show their full beauty, and the time for planting is April and not autumn. Choose a spot which is away from a frost pocket and is sheltered from northerly and easterly winds. Add plenty of peat to the soil and don't plant too deeply. Water the new bush copiously if there is a drought and never dig or plant close to the stem. Each spring mulch with a layer of compost.

VARIETIES: The favourite three (M. stellata, M. soulangiana and M. grandiflora) are beautiful plants but, as described in this section, there are other ones which are less usual but are well worth considering. Where space is limited then the Star Magnolia (**M. stellata**) is the one to pick. It grows about 4–5 ft high and each March or April is covered with fragrant, starry white flowers. The variety **'Water Lily'** has the largest flowers. Late-spring flowerers in the 6–7 ft range of bushes are **M. liliiflora 'Nigra'** (purple/white, May) and **M. loebneri 'Leonard Messell'** (lilac, strap-like petals, May–June). The most popular Magnolia is **M. soulangiana**, a spreading bush which can reach 12 ft but can be kept in check by regular pruning. The flowers appear in April before the leaves — goblet shaped, white within and pink or purple-tinged at the base. There are variations — **'Rustica Rubra'** is all-pink and **'Alba Superba'** is all-white. For the largest flowers (6–7 in. across) choose **'Lennei'** (rosy-purple/white). The most spectacular Magnolia is **M. grandiflora**, an evergreen slow-growing tree which will reach 20 ft or more in time. The creamy-white blooms in July-September are up to 10 in. across, but the tree has to be 20–25 years old before the flowers begin to appear. With the varieties **'Exmouth'** and **'Goliath'** the wait is less than 10 years — grow these plants as wall shrubs. The June-flowering group are large shrubs with nodding white flowers with red anthers — look for **M. sinensis** and **M. wilsonii**.

SITE & SOIL: Any reasonable garden soil will do, but many varieties do not like chalk. Thrives in sun or light shade.

PRUNING: Not necessary. Remove dead wood and unwanted branches after flowering.

PROPAGATION: Layer shoots in early summer. Difficult to raise from cuttings.

Magnolia stellata

Magnolia loebneri 'Leonard Messell'

Magnolia soulangiana

MAHONIA Mahonia

Small or medium shrub

•

Evergreen

•

Colour available

•

Flowering period

JANUARY
FEBRUARY
MARCH
APRIL
MAY
JUNE
JULY
AUGUST
SEPTEMBER
OCTOBER
NOVEMBER
DECEMBER

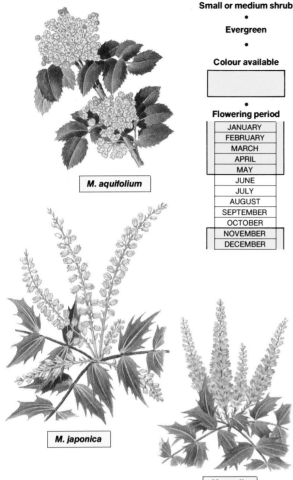

M. aquifolium

M. japonica

M. media 'Charity'

It is not surprising that Mahonia is one of our most popular shrubs. It has year-round interest — evergreen shiny leaves which are often tinged with purple in winter and fragrant flowers between autumn and spring, depending on the variety. After the flowers there are blue-black berries. The popular types grow in shade and in any garden soil — they are ideal as ground cover under trees or close to the north side of the house. The only problem is that the favourite varieties are just a little too popular, and so a few of the more unusual ones are listed below.

VARIETIES: M. aquifolium (Oregon Grape) is the most popular species and you will see it everywhere. It is a low-growing plant (3 ft x 6 ft after 10 years) which is used for ground cover and for retaining soil on sloping banks. The leaflets are Holly-like — dark green in summer and bronze or purple in winter. The yellow flowers are borne in clusters in March and April. **'Apollo'** is a widely-available variety which does not sucker and become invasive like the species — **'Atropurpureum'** has rich purple leaves in winter. Almost matching M. aquifolium in popularity is the taller and more erect **M. japonica** (6 ft). The flower spikes radiate from the stem like the spokes of a wheel. Each pendulous spike bears a mass of lemon yellow flowers with a distinct Lily-of-the-Valley fragrance — the floral display lasts from November to February. The variety **'Bealei'** bears short, erect flower spikes which give a shuttlecock effect. **M. lomarifolia** is perhaps the most imposing species, growing 8 ft tall and bearing terminal clusters of 1 ft high flower spikes. It is unfortunately rather tender, but has given rise to several excellent hybrids grouped together as **M. media. 'Charity'** is a beauty and is highly recommended as a specimen shrub — 6 ft high with tall spikes of flowers from Christmas to February. Other recommended varieties include **'Lionel Fortesque'** and **'Winter Sun'**. All of the Mahonias described so far are widely available — less easy to locate is the low-growing suckering variety **M. nervosa** which waits until May before flowering. **M. undulata** is another of the less-usual Mahonias — it grows about 6 ft high and bears glossy, wavy-edged leaves. For hedging grow the Mahonia x Berberis hybrid **Mahoberberis aquisargentii**.

SITE & SOIL: Any reasonable garden soil will do — thrives in shady situations.

PRUNING: Not necessary — cut back unwanted stems in April.

PROPAGATION: Remove and use rooted suckers of M. aquifolium. For other types plant semi-ripe cuttings in a cold frame in summer.

Mahonia aquifolium

Mahonia lomarifolia

Mahonia media 'Charity'

MENZIESIA Menziesia

Small shrub
•
Deciduous
•
Colours available
•
Flowering period

JANUARY
FEBRUARY
MARCH
APRIL
MAY
JUNE
JULY
AUGUST
SEPTEMBER
OCTOBER
NOVEMBER
DECEMBER

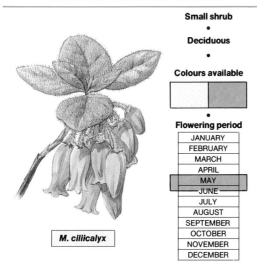

M. ciliicalyx

This rarity is a member of the Erica family, and as with nearly all other Heather-like shrubs it needs acid and moist soil. The clusters of pendent urn-shaped flowers at the tips of the stems make the plant look like a giant Heather, and planting it in a bed of Ericas or Callunas is a useful way of giving height and variety. The leaves, however, are not Heather-like as they are about 3 in. long and oval. Menziesia is a hardy shrub but the flower buds can be damaged by a late frost, so choose a spot sheltered from cold winds. Mulch annually to keep the roots cool.

VARIETIES: The most popular species is **M. ciliicalyx**. It grows about 3 ft high — the branches are sometimes tiered in wedding cake fashion and the leaves are hairy. The waxy flowers are about ½ in. long and appear in May — the colour of the blooms ranges from an insipid creamy-green to pink. The variety **'Purpurea'** is a better choice — the flowers are larger and the colour is an attractive rosy-purple. The flowering period extends from early May to mid June. One or two other species are available from tree and shrub specialist nurseries — some (e.g **M. alba**, **M. polifolia**) are now listed under Daboecia cantabrica (page 38).

SITE & SOIL: Well-drained acid soil is necessary — thrives in partial shade. Add peat at planting time.

PRUNING: Not necessary — cut back dead or damaged shoots in March.

PROPAGATION: Plant semi-ripe cuttings in a propagator in summer.

Menziesia ciliicalyx

MYRICA Bayberry

Medium shrub
•
Deciduous or Evergreen
•
Colours available
•
Berrying period

JANUARY
FEBRUARY
MARCH
APRIL
MAY
JUNE
JULY
AUGUST
SEPTEMBER
OCTOBER
NOVEMBER
DECEMBER

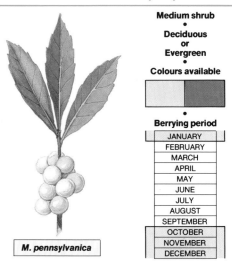

M. pennsylvanica

An unusual plant in a couple of ways. Myrica is unusual as it is rarely seen in gardens or garden centres, and it is unusual in that two species need boggy soil and the other two species need dry, infertile soil. If you have reasonable garden soil, forget about this one! It is not in any way spectacular — the flowers appear on small brownish catkins in April–May. Plants bear either male or female catkins, so you will need types of both sexes if you are to enjoy the most eye-catching thing about this shrub — between autumn and midwinter wax-covered berries appear along the stems.

VARIETIES: The one you are most likely to find is **M. gale** (Sweet Gale, Bog Myrtle). As with other Myricas, the leaves are lance-shaped and aromatic — with this species they have a reddish tinge. It will flourish in boggy land, reaching about 5 ft. The other Myrica for a damp site is the evergreen **M. cerifera** (Wax Myrtle) — 10 ft, with purplish-white berries. Another species with purplish-white berries is **M. pennsylvanica** — 8 ft, deciduous and thrives in acid, dry soil. Poor, dry soil is also required for **M. californica** — 10 ft, deciduous with purple berries.

SITE & SOIL: Depending on species, very moist acid soil or dry, infertile soil. Thrives in partial shade.

PRUNING: Not necessary — avoid cutting back branches unless it is essential.

PROPAGATION: Plant semi-ripe cuttings in a cold frame in spring.

Myrica gale

MYRTUS Myrtle

Small or medium shrub
•
Evergreen
•
Colour available

•
Flowering period

| JANUARY |
| FEBRUARY |
| MARCH |
| APRIL |
| MAY |
| JUNE |
| JULY |
| AUGUST |
| SEPTEMBER |
| OCTOBER |
| NOVEMBER |
| DECEMBER |

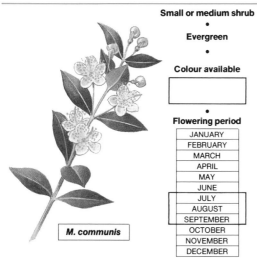

M. communis

This shrub was grown in English gardens in the 16th century, and a sprig was always included in the Victorian bride's bouquet. However, it is not a popular plant nowadays and you will have to go to a larger garden centre to find one. The problem is its lack of hardiness — unless your area is especially mild you will have to plant it against a south- or west-facing wall. Soil is not a problem — it will grow in acid or chalky land. The general form of the Myrtle is a tall bush or small tree with dark leaves and a display of white Rose-like flowers in mid and late summer. These flowers are followed by purple-black berries in autumn.

VARIETIES: The most popular and hardiest species is **M. communis** — the Common Myrtle. It grows about 10 ft high and in July–September the small white flowers with a central boss of fluffy stamens appear. The variety **'Tarentina'** is useful in the small garden as it grows only 3 ft high. There are **'Variegata'** with cream-edged leaves and the rare double-flowered form **'Flore Pleno'**. The leaves of **M. luma** (**Luma apiculata**) are dull and not glossy, and the fruits are edible. You will need a mild location for this one, and also for its gold-variegated variety **'Glanleam Gold'**.

SITE & SOIL: Any well-drained garden soil will do — the site must be sheltered and sunny.

PRUNING: Not necessary, but unwanted growth can be cut back hard in spring.

PROPAGATION: Plant semi-ripe cuttings in a propagator in summer.

Myrtus communis 'Tarentina'

NANDINA Heavenly Bamboo

Small shrub
•
Evergreen
•
Colour available

•
Flowering period

| JANUARY |
| FEBRUARY |
| MARCH |
| APRIL |
| MAY |
| JUNE |
| JULY |
| AUGUST |
| SEPTEMBER |
| OCTOBER |
| NOVEMBER |
| DECEMBER |

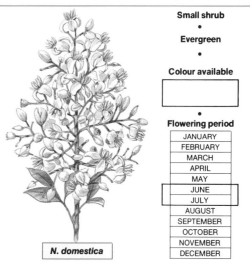

N. domestica

Some years ago Nandina was truly a rarity, but you should now be able to find it at your garden centre. The reason is the recent increase in the use of shrubs in the garden, and ones with coloured foliage are high on the list. Nandina foliage is tinged with red in the spring and flushed with orange in autumn. It is also a flowering and berrying plant — in midsummer large heads of long-stemmed small flowers appear above the leaves, and in autumn there are long-lasting red berries. The stems are upright and the long leaves are made up of numerous oval leaflets. Shoots may die back after a severe winter but new ones will grow up from the base in spring.

VARIETIES: There is just one species — **N. domestica**. When mature it forms a clump about 4 ft high and 3 ft wide. The upright, unbranched stems give it a rather Bamboo-like appearance, but it is a member of the Berberis and not the Bamboo family. The evergreen leaflets are tinged with warm colours in spring and autumn. The variety **'Firepower'** is much more brightly coloured with reds and oranges at the start and at the end of the season. It is also more compact, growing about 3 ft high.

SITE & SOIL: Any well-drained garden soil will do — thrives best in full sun.

PRUNING: Not necessary, but flower-heads should be removed once the berries have gone. After a few years some of the tallest stems can be cut back in early spring.

PROPAGATION: Plant semi-ripe cuttings (plus heel) in a cold frame in late summer.

Nandina domestica

NEILLIA Neillia

Medium shrub
•
Deciduous
•

Colours available

Flowering period

JANUARY
FEBRUARY
MARCH
APRIL
MAY
JUNE
JULY
AUGUST
SEPTEMBER
OCTOBER
NOVEMBER
DECEMBER

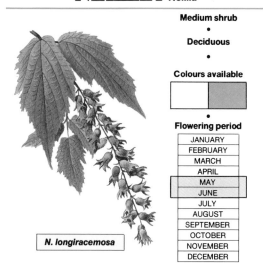

N. longiracemosa

The plant label will tell you that this shrub is easy to grow and bears sprays of attractive flowers in early summer. There are no hidden problems, but Neillia has never caught the public fancy and so remains an uncommon plant for the shrub border. It is a relative of Spiraea, and is a graceful shrub with slender upright stems which branch near the tip. In time a thicket is formed — 6 ft high and 8 ft wide. The leaves often have three lobes with serrated edges and prominent veins, and the pink tubular flowers appear in pendent racemes.

VARIETIES: The most widely available species is **N. longiracemosa** which may be listed as **N. thibetica**. The stems are downy, and in late spring or early summer the flowering sprays appear at the tips of the branches. Each spray is 3–6 in. long and carries 20–30 rosy-pink flowers. A species rather similar to N. longiracemosa is **N. affinis**, which grows to the same height and bears pink-flowered sprays, but these are only 2–3 in. long and bear no more than 10 blooms. The only other species on offer as a garden plant is the 9 ft high **N. sinensis** which produces short sprays of white flowers.

SITE & SOIL: Any reasonable garden soil will do — thrives in full sun or light shade.

PRUNING: After flowering cut back old branches which have borne blooms and shorten the young shoots.

PROPAGATION: Remove rooted pieces or plant semi-ripe cuttings in a cold frame in summer.

Neillia longiracemosa

OLEARIA Daisy Bush

Small or medium shrub
•
Evergreen
•

Colours available

Flowering period

JANUARY
FEBRUARY
MARCH
APRIL
MAY
JUNE
JULY
AUGUST
SEPTEMBER
OCTOBER
NOVEMBER
DECEMBER

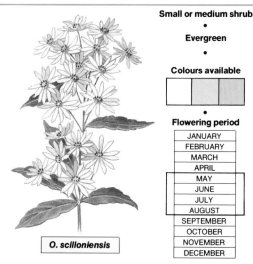

O. scilloniensis

The Daisy Bush is a thing of beauty when in bloom — clusters of Daisy-like flowers may cover the whole bush. These flowers are nearly always white-petalled, but pink and blue varieties are available. When not in bloom, this shrub is not a thing of beauty as its shape and leaves are not particularly interesting. There is a tough side to its character — it does not mind exposed sites, salt-laden air or atmospheric pollution, but all the garden Olearias need full sun to thrive and only two can be regarded as reliably hardy. The taller types are used for hedging in milder coastal areas.

VARIETIES: O. haastii is one of the popular species and has a good reputation for hardiness. It grows about 5 ft high, and in July and August masses of white flowers cover the Box-like leaves. Another hardy species which grows 5 ft high and flowers in July is **O. nummularifolia** — it is distinguished by its small flower-heads and thick yellowish-green leaves. The tall **O. macrodonta** (8 ft, June) is popular — look for the sage-green Holly-like leaves. For May flowers grow **O. scilloniensis** — for coloured blooms grow **O. phlogopappa 'Comber's Blue'** or **'Comber's Pink'**.

SITE & SOIL: Any well-drained reasonable soil will do — thrives best in full sun.

PRUNING: Dead-head the faded blooms with shears after flowering. Remove dead branches in April.

PROPAGATION: Plant semi-ripe cuttings in a cold frame in summer.

Olearia haastii

OSMANTHUS Osmanthus

Medium shrub
•
Evergreen
•
Colours available
•
Flowering period

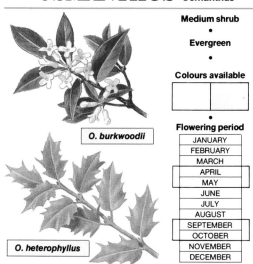

O. burkwoodii

O. heterophyllus

JANUARY	
FEBRUARY	
MARCH	
APRIL	
MAY	
JUNE	
JULY	
AUGUST	
SEPTEMBER	
OCTOBER	
NOVEMBER	
DECEMBER	

Osmanthus is an excellent bush to plant between shrubs with large and colourful flowers. It has a neat and rounded growth habit, and is densely covered with evergreen leaves. The white or creamy tubular blooms are small, but they have a Jasmine-like fragrance. The period of flowering is either spring or autumn, depending on the species you have chosen. Osmanthus does not have to be pruned, but it can be cut back regularly without harm and makes an excellent hedge. No problems, but the leaves are scorched by cold northerly winds in winter.

VARIETIES: The most popular species is **O. delavayi** — a 5 ft shrub with arching stems, Box-like foliage and masses of white blooms in April. It is a parent of **O. burkwoodii** (**Osmarea burkwoodii**) which bears leathery glossy foliage — dark green and an attractive foil for the clusters of tubular white flowers in April and May. The most popular of the autumn-flowering species is **O. heterophyllus** which is easily recognised by its Holly-like foliage. There are several interesting varieties, including **'Purpureus'** (purple-tinged leaves) and **'Variegatus'** (creamy white-edged leaves). The flowers, half hidden by the foliage, appear in September–October.

SITE & SOIL: Any well-drained reasonable soil will do — thrives in sun or partial shade. Light shade is best.

PRUNING: Not necessary — remove dead or unwanted branches immediately after flowering.

PROPAGATION: Layer branches in autumn or plant semi-ripe cuttings in a cold frame in summer.

Osmanthus delavayi

OZOTHAMNUS Ozothamnus

Small shrub
•
Evergreen
•
Colour available
•
Flowering period

O. rosmarinifolius

JANUARY	
FEBRUARY	
MARCH	
APRIL	
MAY	
JUNE	
JULY	
AUGUST	
SEPTEMBER	
OCTOBER	
NOVEMBER	
DECEMBER	

This small Australasian shrub was once classed with and is still sometimes listed as Helichrysum — see page 55. As you would expect, there are many shared features such as narrow leaves, small flowers surrounded by 'everlasting' bracts and a need for good drainage and full sun. The distinguishing characteristics of Ozothamnus are the presence of red or reddish flower buds which open to form white flowers with brown or red bracts beneath. The fluffy seed heads which form when flowering is over are quite decorative. Once thought to be rather tender, the two species described below have proved to be quite hardy.

VARIETIES: Several species are obtainable from specialist nurseries, but only two are reasonably widely available. **O. ledifolius** is the Kerosene bush, so called because the gum on the underside of the ½ in. long leaves and on the stems is inflammable. The foliage is yellowish below and the seed heads have a honey-like fragrance. It is a rounded bush about 3 ft high — **O. rosmarinifolius** is larger, reaching nearly 5 ft and with leaves about 1½ in. long. This narrow foliage has a bluish-green hue like Rosemary, and the young stems are covered with white wool.

SITE & SOIL: Requires light, well-drained soil — full sun is essential.

PRUNING: Not necessary, but can be cut back to maintain bushy growth habit.

PROPAGATION: Plant semi-ripe cuttings in a cold frame in summer.

Ozothamnus ledifolius

PAEONIA Tree Peony

Medium shrub
•
Deciduous
•
Colours available

•
Flowering period

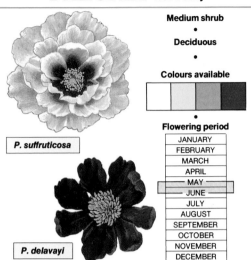

P. suffruticosa

| JANUARY |
| FEBRUARY |
| MARCH |
| APRIL |
| MAY |
| JUNE |
| JULY |
| AUGUST |
| SEPTEMBER |
| OCTOBER |
| NOVEMBER |
| DECEMBER |

P. delavayi

Peonies are much more familiar as herbaceous border plants than as shrubs, but there are several woody forms. They are spectacular bushes in both leaf and flower, but you do need the right conditions. Peonies will fail in poorly-drained clays or infertile sands. The leaves of some species are up to 1 ft long and deeply divided so as to be ornamental, but the real glory is the flowers — large cups or balls of papery petals. A fine sight, but the flowering period is short. It is usually best to choose a single or semi-double variety — the heavy blooms of double-flowering types often need individual staking.

VARIETIES: For white, pink or red cup-shaped flowers which are up to 6 in. across, choose a variety of **P. suffruticosa** (Moutan Peony) which grows about 6 ft high. Examples include **'Rock's Variety'** (single, pale pink), **'Higurashi'** (semi-double, crimson) and **'Hodai'** (double, rosy-red). For saucer-shaped flowers in golden yellow pick the popular **P. lutea ludlowii**. If you want really large yellow blooms then you will have to grow one of the **P. lemoinei** varieties, such as **'Alice Harding'**. The suckering shrub **P. delavayi** (5 ft) bears single crimson flowers — the leaves are highly ornamental.

SITE & SOIL: Well-drained, fertile soil is necessary. Choose a sunny and sheltered site.

PRUNING: When the bush is mature remove a few of the oldest stems in early spring.

PROPAGATION: Sow seed in spring for species — for named varieties buy container-grown plants.

Paeonia lutea ludlowii

PARAHEBE Parahebe

Prostrate shrub
•
Evergreen
•
Colours available

•
Flowering period

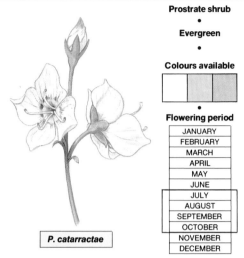

P. catarractae

| JANUARY |
| FEBRUARY |
| MARCH |
| APRIL |
| MAY |
| JUNE |
| JULY |
| AUGUST |
| SEPTEMBER |
| OCTOBER |
| NOVEMBER |
| DECEMBER |

Some time ago the genus Veronica was split into the Hebes (woody plants) and the Veronicas (herbaceous plants). A few, the Parahebes, didn't fit neatly into either group, so at the garden centre you may find them with the shrubs, alpines or perennials. They are in fact semi-woody shrubs and are useful as ground cover or specimen plants in the rock garden. Parahebes generally grow less than 1 ft high and produce small white, blue or pink Speedwell-like flowers. These blooms are borne in loose erect clusters and appear in late summer or early autumn.

VARIETIES: The most popular species is **P. catarractae** — a dwarf and spreading bush which grows about 10 in. high. The flowers are white or pale purple with a crimson central ring and appear in August–October. Mauve-veined and blue varieties are available — **'Diffusa'** is a pink-veined, white-flowering variety which forms a prostrate mat. **P. lyallii** is another species which is available in spring from large garden centres and is an easier plant to grow. It is a spreading bush 8 in. high with leathery leaves and pink-veined white flowers in July and August. Another easy-to-grow one is **P. bidwillii** (6 in.) but it may be difficult to find.

SITE & SOIL: Any well-drained garden soil will do — thrives best in full sun.

PRUNING: Not necessary — cut back dead or unwanted branches in spring.

PROPAGATION: Plant softwood cuttings in a cold frame in early summer.

Parahebe catarractae

PASSIFLORA Passion Flower

Climbing shrub
•
Deciduous
or
Semi-evergreen

Colours available

•

Flowering period

JANUARY
FEBRUARY
MARCH
APRIL
MAY
JUNE
JULY
AUGUST
SEPTEMBER
OCTOBER
NOVEMBER
DECEMBER

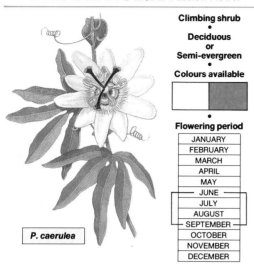

P. caerulea

Sometimes described as one of the most exotic blooms in the garden, this claim to fame is based on its interesting and unusual structure rather than colour or size. The flower parts resemble in shape or number the various features of Christ's Passion. Very few forms of Passiflora can be grown outdoors and even these moderately hardy ones must be grown against a south- or west-facing wall. Stems may be cut down by frost, but new ones should appear in spring.

VARIETIES: The only popular species is the Blue Passion Flower **P. caerulea**. It is a vigorous climber which can reach 20 ft — provide a stout support for its tendrils. The leaves are large with five to seven lobes — the slightly fragrant flowers are 3 in. across. The petals and sepals are similar, forming a white or greenish-white ring around the intricate centre. Stamens, styles and stigmas are all prominent, and there is a corona of coloured filaments — in August the orange egg-shaped fruits appear. **'Constance Elliott'** is an all-white variety and is claimed to be a little hardier. Only one other species should be tried outdoors — the violet-flowered **P. umbilicata**.

SITE & SOIL: Free-draining soil in full sun is essential — provide young plants with maximum frost protection in winter.

PRUNING: Cut back all frost-damaged and unwanted growth in April.

PROPAGATION: Layer stems in spring or plant semi-ripe cuttings in a cold frame in summer.

Passiflora caerulea

PERNETTYA Prickly Heath

Dwarf shrub
•
Evergreen
•

Colours available

•

Berrying period

JANUARY
FEBRUARY
MARCH
APRIL
MAY
JUNE
JULY
AUGUST
SEPTEMBER
OCTOBER
NOVEMBER
DECEMBER

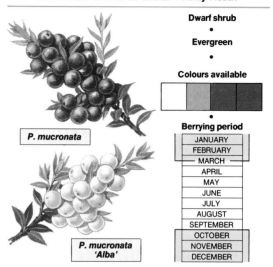

P. mucronata

P. mucronata 'Alba'

One of the best of all the berrying bushes. Birds don't like the large, porcelain-like fruits and so they remain on the suckering bush from early autumn until early spring. The bush grows about waist-high and spreads steadily to form a dense thicket. In May or June the creamy-white flowers appear — bell-shaped and pendent. These blooms are either male or female and are nearly always borne on separate plants, so you have to grow a group (one male to three to five female varieties) to make sure that berries will be produced. The dark green leaves are about ½ in. long and are stiff and prickly.

VARIETIES: The only species you will find at your local garden centre is **P. mucronata**. It rarely exceeds 3 ft in height and the wiry stems bear masses of blooms. There is just one hermaphrodite (male- and female-flowering) variety — **'Bell's Seedling'** (dark pink berries). For male plants look for one of the following labels — **'Edward Balls'**, **'Male'**, **'Thymifolia'** or **'Masculata'**. Popular female varieties include **'Cherry Ripe'** (cherry red berries), **'Lilian'** (pink), **'Mother of Pearl'** (pale pink), **'Mulberry Wine'** (purple) and the white-berried **'Alba'** and **'White Pearl'**.

SITE & SOIL: Acid soil is essential — add peat at planting time. Thrives in sun or partial shade.

PRUNING: Not necessary — trim back unwanted branches in spring or summer.

PROPAGATION: Sow seed in spring or remove rooted suckers and plant in autumn.

Pernettya mucronata 'Bell's Seedling'

PEROVSKIA Russian Sage

Small shrub
•
Deciduous
•
Colour available

•
Flowering period

JANUARY	
FEBRUARY	
MARCH	
APRIL	
MAY	
JUNE	
JULY	
AUGUST	
SEPTEMBER	
OCTOBER	
NOVEMBER	
DECEMBER	

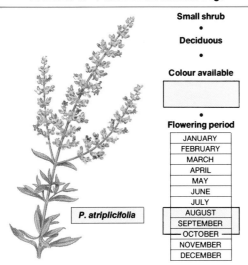

P. atriplicifolia

Perovskia is not widely grown and from a distance it is sometimes mistaken for an overgrown Lavender bush. The similarities include stiff, erect stems with small grey leaves and in late summer a display of tiny blue flowers borne on long spikes. On closer inspection the two plants are quite different — the leaves of Russian Sage are either deeply toothed or finely cut and when crushed emit a Sage-like aroma. The flowers are borne in branching sprays which give the plant an airy, open look. Some form of light staking may be necessary.

VARIETIES: The only species you will find at the garden centre is **P. atriplicifolia**. The stems grow about 3 ft tall and the sprays of Lavender-blue flowers are about 1 ft long. It is a plant for the herbaceous or mixed border where it provides end-of-season colour with its blue flower-heads and yellow autumn leaves. Its major drawback is that it is a late starter — being cut back each spring means that there is little to see until early summer. This is not a serious disadvantage if used in the middle or back of an herbaceous border. The variety **'Blue Spire'** with its larger flower-heads is more popular than the species.

SITE & SOIL: Any well-drained garden soil will do — full sun is essential.

PRUNING: Cut back the stems to a few inches above the ground in April.

PROPAGATION: Plant semi-ripe cuttings in a cold frame in summer.

Perovskia atriplicifolia 'Blue Spire'

PHLOMIS Jerusalem Sage

Dwarf or small shrub
•
Evergreen
•
Colours available

•
Flowering period

JANUARY	
FEBRUARY	
MARCH	
APRIL	
MAY	
JUNE	
JULY	
AUGUST	
SEPTEMBER	
OCTOBER	
NOVEMBER	
DECEMBER	

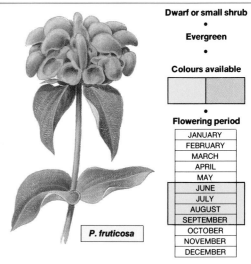

P. fruticosa

This shrub is grown for its distinctive foliage as well as for its attractive summer flowers. The rather coarse leaves are generally covered with dense woolly hairs and the stalk-less hooded blooms are borne in whorls along the stems. Phlomis makes a useful addition to the border where its greyish foliage provides an attractive contrast to the green leaves borne by so many other plants. With age Phlomis plants tend to become loose and floppy, and they can be killed in a cold and wet winter.

VARIETIES: The hardiest species is **P. fruticosa**, and it is the only one you are likely to find at the garden centre. It is low-growing, reaching about 3 ft, but it is wide-spreading. The deep yellow flowers appear in June and July and the grey-green foliage is furry. **P. 'Edward Bowles'** is a larger plant with 4–5 ft stems and sulphur yellow flowers which appear later in August and September. **P. chrysophylla** is a yellow, June-flowering Phlomis like P. fruticosa, but its soft grey leaves take on a distinct yellow tinge after July. **P. italica** is a 2 ft dwarf which is quite different from the others described above — the summer flowers are borne in terminal spikes and they are pale lilac in colour.

SITE & SOIL: Any well-drained soil will do — full sun is essential. Choose a sheltered site.

PRUNING: Cut back branches by about one-third in late spring. Remove frost-damaged stems.

PROPAGATION: Sow seed under glass in spring or plant softwood cuttings in a cold frame in summer.

Phlomis fruticosa

PHILADELPHUS Mock Orange

Tall and Medium Groups

P. 'Virginal'

P. coronarius

P. 'Beauclerk'

P. 'Belle Etoile'

Dwarf, small, medium or large shrub

•

Deciduous

•

Colours available

Flowering period

JANUARY
FEBRUARY
MARCH
APRIL
MAY
JUNE
JULY
AUGUST
SEPTEMBER
OCTOBER
NOVEMBER
DECEMBER

Low Group

P. 'Sybille'

P. microphyllus

Mock Orange is a great favourite and quite rightly so. White or creamy-white flowers appear in great profusion during June and July, and their Orange-blossom fragrance is quite strong. The usual height is about 6 ft, but there are dwarfs for the rockery and front of the bed as well as tall-growing varieties for the back of the border. The oval leaves are usually a pale shade of green and the flowers measure ¾–1½ in. across, depending on the variety. The great virtue of Philadelphus is that it provides abundant blooms in the high-summer gap between the spring floral display and the bright colours of autumn. Its other virtue is that it is fully hardy and will grow almost anywhere — in poor soil, windy sites and salt-laden air. It does not like too much shade, however, and you must prune it properly each year. Every shrub border needs at least one Philadelphus but don't call it Syringa — that is the latin name for Lilac.

VARIETIES: Plants in the *Tall Group* reach 10 ft or more if lightly pruned. **P. 'Virginal'** is the most popular one — the pure white flowers are double and are borne in pendent clusters. Equally tall but rather more spreading is the old favourite **P. coronarius** which has creamy-white single flowers. The *Medium Group* (5–10 ft) contains the largest number of varieties. For something different in foliage you can grow **P. coronarius 'Aureus'** in a sunny spot — the single white flowers are partly hidden by the golden yellow leaves. For something different in floral display you can choose a hybrid with flowers which are flushed with purple at the centre — two popular examples are **P. 'Beauclerk'** and **P. 'Belle Etoile'**. Other popular Mock Oranges in this Medium Group are the single-flowered **P. 'Erectus'** and **P. 'Innocence'** — for masses of double flowers choose **P. 'Enchantment'**. Varieties in the *Low Group* grow less than 5 ft high — here you will find the purple-blotched flowers of **P. 'Sybille'** and the white-edged leaves of **P. coronarius 'Variegatus'**. These two grow about 4–5 ft high — for something a little more compact you can grow **P. 'Silver Showers'** or **P. microphyllus** (single, very fragrant, 3 ft). The popular dwarf for the rock garden is **P. 'Manteau d'Hermine'** which grows 2 ft high and bears double flowers which are creamy-white.

SITE & SOIL: Any reasonable garden soil will do — it can be acid or chalky. Pick a sunny or lightly-shaded spot.

PRUNING: Immediately after flowering cut out about one-third of the old stems which have bloomed. Make sure the bush is not overcrowded with branches.

PROPAGATION: Plant semi-ripe cuttings in a cold frame in summer or hardwood cuttings in the open in late autumn.

Philadelphus 'Virginal'

Philadelphus 'Erectus'

Philadelphus coronarius 'Variegatus'

PHYGELIUS Cape Figwort

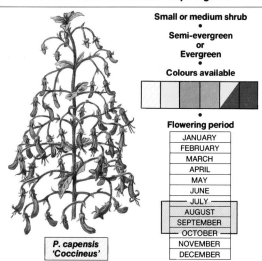

Small or medium shrub
•
Semi-evergreen
or
Evergreen
•
Colours available
•

Flowering period

| JANUARY |
| FEBRUARY |
| MARCH |
| APRIL |
| MAY |
| JUNE |
| JULY |
| AUGUST |
| SEPTEMBER |
| OCTOBER |
| NOVEMBER |
| DECEMBER |

P. capensis 'Coccineus'

An attractive shrub from South Africa which you will now find in many catalogues but in very few gardens. The problem is that it is susceptible to frost, but this need not put you off if you live in a relatively mild area. You can treat it as a border perennial, cutting off all the stems each spring and allowing new ones to grow up from the base. Alternatively you can grow it against a south wall and trim the frost-affected side shoots away from the main stems each year. It is certainly worth trying if you have succeeded with rather delicate plants in the past.

VARIETIES: P. aequalis is one of the widely available species. The shrub grows about 3 ft high and produces one-sided flower-heads bearing numerous yellow-throated pink or red blooms — the variety **'Yellow Trumpet'** has all-yellow flowers. **P. capensis 'Coccineus'** (8 ft or more as a wall shrub) differs in having its nodding flowers all round the spike, and each yellow-throated red bloom has reflexed lobes at the mouth. The hybrid of the two basic species is **P. rectus** and a number of named varieties are listed — look for **'African Queen'** (pale red), **'Moonraker'** (yellow), **'Salmon Leap'** (orange) and **'Devil's Tears'** (dark pink).

SITE & SOIL: Any well-drained garden soil will do — thrives in sun or light shade.

PRUNING: Prune to ground level in early April — with wall shrubs remove all side shoots killed by frost.

PROPAGATION: Sow seed under glass or plant semi-ripe cuttings in a cold frame in summer.

Phygelius aequalis 'Yellow Trumpet'

PHYSOCARPUS Nine Bark

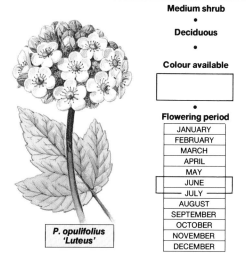

Medium shrub
•
Deciduous
•
Colour available
•

Flowering period

| JANUARY |
| FEBRUARY |
| MARCH |
| APRIL |
| MAY |
| JUNE |
| JULY |
| AUGUST |
| SEPTEMBER |
| OCTOBER |
| NOVEMBER |
| DECEMBER |

P. opulifolius 'Luteus'

The three-lobed leaves are usually yellow or golden, and in summer there are dome-shaped heads of white or pink-tinged white flowers. In autumn there are small red fruits and in winter pieces of the bark peel away to reveal the coloured wood below. It presents no problems — there is no worry about frost damage and Nine Bark will grow in almost any soil apart from shallow chalk. Flowering stems with their display of brightly-coloured leaves and tightly-packed clusters of flowers are excellent material for flower arranging.

VARIETIES: There is just one species which is sold for garden use — **P. opulifolius**. It is occasionally listed as **Spiraea opulifolia** — each individual bloom is similar in form to that of a spring-flowering Spiraea. The basic species has green foliage and it is very difficult to locate a supplier. It is not worth searching for, as the coloured-leaved varieties are much more desirable. The first one was **'Luteus'** (8 ft) with its foliage which remains clear yellow until midsummer. **'Dart's Gold'** is a definite improvement — leaves are more plentiful, the shrub (6 ft) is more compact and the golden-yellow colour of the foliage lasts longer.

SITE & SOIL: Any well-drained garden soil will do — thrives in sun or light shade.

PRUNING: Immediately after flowering cut to ground level about one-third of the old shoots which have flowered.

PROPAGATION: Plant semi-ripe cuttings in a cold frame in summer or hardwood cuttings in the open in late autumn.

Physocarpus opulifolius 'Dart's Gold'

PIERIS Andromeda

Small or medium shrub
•
Evergreen
•

Colours available

Flowering period

JANUARY	
FEBRUARY	
MARCH	
APRIL	
MAY	
JUNE	
JULY	
AUGUST	
SEPTEMBER	
OCTOBER	
NOVEMBER	
DECEMBER	

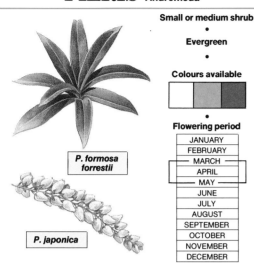

P. formosa forrestii

P. japonica

Not too many years ago you would find only one or two varieties on offer at the average garden centre, but nowadays you can often find a range of different types. Pieris has become increasingly popular as gardeners have realised what a useful shrub it is. In spring there are the long sprays of bell-shaped blooms which look like Lily-of-the-Valley, and with the more popular varieties there is a bright red display of young foliage. Neat, slow-growing and requiring little attention.

VARIETIES: The boldest display is provided by the varieties of **P. formosa forrestii. 'Wakehurst'** (8–10 ft) is the most popular one, with vivid red young foliage and white flowers in April and May. **'Jermyns'** has the added benefit of red flower buds all winter. For a similar but less frost-sensitive plant, choose **P. 'Forest Flame'** (6 ft) or its sport **P. 'Flaming Silver'** which bears white-edged mature leaves. Turn to **P. japonica** (6 ft) if you want March–April drooping flower-heads and colours other than white. Young foliage is coppery — varieties include **'Flamingo'** (pink flowers), **'Pygmaea'** (3 ft high) and **'Variegata'** (silver-edged leaves). **'Valley Valentine'** bears red flowers which are white at the base.

SITE & SOIL: Acid soil is essential — add peat at planting time. Shade from morning sun is beneficial.

PRUNING: Not necessary — remove unwanted branches in late winter and dead flowers in May.

PROPAGATION: Sow seed under glass in spring or layer branches in early summer.

Pieris formosa forrestii 'Wakehurst'

PIPTANTHUS Evergreen Laburnum

Large shrub
•
Semi-evergreen
•

Colour available

Flowering period

JANUARY	
FEBRUARY	
MARCH	
APRIL	
MAY	
JUNE	
JULY	
AUGUST	
SEPTEMBER	
OCTOBER	
NOVEMBER	
DECEMBER	

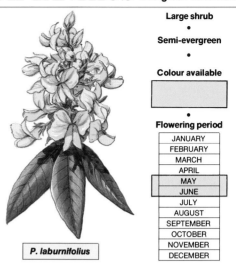

P. laburnifolius

You will find this shrub in lots of tree and shrub catalogues but it is rarely available at the garden centre. Like the Laburnum tree it has leaves which are made up of three leaflets and in spring there is a bright display of large Pea-like flowers. These blooms, however, are borne in erect flower-heads and not in drooping racemes like a Laburnum. In addition it is a somewhat tender plant which needs a warm spot in the garden. It has its good points — Piptanthus makes a change from the over-popular Laburnum and it has excellent resistance to drought, but it is not a long-lived plant.

VARIETY: There is just one species — **P. laburnifolius** (**P. nepalensis**). When planted in the open it will eventually become an 8 ft x 8 ft bush, but it is better to grow it against a south-facing wall where it may reach 10 ft or more. The 4 in. long leaflets are glossy on the upper surface and despite the common name some or all of them may fall if the winter weather is severe. Grey pods are formed in the autumn and seed can be saved, but it is easier to raise new plants from layers or cuttings. A plant to buy if you like unusual shrubs, but one to avoid if you live in a cold area.

SITE & SOIL: Any well-drained garden soil will do — thrives best in full sun.

PRUNING: Not essential — remove unwanted or frost-damaged branches in spring.

PROPAGATION: Layer branches in early summer or plant semi-ripe cuttings in a cold frame in summer.

Piptanthus laburnifolius

PITTOSPORUM Pittosporum

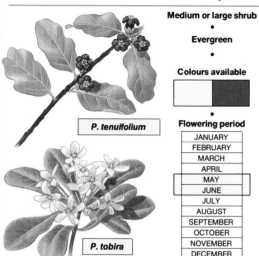

Medium or large shrub

•

Evergreen

•

Colours available

Flowering period

JANUARY
FEBRUARY
MARCH
APRIL
MAY
JUNE
JULY
AUGUST
SEPTEMBER
OCTOBER
NOVEMBER
DECEMBER

P. tenuifolium

P. tobira

The most popular species is P. tenuifolium, but it is a poor choice for most gardeners. The small purple flowers appear only in mild coastal areas and part or all of the bush may die in a severe winter. It makes an attractive hedge in southern coastal districts but its greatest appeal is to the flower arranger — the black twigs with their wavy-edged leathery leaves are excellent material for indoor decoration. For floral display grow P. tobira — a rather tender plant which needs the shelter of a warm wall.

VARIETIES: The only Pittosporum which can be regarded as hardy is **P. dallii**, but this large shrub rarely flowers. Another shy-flowerer is the much more common **P. tenuifolium** — this slow-growing shrub will eventually reach 12 ft or more and may flower in May in exceptionally mild parts of the country. The leaf colour is grey-green — for white-edged foliage grow the variety **'Garnettii'** and for purple leaves pick **'Purpureum'**. **P. tobira** (Japanese Pittosporum) does produce its creamy flowers with their Orange blossom scent every May and June, but it is only reliable in mild areas. For other areas choose Choisya if you want a shrub which produces white flowers with an Orange fragrance.

SITE & SOIL: A well-drained soil in a warm and sheltered spot is necessary — salt-laden air is not a problem.

PRUNING: Not essential — remove unwanted or frost-damaged branches in spring.

PROPAGATION: Plant semi-ripe cuttings in a cold frame in summer.

Pittosporum tobira

POLYGONUM Russian Vine

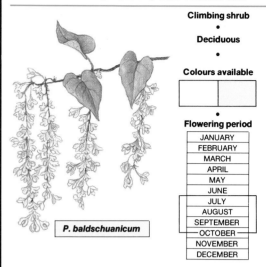

Climbing shrub

•

Deciduous

•

Colours available

Flowering period

JANUARY
FEBRUARY
MARCH
APRIL
MAY
JUNE
JULY
AUGUST
SEPTEMBER
OCTOBER
NOVEMBER
DECEMBER

P. baldschuanicum

The Russian or Mile-a-Minute Vine has been described as a commonplace climber, but it has an extremely useful part to play in many gardens. No other plant can be relied upon to cover an unsightly wall, ugly fence, dead tree or old shed as quickly as P. baldschuanicum. Throughout the summer and autumn there are masses of white or creamy flowers covering the oval or heart-shaped leaves on the upper part of the plant. Obviously a good screening plant but it does lose its leaves in the winter, grows relatively slowly in exposed coastal areas and must be kept in check in good soil and favourable conditions by regular pruning.

VARIETIES: In the garden centre you will find Russian Vine with the name **P. baldschuanicum** on the label, but the experts tell us that the flowers in the floral sprays of the true P. baldschuanicum are creamy-white tinged with pink — the more common white-flowered form is really **P. aubertii**. To make matters even more complicated some nurseries now sell climbing Polygonum as **Fallopia baldschuanica**! Whatever the latin name, Russian Vine will grow at the rate of 15 ft or more each year and eventually reaches 40 ft if left unpruned. Support is necessary.

SITE & SOIL: Any reasonable garden soil will do — thrives in sun or partial shade.

PRUNING: Cut back stems in spring to keep growth in check — tolerates hard pruning.

PROPAGATION: Plant semi-ripe cuttings in a cold frame in summer.

Polygonum baldschuanicum

PONCIRUS Japanese Bitter Orange

Medium shrub

•

Deciduous

•

Colour available

•

Flowering period

JANUARY
FEBRUARY
MARCH
APRIL
MAY
JUNE
JULY
AUGUST
SEPTEMBER
OCTOBER
NOVEMBER
DECEMBER

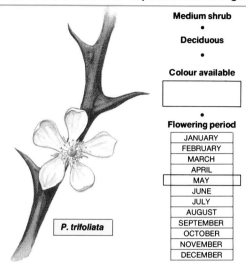

P. trifoliata

And now for something quite different — even when not in flower nor fruit this shrub always attracts attention. The dome-shaped bush is made up of tangled stems, twisted and olive-green with fearsome spines along their lengths. Apart from its architectural interest, large flowers appear in late spring provided the previous autumn has been warm. The flowers are followed in late summer by the unusual fruits — small, wrinkled and thick-skinned miniature 'Oranges' which are about 1½ in. in diameter. Obviously a 'must' if you collect novelty shrubs.

VARIETY: There is just one species — **P. trifoliata**, which may be listed as **Citrus trifoliata** or **Aegle sepiaria**. It is a slow-growing plant, reaching 6 ft x 6 ft after many years. The sweetly-scented white flowers measure about 2 in. across and are borne along the stems. After flowering the leaves appear in the axils of the 1 in. long spines — these 2 in. long leaves are borne in threes and their production is sparse. This is a plant of angular stems and prominent spines with hardly any foliage cover. It is closely related to the familiar Orange, but the fruits (green at first and then yellow) are bitter and inedible.

SITE & SOIL: Well-drained, light soil is necessary — thrives in full sun or light shade.

PRUNING: Not necessary nor desirable — only cut back if the growth is getting out of hand.

PROPAGATION: Purchase container-grown plants from a garden centre or nursery.

Poncirus trifoliata

POTENTILLA Shrubby Cinquefoil

Dwarf or small shrub

•

Deciduous

•

Colours available

•

Flowering period

JANUARY
FEBRUARY
MARCH
APRIL
MAY
JUNE
JULY
AUGUST
SEPTEMBER
OCTOBER
NOVEMBER
DECEMBER

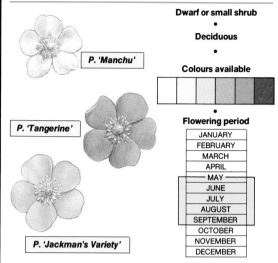

P. 'Manchu'

P. 'Tangerine'

P. 'Jackman's Variety'

This shrub is as 'ordinary' as its neighbour on this page is 'different'. Ordinary it may well be, but it is an indispensable part of millions of shrub and mixed borders throughout the country. It is not spectacular and the leaves and flowers are neither large nor particularly eye-catching. But it is in bloom from May until September, providing floral colour as so many showier displays around it come and go. Another important virtue is that it will grow in any type of soil and requires little attention.

VARIETIES: The naming of the species of Potentilla has got into a muddle over the years — the best plan is to just look for the variety name. Most of the named types have **P. fruticosa** as a parent — look for **'Abbotswood'** (2½ ft, white), **'Elizabeth'** (3 ft, yellow), **'Jackman's Variety'** (4 ft, yellow), **'Katherine Dykes'** (5 ft, yellow), **'Manchu'** (1 ft, white), **'Primrose Beauty'** (3 ft, yellow), **'Princess'** (2 ft, pink), **'Red Ace'** (2 ft, vermilion), **'Tangerine'** (2 ft, coppery yellow) and **'Tilford Cream'** (1½ ft, creamy-white). **P. vilmoriniana** is a rather difficult late flowerer with cream blooms and silky leaves — **P. arbuscula 'Beesii'** (1½ ft) has golden flowers and silvery foliage.

SITE & SOIL: Any well-drained garden soil will do — thrives in sun or light shade.

PRUNING: Remove unwanted or damaged branches in spring — cut back young strong growth by about one-third.

PROPAGATION: Plant semi-ripe cuttings in a cold frame in summer.

Potentilla 'Red Ace'

PRUNUS Prunus

Prostrate, dwarf, small, medium or large shrub
•
Deciduous or Evergreen
•
Colours available

Evergreen Group

P. laurocerasus

•

Flowering period

JANUARY
FEBRUARY
MARCH
APRIL
MAY
JUNE
JULY
AUGUST
SEPTEMBER
OCTOBER
NOVEMBER
DECEMBER

P. lusitanica

Deciduous Group

P. triloba

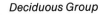

P. incisa

The most spectacular varieties of flowering Prunus are trees, commonly referred to as 'Flowering Cherries'. There are, however, a number of shrubby forms which can serve a useful purpose in the garden. The main role is for hedging and screening, but they can also be employed as specimen plants and there are dwarfs suitable for containers. There are two basic groups — the evergreens (Laurels) which are so popular as large hedges and the deciduous types used for either hedging or as bushes in the shrub border.

VARIETIES: The *Evergreen Group* consists of two tall-growing, glossy-leaved species which are easily confused when not in flower or fruit. **P. laurocerasus** (Cherry or Common Laurel) is very popular, reaching 15 ft if left unpruned but much more commonly trimmed to form a wide hedge or screen. In April the small white flowers appear on erect candles and are followed by red Cherry-like fruits which turn black with age. Prune with secateurs and not shears, and remember that Laurel leaves are poisonous. There are a number of interesting varieties — **'Otto Luyken'** and **'Zabeliana'** (4 ft) can be used for ground cover and **'Castlewellan'** has white-marbled leaves. **P. lusitanica** (Portugal Laurel) has smaller leaves than the Cherry Laurel, and is also hardier and more tolerant of chalk. It will grow 15 ft or more if left unpruned — recognise it by its red leaf stalks. In June the Hawthorn-scented white flowers are borne in tassels — oval purple fruits appear later. **'Azorica'** has larger leaves and **'Variegata'** has white-margined leaves. The *Deciduous Group* contains several types which are used for hedging. For a low hedge grow the red-leaved **P. cistena** (Crimson Dwarf) with white flowers in spring — for a taller hedge there are **P. cerasifera** (Cherry Plum), which bears its white flowers in February-March, and its purple-leaved variety **'Pissardii'**. The Blackthorn or Sloe (**P. spinosa**) can be planted as a spiny hedge with white flowers in March and black fruits in autumn. When choosing a specimen shrub rather than hedging material, beauty of flower rather than leaf is the prime consideration. There are **P. tenella 'Fire Hill'** (4 ft, rosy-red, April), **P. glandulosa 'Alba Plena'** (5 ft, double white, May), **P. glandulosa 'Sinensis'** (double pink), **P. triloba** (6 ft, double pink, April), and **P. incisa** (9 ft, white or pale pink, March). For ground cover there is the 9 in. high **P. pumila depressa** which bears white flowers in May. **P. prostrata** is a taller ground-covering species.

SITE & SOIL: Any well-drained garden soil will do. Pick a sunny spot for deciduous types — partial shade for evergreens.

PRUNING: Prune in late summer — never in winter. Cut out damaged and unwanted shoots.

PROPAGATION: Plant semi-ripe cuttings of evergreen varieties in a cold frame in summer. Deciduous types should be bought as container-grown specimens from a garden centre or nursery.

Prunus lusitanica

Prunus cistena

Prunus tenella 'Fire Hill'

PYRACANTHA Firethorn

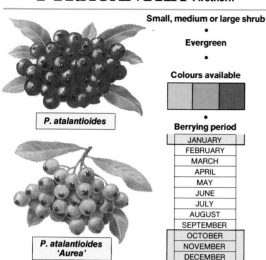

P. atalantioides

P. atalantioides 'Aurea'

Small, medium or large shrub
•
Evergreen
•
Colours available
•
Berrying period

JANUARY
FEBRUARY
MARCH
APRIL
MAY
JUNE
JULY
AUGUST
SEPTEMBER
OCTOBER
NOVEMBER
DECEMBER

Firethorn is a popular wall shrub, displaying its colourful berries from early autumn until midwinter. It can also be used as a free-standing specimen plant or an informal hedge, but remember it is a quick-growing bush and will need to be cut back regularly if planted in a confined space. It is rather similar to Cotoneaster, but the leaves are toothed and the stems are spiny — wear gloves when pruning. Pyracantha is a tough and hardy shrub — it will flourish in an exposed site or against a shady wall.

VARIETIES: **P. coccinea 'Lalandei'** (12 ft) used to be the favourite choice, but not any more. In autumn the branches are covered by orange-red berries, but it is susceptible to disease. **P. 'Orange Glow'** is a better choice as it is more resistant to scab and berry-seeking birds. For red berries there is **P. atalantioides** (12 ft) — for orange fruit you can choose **P. 'Orange Charmer'**. The golden-yellow types include **P. atalantioides 'Aurea'** (10 ft), **'Golden Charmer'** (10 ft) and **'Soleil d'Or'** (8 ft). For fire-blight resistance you will have to choose one of the American varieties such as **P. 'Mojave'**, **P. 'Shawnee'** or **P. 'Teton'**. The dwarf is the 3 ft high **P. 'Red Cushion'**.

SITE & SOIL: Any reasonable garden soil will do, including chalk. Thrives in sun or partial shade.

PRUNING: Remove unwanted and damaged branches in late winter or early spring.

PROPAGATION: Sow seed under glass in winter or plant semi-ripe cuttings in a cold frame in summer.

Pyracantha coccinea 'Lalandei'

RHAPHIOLEPIS Rhaphiolepis

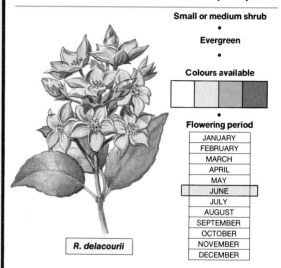

R. delacourii

Small or medium shrub
•
Evergreen
•
Colours available
•
Flowering period

JANUARY
FEBRUARY
MARCH
APRIL
MAY
JUNE
JULY
AUGUST
SEPTEMBER
OCTOBER
NOVEMBER
DECEMBER

Unlike its partner on this page Rhaphiolepis is an unusual plant with a slow growth habit, reaching its mature height of about 5 ft after many years. Unfortunately it also differs by not being fully hardy, although R. umbellata will be harmed in only an abnormally severe winter. Growth is neat and dome-shaped, and the glossy oval leaves are slightly serrated. For the best floral display grow it in the shelter of a south-facing wall — the flowers which measure about ½ in. across are star-shaped and are borne in erect clusters.

VARIETIES: The only species which appears in numerous catalogues is **R. umbellata**. The white flowers appear in early summer and are followed by near-black berries. It is a compact bush growing about 4 ft high. **R. delacourii** is a taller plant, growing 6 ft or more in time against a sunny wall, but it is also rather more tender. The upright flower-heads bear blooms which are an attractive shade of pink — for a lighter shade grow the variety **'Spring Song'** and for a darker near-red shade choose **'Coate's Crimson'**. You may find **R. indica** in the catalogue, but it belongs in the conservatory rather than the garden.

SITE & SOIL: Any well-drained garden soil will do — thrives in sun or partial shade.

PRUNING: Not necessary — remove unwanted or damaged branches in early spring.

PROPAGATION: Plant semi-ripe cuttings in a cold frame in summer.

Rhaphiolepis umbellata

RHODODENDRON Rhododendron

Large-flowered Hybrid Group

R. 'Britannia'

R. 'Pink Pearl'

R. 'Purple Splendour'

R. 'Sappho'

Dwarf, small, medium or large shrub
•
Evergreen
•
Colours available

•
Flowering period

| JANUARY |
| FEBRUARY |
| MARCH |
| APRIL |
| MAY |
| JUNE |
| JULY |
| AUGUST |
| SEPTEMBER |
| OCTOBER |
| NOVEMBER |
| DECEMBER |

Dwarf Hybrid Group

R. 'Elizabeth'

R. 'Carmen'

Species Group

R. macabeanum

Some garden centres seem to be overwhelmed by containers of Rhododendrons in spring, which may seem a little surprising as it is not a grow-anywhere plant. It will fail miserably in alkaline soil, may do reasonably well in neutral soil but needs an acid home if it is to flourish. Despite this fussiness it is one of our favourite shrubs and there are thousands of species and hybrids. We now see Rhododendrons almost everywhere and they seem to be part of our countryside, but another surprise is that it only became a popular garden plant in Victorian times. The reasons for its universal appeal are easy to see. The glossy evergreen foliage is attractive all the year round, and in the flowering season the clusters of blooms may be numerous enough to almost cover the plant. Each flower is either bell- or trumpet-shaped and the whole of the floral colour range is covered apart from true blue and true black. The most popular garden Rhododendrons are about 6 ft tall and bloom in May, but there are many variations. You can buy tiny 1 ft high rockery types as well as wide-spreading 20 ft trees. There are varieties which flower as early as February and others which bloom as late as August. Rhododendrons are shallow-rooted — do not plant too deeply and mulch with peat each autumn. Water copiously in prolonged dry weather. Some Rhododendrons are popularly described as 'Azaleas' and are labelled with this name — they are described on page 86.

VARIETIES: The most popular Rhododendrons belong to the *Large-flowered Hybrid Group*. The basic ones are the 'Hardy Hybrids' — noted for their toughness and ability to flourish in an exposed site. During this century many other hybrids have been introduced — often more colourful but a little less hardy. The usual height range is 5–8 ft and depending on variety the time of flowering is between April and July. Only a few of the popular varieties can be mentioned here — there are many more. Look for **'Betty Wormald'** (large, deep rose, May–June), **'Britannia'** (crimson, May–June), **'Cunningham's White'** (white, pale purple markings, May–June), **'Cynthia'** (crimson, dark markings, May–June), **'Doncaster'** (scarlet, dark markings, May–June), **'Fastuosum Flore Pleno'** (semi-double, mauve, May–June), **'Goldsworth Orange'** (pink-tinged orange, July), **'John Walter'** (cherry red, July), **'Lord Roberts'** (dark crimson, June), **'Mrs G. W. Leak'** (pink, dark markings, May–June), **'Pink Pearl'** (very popular, white-edged pink, May–June), **'Purple Splendour'** (deep purple, June) and **'Sappho'** (purple-centred white, May–June). For the small garden the *Dwarf Hybrid Group* is becoming increasingly popular. The plants grow 2–3 ft high and bear a mass of small flower clusters in April–May. **'Elizabeth'** (red) is the most popular, but there are many others — **'Baden Baden'** (scarlet), **'Blue Diamond'** (violet-blue), **'Blue Tit'** (lavender-blue), **'Bow Bells'** (pink), **'Carmen'** (crimson), **'Pink Drift'** (lavender-rose), **'Princess Anne'** (yellow), **'Scarlet Wonder'** (ruby red) and **'Yellow Hammer'** (lemon yellow) are examples of widely available Dwarf Hybrids. For something more unusual pick a plant from the *Species Group*, such as the March-flowering **R. macabeanum** (pale yellow), the tree-like **R. arboreum** (various colours) or the flat-flowered **R. quinquefolium** (white). **R. yakushimanum** (3 ft, pink flowers fading to white) is an important species as it has given rise to a number of excellent low-growing hybrids, such as **'Percy Wiseman'**, **'Surrey Heath'** and the Snow White dwarfs **'Doc'**, **'Grumpy'**, **'Dopey'** etc.

SITE & SOIL: Acid soil is essential. In chalky soil the leaves turn yellow — watering with a sequestered iron compound will help. Thrives best in partial shade.

PRUNING: Break off dead blooms from large-flowered types with finger and thumb — do not damage buds at the base of the flower. Cut back leggy stems hard in late winter.

PROPAGATION: The most reliable method is layering branches in autumn, but it is generally better to buy new plants.

Rhododendron 'Betty Wormald'

Rhododendron 'Cynthia'

Rhododendron 'Fastuosum Flore Pleno'

Rhododendron 'Doncaster'

Rhododendron 'Mrs G. W. Leak'

Rhododendron 'Baden Baden'

Rhododendron 'Blue Diamond'

Rhododendron 'Yellow Hammer'

Rhododendron 'Percy Wiseman'

RHODODENDRON Azalea

Evergreen Group

R. 'Blue Danube'

R. 'Palestrina'

R. 'Vuyk's Scarlet'

Small or medium shrub
•
Deciduous
or
Evergreen

Colours available

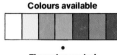

•
Flowering period

JANUARY
FEBRUARY
MARCH
APRIL
MAY
JUNE
JULY
AUGUST
SEPTEMBER
OCTOBER
NOVEMBER
DECEMBER

Deciduous Group

R. 'Cecile'

Some Rhododendron varieties are traditionally referred to as 'Azaleas', but there is no simple way of always being able to distinguish an Azalea from a Rhododendron. Azaleas are often daintier and with smaller leaves, but not always — there are 10 ft high Azaleas and ground-hugging Rhododendrons. Many Azaleas lose their leaves in winter, but some of the most beautiful ones are evergreen like a Rhododendron. It seems that Rhododendrons have ten stamens and Azaleas have a smaller number, but many purists say that the separation into Rhododendrons and Azaleas is wholly artificial. Still, the plant labels say 'Azalea' on many lovely Rhododendron varieties, and it is some of these plants which are considered here.

VARIETIES: The *Evergreen Group* are known as Japanese Azaleas. They are low-growing, reaching about 2–4 ft when mature, and bear oval leaves which are about 1½ in. long. The bell-shaped flowers appear in April or May, covering the spreading branches in sheets of colour. There are a number of types — the Glenn Dale (GD) and Vuyk (V) hybrids have the largest (2–3 in.) flowers, Kaempferi (KF) hybrids have medium-sized blooms and Kurume (K) hybrids have small (1–1½ in.) flowers. Examples include **'Addy Wery'** (K, red), **'Blaauw's Pink'** (K, salmon pink), **'Blue Danube'** (V, violet), **'Hatsugiri'** (K, crimson-purple), **'Hino-mayo'** (K, pink), **'John Cairns'** (KF, orange-red), **'Louise Dowdle'** (GD, pink), **'Mother's Day'** (rose-red), **'Orange Beauty'** (KF, orange), **'Palestrina'** (V, white), **'Rosebud'** (K, rose-pink) and **'Vuyk's Scarlet'** (V, red). The *Deciduous Group* are taller with an average height of 5–8 ft. The trumpet-shaped flowers in May or June are followed by rich autumn foliage colours. There are a number of types — the Ghent (Gh) hybrids have sweet-smelling Honeysuckle-like flowers, Knap Hill and Exbury (Kn) hybrids bear unscented trumpet-shaped flowers and Mollis (M) hybrids are noted for their bright flower colours and large trusses which appear before the leaves. Examples include **'Berryrose'** (Kn, yellow-tinged pink), **'Cecile'** (Kn, yellow-tinged pink), **'Daviesii'** (Gh, yellow-tinged white), **'Glowing Embers'** (Kn, reddish-orange), **'Homebush'** (Kn, semi-double, pink), **'Klondyke'** (Kn, red-tinged golden yellow), **'Koster's Brilliant Red'** (M, orange-red), **'Lemonara'** (M, yellow), **'Persil'** (Kn, orange-tinted white), **'Satan'** (Kn, red), **'Spek's Orange'** (M, orange) and **'Strawberry Ice'** (Kn, gold-tinted pink).

SITE & SOIL: Acid soil is essential — see Rhododendron on page 84. Choose a sheltered site in partial shade. Water copiously in prolonged dry weather.

PRUNING: Not necessary — remove unwanted or damaged branches after flowering.

PROPAGATION: The most reliable method is layering branches in autumn, but it is generally better to buy new plants.

Rhododendron 'Addy Wery'

Rhododendron 'Rosebud'

Rhododendron 'Glowing Embers'

RIBES Ornamental Currant

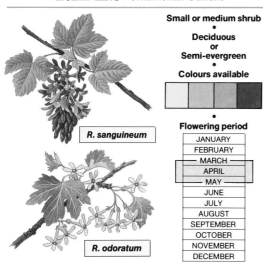

R. sanguineum

R. odoratum

Small or medium shrub
•
Deciduous
or
Semi-evergreen

Colours available

•

Flowering period

| JANUARY |
| FEBRUARY |
| MARCH |
| APRIL |
| MAY |
| JUNE |
| JULY |
| AUGUST |
| SEPTEMBER |
| OCTOBER |
| NOVEMBER |
| DECEMBER |

Several Ornamental Currants and Gooseberries are grown as decorative plants in the shrub border — by far the most popular one is the Flowering Currant which can be seen flowering in the spring in gardens everywhere. It has become a great favourite because small plants are inexpensive and they are quick-growing. In clay soil or sandy ground, in sun or semi-shade, a sizeable bush or hedge is produced in a short time.

VARIETIES: The Flowering Currant is **R. sanguineum**. It is an upright bush about 6 ft high which bears drooping clusters of small flowers in March and April. These blooms are followed by black fruits. The flower colour is an insipid pink and it is usual to pick one of the more colourful varieties rather than the species. There are **'Purloborough Scarlet'** (red flowers), **'King Edward VII'** (4 ft, crimson flowers) and the compact **'Brocklebankii'** (3 ft, pink flowers, golden leaves). **R. odoratum** (6 ft) bears fragrant yellow flowers in April and purple leaves in autumn — the uncommon **R. gordonianum** has orange flowers. The rather tender **R. speciosum** (5 ft) should be grown against a wall — small, red Fuchsia-like flowers appear in spring.

SITE & SOIL: Any reasonable garden soil will do — thrives in full sun or partial shade.

PRUNING: After flowering cut back shoots which have bloomed and remove old and unproductive wood.

PROPAGATION: Plant semi-ripe cuttings in a cold frame in summer or hardwood cuttings in the open in late autumn.

Ribes sanguineum 'Brocklebankii'

ROMNEYA Tree Poppy

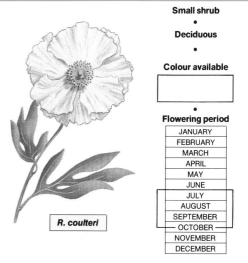

R. coulteri

Small shrub
•
Deciduous
•

Colour available

•

Flowering period

| JANUARY |
| FEBRUARY |
| MARCH |
| APRIL |
| MAY |
| JUNE |
| JULY |
| AUGUST |
| SEPTEMBER |
| OCTOBER |
| NOVEMBER |
| DECEMBER |

From midsummer until autumn there are white fragrant Poppies which are 4–6 in. across, and the deeply cut leaves are an attractive shade of bluish-grey. The problem is that it is slow to establish, but once established it spreads quickly and can be invasive. Another problem is that some of the stems may be killed by frost, but new growth is rapidly produced.

VARIETIES: The basic species is **R. coulteri**, a thicket-forming plant which grows 4–5 ft high. The large, solitary blooms have a prominent central boss of golden stamens and are borne at the tips of the upright stems. The variety **'Trichocalyx'** is sometimes listed but is very similar to the species. Choose **R. hybrida 'White Cloud'** if you can find it — the flowers are larger than the blooms of R. coulteri.

SITE & SOIL: Requires well-drained, light soil in full sun.

PRUNING: Cut down stems to a few inches in March.

PROPAGATION: Plant rooted suckers in spring.

Romneya coulteri

ROSA Shrub Rose

Shrub Roses do not have the popular appeal of Hybrid Teas and Floribundas, but are well worth considering for the shrub border. They come in all sorts of shapes and sizes, and there is one to suit nearly every garden. See The Rose Expert for details.

ROSMARINUS Rosemary

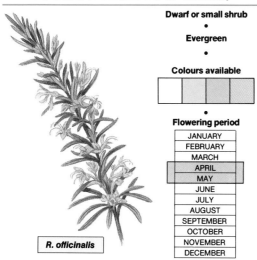

Dwarf or small shrub

•

Evergreen

•

Colours available

Flowering period

| JANUARY |
| FEBRUARY |
| MARCH |
| APRIL |
| MAY |
| JUNE |
| JULY |
| AUGUST |
| SEPTEMBER |
| OCTOBER |
| NOVEMBER |
| DECEMBER |

R. officinalis

Rosemary has been grown as a herb for hundreds of years, but it also has a place in the shrub border. It is generally an upright bush with masses of small flowers. The main blooming period is spring, but summer and autumn flowers occasionally appear. Rosemary is an easy plant to grow but it will not thrive if the soil is heavy and wet. Use it as a grey-blue foil between more colourful plants.

VARIETIES: There is just one species which is widely available — **R. officinalis**. It grows about 5 ft high and the leaves are grey-green above, powdery white below. The pale blue-violet flowers appear in clusters along the stems. There are a number of interesting varieties, such as **'Aureus'** with white flowers and **'Variegatus'** with yellow-splashed leaves. The favourite blue variety is the erect **'Miss Jessop's Upright'** (**'Fastigiata'**) which grows 5–6 ft high. For the brightest blue flowers and dark green leaves grow **'Benenden Blue'** — for pinkish flowers grow **'Majorcan Pink'** or **'Roseus'**. There are also several compact varieties, including **'Severn Sea'** (2 ft), **'Tuscan Blue'** (2 ft) and **'Prostratus'** (**'Lavandulaceus'**) which grows 1–1½ ft high.

SITE & SOIL: The soil must be well drained and not clayey — thrives best in full sun.

PRUNING: Trim the bush lightly with garden shears as soon as flowering is over in spring.

PROPAGATION: Plant semi-ripe cuttings in a cold frame in summer.

Rosmarinus officinalis 'Prostratus'

RUBUS Ornamental Bramble

Small or medium shrub

•

Deciduous

•

Colours available

Flowering period

| JANUARY |
| FEBRUARY |
| MARCH |
| APRIL |
| MAY |
| JUNE |
| JULY |
| AUGUST |
| SEPTEMBER |
| OCTOBER |
| NOVEMBER |
| DECEMBER |

R. tridel 'Benenden'

Some of the Ornamental Brambles are grown for their colourful stems in winter — the white-stalked R. cockburnianus is the most popular one. Others are grown for their floral display or their fruits. They are all arching bushes and easy to grow with flowers which look like single Roses with a central boss of golden stamens. The flowering period depends on the species, and so does the presence of prickles. They are tall rambling plants, reaching 8–10 ft and not easy to fit comfortably in many borders. The Bramble-like fruits are tasteless.

VARIETIES: The best of the flowering types is **R. tridel 'Benenden'**. It has tall shoots (10 ft) which are thornless. In May 2 in. wide fragrant white blooms are borne along the peeling brown stems — fruit is rarely formed. **R. odoratus** is different in a number of ways. The thornless stems do not arch and the leaves are velvety — the fragrant flowers are purplish-rose and appear in clusters in June-September. **R. spectabilis** has 5 ft high prickly stems and bears its pink flowers in April. A double-flowered form is available. **R. illecebrosus** is a low-growing species which produces white flowers and large red fruit.

SITE & SOIL: Any reasonable garden soil will do — thrives in sun or partial shade.

PRUNING: Remove some of the older stems in autumn — cut away dead and damaged branches.

PROPAGATION: Plant semi-ripe cuttings in a cold frame in summer.

Rubus odoratus

SALIX Shrubby Willow

Prostrate, dwarf, small or medium shrub

•

Deciduous

•

Colours available

•

Flowering period

| JANUARY |
| FEBRUARY |
| MARCH |
| APRIL |
| MAY |
| JUNE |
| JULY |
| AUGUST |
| SEPTEMBER |
| OCTOBER |
| NOVEMBER |
| DECEMBER |

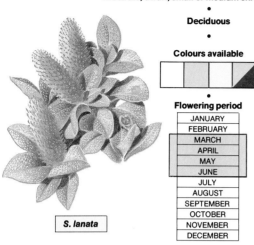

S. lanata

Most garden Willows are trees and so are outside the scope of this book, but there are a number of Shrubby Willows which bear an interesting or impressive display of catkins. These plants are usually quite small and are suitable for the larger rockery or front of the border, but there are also a few taller types which are grown primarily for their catkin display. It is true that Willows prefer damp soils, but wet ground is not essential. Most soil types will do, but copious watering may be necessary in a period of prolonged drought.

VARIETIES: S. lanata (Woolly Willow) is a spreading 3 ft high bush with silvery-grey leaves and yellowish-grey catkins in spring. These erect catkins may be up to 4 in. long — for even longer catkins grow the variety **'Stuartii'. S. repens argentea** is a creeping variety with silvery leaves and yellow catkins in early spring. Even more prostrate is **S. retusa** which grows only a few inches high, but its catkins in May–June are 5–7 in. long. **S. hastata 'Wehrhahnii'** (4 ft) has silvery-white catkins covering the branches in spring. **S. gracistyla** (8 ft) is a taller Shrubby Willow grown for its showy red and grey catkins.

SITE & SOIL: Any reasonable soil apart from light sands will do — thrives in sun or partial shade.

PRUNING: Not necessary — remove damaged or unwanted branches in late winter.

PROPAGATION: Easy — plant hardwood cuttings in the open in late autumn.

Salix gracistyla

SAMBUCUS Elder

Medium or large shrub

•

Deciduous

•

Colours available

•

Flowering period

| JANUARY |
| FEBRUARY |
| MARCH |
| APRIL |
| MAY |
| JUNE |
| JULY |
| AUGUST |
| SEPTEMBER |
| OCTOBER |
| NOVEMBER |
| DECEMBER |

S. nigra

The pungent flat heads of tiny cream-coloured flowers of the Common Elder and the large bunches of shiny black berries which follow are a familiar sight in the countryside. It is an upright tall shrub or small tree with large leaves made up of a number of green saw-edged leaflets. The effect is quite plain and for garden use there are much better ones — some of these desirable ones are varieties of the Common Elder and the rest are other species. Do not use red berries for winemaking.

VARIETIES: The Common Elder is **S. nigra** — a quick-growing shrub (20 ft) which flowers in June. The variety **'Aurea'** (8 ft) has yellow leaves — for purple foliage grow **'Purpurea'**. There are two variegated forms — **'Marginata'** has cream-edged leaves and **'Aureomarginata'** has bright golden edges. Finally there is **'Laciniata'** with finely-divided, fern-like foliage. The American Elder (**S. canadensis**) has domed rather than flat flower-heads in July — **'Aurea'** has yellow leaves and red berries. **S. racemosa 'Plumosa Aurea'** is perhaps the best of the garden Elders. It grows about 6 ft high and has deeply cut golden leaves, conical yellow flower-heads in May and red berries.

SITE & SOIL: Any garden soil will do, including clay. Yellow-leaved varieties need a sunny spot.

PRUNING: Remove about one-third of the oldest stems in early spring.

PROPAGATION: Plant hardwood cuttings in the open in late autumn.

Sambucus nigra 'Aureomarginata'

SANTOLINA Cotton Lavender

Dwarf shrub
•
Evergreen
•
Colours available

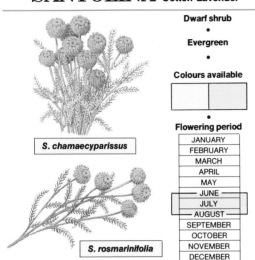

S. chamaecyparissus

S. rosmarinifolia

Flowering period

| JANUARY |
| FEBRUARY |
| MARCH |
| APRIL |
| MAY |
| JUNE |
| JULY |
| AUGUST |
| SEPTEMBER |
| OCTOBER |
| NOVEMBER |
| DECEMBER |

Santolina is a low-growing, mound-forming bush for use at the front of the shrub border or as low hedging. It is usually grown for both its flowers and its foliage, although the flower buds are sometimes removed to improve the foliage display. The leaves are long and finely-divided, giving a ferny effect which is silvery-grey or green, depending on the species. The small button-like flower-heads appear in summer on thin stalks above the foliage — colours range from cream to bright yellow. Santolina detests waterlogging and shade.

VARIETIES: The most popular species is **S. chamaecyparissus** — a 2 ft high plant with a fine display of silvery foliage but a rather poor showing of lemon yellow flowers. The variety **'Nana'** (1 ft) is a good choice for the rock garden. For a taller species choose **S. pinnata** (2½ ft) with creamy flowers and feathery foliage. It has two fine varieties — **'Neapolitana'** with bright yellow flowers and **'Edward Bowles'** with creamy ones. The best floral display is provided by **S. rosmarinifolia**, sometimes listed as **S. virens** or **S. viridis**. The thread-like leaves are bright green and the massed flower-heads are lemon yellow.

SITE & SOIL: Thrives in any well-drained reasonable soil — full sun is essential.

PRUNING: Trim after flowering — every two or three years cut back hard in April.

PROPAGATION: Plant semi-ripe cuttings in a cold frame in summer.

Santolina pinnata 'Neapolitana'

SARCOCOCCA Christmas Box

Dwarf or small shrub
•
Evergreen
•
Colours available

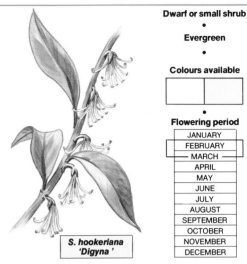

S. hookeriana 'Digyna'

Flowering period

| JANUARY |
| FEBRUARY |
| MARCH |
| APRIL |
| MAY |
| JUNE |
| JULY |
| AUGUST |
| SEPTEMBER |
| OCTOBER |
| NOVEMBER |
| DECEMBER |

This evergreen shrub is of little interest during the spring and summer months — it is low-growing and the lance-shaped or oval leaves are nothing special. But in late winter or early spring it becomes a plant much loved by flower arrangers. Clusters of white- or cream-petalled male flowers and insignificant female flowers are borne all along the stems — a key feature is the very strong fragrance. The blooms are followed by berries — black or red depending on the species. Most types sucker quite freely, so Sarcococca is a spreading plant.

VARIETIES: S. confusa (2½ ft) is a dark green plant which looks rather like a Privet. The cream-coloured flowers are followed by black berries. The favourite Sarcococca is **S. hookeriana 'Digyna'** (4 ft) which is taller than S. confusa and has narrower, purple-tinged leaves. The flowers are white and the berries are black. **S. hookeriana 'Humilis'** is a variety with similar flowers and berries, but it is a dwarf with dark green leaves — 1 ft high and suckering to form a thicket 3 ft wide. **S. ruscifolia** is a 3 ft x 3 ft bush when mature — it differs from the varieties listed above by having broad leaves and red berries.

SITE & SOIL: Any reasonable garden soil will do — thrives in sun or partial shade.

PRUNING: Not necessary — remove damaged or unwanted branches immediately after flowering.

PROPAGATION: Remove rooted suckers or plant semi-ripe cuttings in a cold frame in summer.

Sarcococca hookeriana 'Digyna'

SENECIO Shrubby Ragwort

Small, medium or climbing shrub
•
Evergreen
•
Colours available

•
Flowering period

JANUARY
FEBRUARY
MARCH
APRIL
MAY
JUNE
JULY
AUGUST
SEPTEMBER
OCTOBER
NOVEMBER
DECEMBER

S. 'Sunshine'

Like Santolina, this low and spreading shrub is often grown for its foliage rather than its flowers. The leathery oval leaves are covered with silvery hairs, especially when young. The Daisy-like flowers which are borne in loose heads are attractive enough in several species, but the flowering period in early summer is short. Senecios are not troubled by wind or salt-laden air but they are not completely hardy — most require a sheltered site.

VARIETIES: The Shrubby Ragworts are from New Zealand and their naming in the catalogues and garden centres is a mess. The purists want to change their genus name to **Brachyglottis**, but 'Senecio' remains on most labels. The popular species with smooth-edged leaves has long been listed as **S. laxifolius** or **S. greyi**, but it seems that these species are actually quite rare. Our Common Senecio is really **S. 'Sunshine'** — 3 ft high with lots of bright yellow flowers. **S. monroi** (3 ft) is another popular species — the grey leaves have crinkled edges and are covered with white felt below. The rare white-flowered **S. hectori** (8 ft) is rather tender — the climbing **S. scandens** (10 ft) needs a south wall.

SITE & SOIL: Any well-drained garden soil will do — full sun is necessary.

PRUNING: Remove dead and straggly shoots after flowering to maintain bushiness.

PROPAGATION: Plant semi-ripe cuttings in a cold frame in summer.

Senecio monroi

SKIMMIA Skimmia

Small shrub
•
Evergreen
•
Colour available

•
Flowering period

JANUARY
FEBRUARY
MARCH
APRIL
MAY
JUNE
JULY
AUGUST
SEPTEMBER
OCTOBER
NOVEMBER
DECEMBER

S. japonica

A neat, domed evergreen — a good choice for the small border or for growing in a tub. Everybody agrees that it is a tough little plant, standing up to salt spray, air pollution and shade but not waterlogging. Not all the experts, however, agree over its ability to grow in chalk — the standard textbooks say that it needs neutral or acid soil, but some claim that the most popular species (S. japonica) will succeed in alkaline soil. Skimmia grows about 2–3 ft high and the large leathery leaves are silvery below. In spring the prominent clusters of tiny white flowers appear above the foliage and in autumn the glossy red (rarely white) berries are present and persist all winter.

VARIETIES: S. japonica is the usual species — you will need a male variety close to female ones if you want an autumn display of red berries. **'Nymans'** (female) produces an abundance of large berries, **'Foremanii'** (female) has the largest bunches and **'Rubella'** bears clusters of red flower buds all winter long. **'Fragrans'** (male) has the most fragrant flowers and **'Fructu-albo'** is a rare form which produces white fruits. For the largest flower-heads grow **S. confusa** — if you can only have one plant, buy the bisexual **S. reevesiana**.

SITE & SOIL: Any well-drained neutral or acid soil will do — thrives in full sun or partial shade.

PRUNING: Not necessary — remove damaged or unwanted branches in spring.

PROPAGATION: Plant semi-ripe cuttings in a cold frame in summer.

Skimmia japonica 'Rubella'

SOLANUM Perennial Nightshade

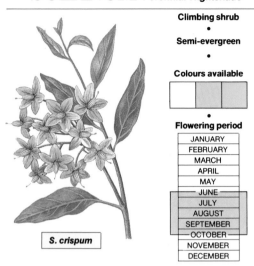

Climbing shrub
•
Semi-evergreen
•

Colours available

Flowering period

JANUARY
FEBRUARY
MARCH
APRIL
MAY
JUNE
JULY
AUGUST
SEPTEMBER
OCTOBER
NOVEMBER
DECEMBER

S. crispum

Potato, Tomato and Deadly Nightshade are all members of the genus Solanum, and so are two colourful climbing species. Both bear small attractive blooms in large clusters from midsummer to autumn, but the flower colours are different and so are their climbing habits. Each flower has a central cone of yellow stamens, and berries appear after the blooms have faded — these fruits are poisonous, as you would expect from the common name. Worth a try, as there are not many unusual climbers to choose from. Rather tender, but Solanum quickly produces new shoots to replace ones killed by frost.

VARIETIES: The more reliable species is **S. crispum**, the Chilean Potato Vine. It is a vigorous plant which grows quickly and soon reaches a height of 15 ft or more. It is a weak-stemmed scrambler rather than a true climber, and it produces masses of 1 in. wide mauve flowers in loose clusters between July and September. The variety **'Glasnevin'** is hardier and bears larger flowers. **S. jasminoides** is a true climber — its twining stems may grow over 20 ft high. It is a more tender plant than S. crispum, but it should succeed in southern counties. The June–October flowers are pale blue — for white flowers grow the variety **'Album'**.

SITE & SOIL: Any well-drained reasonable soil will do — plant in full sun against a south or west wall.

PRUNING: Cut back unwanted growth in April.

PROPAGATION: Layer stems in summer.

Solanum jasminoides 'Album'

SOPHORA Sophora

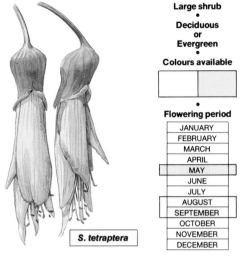

Large shrub
•
Deciduous
or
Evergreen
•

Colours available

Flowering period

JANUARY
FEBRUARY
MARCH
APRIL
MAY
JUNE
JULY
AUGUST
SEPTEMBER
OCTOBER
NOVEMBER
DECEMBER

S. tetraptera

A large and unusual shrub for a mild area and for growing against a sunny wall. Nearly all the types which are listed in the catalogues grow to 10 ft or more, and some turn into small trees when mature. This plant is noted for its attractive foliage — long leaves made up of many small and oval leaflets. This foliage indicates that Sophora is a member of the Legume family, but the flowers in some species are tubular rather than Pea-like. These blooms are borne in trusses which hang down from the drooping branches, and they are followed by showy pods.

VARIETIES: The most widely available species is the Kowhai or New Zealand Laburnum **S. tetraptera**. It is a bushy plant reaching 12 ft or more and the 1 ft long leaves with scores of tiny leaflets provide excellent material for the flower arranger. The yellow flowers are about 2 in. long and are tubular. When they fade the seed pods appear — 6 in. long with four distinct wings. May is the flowering period, as it is for **S. microphylla**, which is very similar in appearance but with leaves and flowers which are smaller. Both plants are evergreen — the tree-like **S. japonica** is deciduous and bears creamy flowers in late summer.

SITE & SOIL: Requires light, well-drained soil — full sun is essential.

PRUNING: Not necessary — cut back dead or unwanted branches in early spring.

PROPAGATION: Plant semi-ripe cuttings in a cold frame in summer.

Sophora microphylla

SORBARIA Tree Spiraea

Medium or large shrub
•
Deciduous
•
Colours available
•
Flowering period

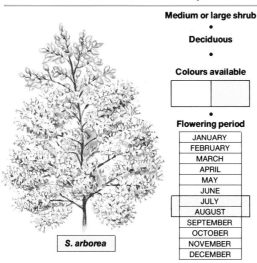

S. arborea

Flowering period
JANUARY
FEBRUARY
MARCH
APRIL
MAY
JUNE
JULY
AUGUST
SEPTEMBER
OCTOBER
NOVEMBER
DECEMBER

A shrub for the large or woodland garden where the tall branches and suckering growth habit will not be a problem. It is sometimes listed as a Spiraea, but Sorbaria can be recognised by its large ferny leaves bearing 10–25 oval leaflets. These 8–12 in. long leaves are generally silvery below and turn yellow in winter. The crowning glory of Sorbaria are the large and generally wide-spreading spikes of tiny white or creamy-white flowers which are borne in midsummer and late summer. In winter there is a thicket of reddish-brown stems and seed heads.

VARIETIES: S. aitchisonii (S. tomentosa) is an elegant plant with tall, spreading stems which may reach 10 ft or more in time. The leaflets are sharply serrated and in July and August the 1 ft high creamy-white floral spikes are present. **S. arborea (S. kirilowii)** is another 10 ft tall robust species with narrow leaflets which are downy below. The summer flower-heads are white. **S. sorbifolia (S. sorbarifolia)** is not as tall as the others and rarely grows more than 5–6 ft high, but it suckers more freely and can be invasive. The flower-heads are smaller (5–8 in.) and are quite narrow.

SITE & SOIL: Any well-drained garden soil will do — thrives best in full sun.

PRUNING: Cut out about one-third of the old stems in early spring.

PROPAGATION: Use rooted suckers or plant semi-ripe cuttings in a cold frame in summer.

Sorbaria aitchisonii

SORBUS Creeping Rowan

Dwarf shrub
•
Deciduous
•
Colours available
•
Fruiting period

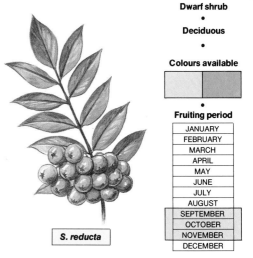

S. reducta

Fruiting period
JANUARY
FEBRUARY
MARCH
APRIL
MAY
JUNE
JULY
AUGUST
SEPTEMBER
OCTOBER
NOVEMBER
DECEMBER

It will seem strange for many readers to find Sorbus listed in a book on flowering shrubs. Sorbus is generally known as a popular tree — scores of different varieties of Mountain Ash, Rowan and Whitebeam are grown. There is, however, one diminutive shrubby species which is widely available and is useful for a large rockery or the front of a shrub border. Like its tall relatives it is grown for its pinnate foliage which colours up brightly in autumn and for its berry-like fruits which appear in late summer.

VARIETY: There is just one low-growing Sorbus shrub you will find in the catalogues — **S. reducta**, which came to this country during World War II. It is a suckering plant, producing a thicket of 1–2 ft high stems. The 4 in. long leaves have red stalks and about a dozen saw-edged leaflets which turn bronzy-purple in autumn. Clusters of white flowers are borne in May or June, and these are followed by small round fruits which may be white tinged with pink or distinctly pink, depending on the stock you buy. Attractive to birds, but less so than the red-fruited Mountain Ash tree.

SITE & SOIL: Any well-drained non-chalky soil will do — thrives in full sun or light shade.

PRUNING: Not necessary. Remove dead or unwanted branches in early spring — cut out badly diseased branches immediately.

PROPAGATION: Plant rooted suckers or sow seed under glass in spring.

Sorbus reducta

SPIRAEA Spiraea

Summer-flowering Group

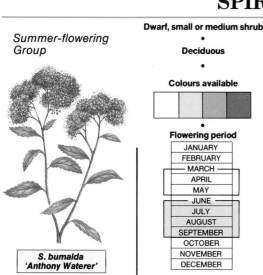

S. bumalda 'Anthony Waterer'

S. billardii 'Triumphans'

Dwarf, small or medium shrub
•
Deciduous
•
Colours available

•
Flowering period

| JANUARY |
| FEBRUARY |
| MARCH |
| APRIL |
| MAY |
| JUNE |
| JULY |
| AUGUST |
| SEPTEMBER |
| OCTOBER |
| NOVEMBER |
| DECEMBER |

Spring-flowering Group

S. vanhouttei

The Spiraeas are a large and varied group. There are a few, such as the over-used 'Anthony Waterer', which are included in almost every bargain collection — there are also others which are unusual enough to be classed as rarities. There are tall varieties which flower in March before the leaves appear and at the other end of the scale there are Spiraeas which are in bloom in autumn. The popularity of these shrubs is due to their quick-growing and free-flowering nature. They are easy to grow and generally provide no problems, but some of the large suckering varieties can form dense thickets and all require annual pruning. The Spring-flowering Group bears tiny, white flowers which are massed in clusters on arching stems. The flowers of the Summer-flowering Group are usually pink or red, the small blooms appearing in flat heads, round domes or upright spikes.

VARIETIES: The favourite Spiraea in the *Spring-flowering Group* is the Bridal Wreath (**S. arguta**). It grows about 6 ft high with arching sprays of white flowers in April and May. **S. thunbergii** is earlier with leafless arching sprays covered with starry flowers in March. April–May flowerers include **S. cinerea 'Grefsheim'** (5 ft), which bears greyish downy leaves in spring, and **S. prunifolia** with masses of small double flowers and foliage which turns bright red in autumn. For the latest flowers in this group (June) and the most compact growth habit (3 ft x 3 ft) grow **S. nipponica 'Snowmound'**. For the tallest stems (8 ft) for hedging there is the thicket-forming **S. vanhouttei**. The favourite Spiraea in the *Summer-flowering Group* is **S. bumalda 'Anthony Waterer'** — 3 ft high with flat heads of carmine-pink flowers in July–September. The leaves are sometimes tinged with pink or cream — for foliage which is bright gold in spring there are the varieties **'Goldflame'** (3 ft) and **'Goldmound'** (1 ft). These S. bumalda varieties are sometimes listed under S. japonica — varieties which are always or nearly always listed under **S. japonica** include **'Albiflora'** (2 ft, white, August–September), **'Alpina'** (1½ ft, pink, June), **'Little Princess'** (2 ft, pink, July–September), **'Bullata'** (2 ft, deep pink, July–September) and **'Shirobana'** (4 ft, mixture of white and pink flowers, July–September). The showiest plant in this section is **S. billardii 'Triumphans'** (8 ft, purple-rose spikes, July–August).

SITE & SOIL: Any reasonable garden soil will do — thrives in sun or light shade.

PRUNING: The Spring-flowering Group should have old and weak stems removed when blooms have faded. The Summer-flowering Group should be pruned more severely — cut back the stems to a few inches above the ground in early spring.

PROPAGATION: Plant semi-ripe cuttings in a cold frame in summer or hardwood cuttings in the open in late autumn.

Spiraea arguta

Spiraea nipponica 'Snowmound'

Spiraea bumalda 'Goldflame'

SPARTIUM Spanish Broom

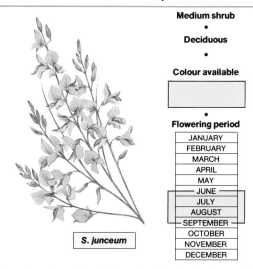

Medium shrub

•

Deciduous

•

Colour available

•

Flowering period

| JANUARY |
| FEBRUARY |
| MARCH |
| APRIL |
| MAY |
| JUNE |
| JULY |
| AUGUST |
| SEPTEMBER |
| OCTOBER |
| NOVEMBER |
| DECEMBER |

S. junceum

Spartium is a tall and showy bush when in flower. The green Rush-like stems are clothed with bright yellow Pea-like flowers throughout the summer, and there are very few leaves to mask this sea of gold. The situation is different when the shrub is not in flower — the appearance is often leggy, and so you should place this plant with care in the border. The experts disagree about pruning. Some say that the plant should be cut back in spring to keep it bushy — others say that it *is* a gaunt plant and it is spoilt by pruning. Perhaps both views are right — when grown in full sun and especially in a coastal garden the plant remains attractive. In a partly shady or damp site, however, the stems become distinctly unattractive, and here annual pruning is essential.

VARIETY: S. junceum is the only species. The upright stems may reach 9 ft or more, but can be kept in check by pruning. It is usually grown as a loose bush but can be trained as a standard. The leaves are small, narrow and infrequent but the 1 in. long Pea-like blooms are plentiful and are borne in spreading flower-heads over a long period.

SITE & SOIL: Requires well-drained, light soil — full sun is necessary.

PRUNING: Dead-head faded blooms. The previous season's growth can be cut back to 2 in. from the old wood in March.

PROPAGATION: Plant semi-ripe cuttings in a cold frame in summer.

Spartium junceum

STACHYURUS Stachyurus

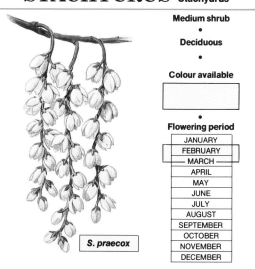

Medium shrub

•

Deciduous

•

Colour available

•

Flowering period

| JANUARY |
| FEBRUARY |
| MARCH |
| APRIL |
| MAY |
| JUNE |
| JULY |
| AUGUST |
| SEPTEMBER |
| OCTOBER |
| NOVEMBER |
| DECEMBER |

S. praecox

The shrubs we see in flower in late winter or early spring are so often restricted to the universally popular ones such as Hazel, Witch Hazel and Winter Jasmine. To provide a change there is no reason why you should not grow Stachyurus, which will thrive in any fertile soil and produce an abundance of pale yellow flowers in February-March or even earlier in some seasons. These cup-shaped blooms are borne on the stiff and pendent racemes which first appear on the branches in autumn. It is a hardy plant and the branchlets can be used for indoor winter decoration.

VARIETIES: The more popular species is **S. praecox**. It grows about 8 ft high and the 2–3 in. long catkin-like racemes bear about 20 small flowers. These blooms appear among the reddish-brown branches before the foliage opens — the leaves are about 4 in. long and broadly oval. The less widely available **S. chinensis** is quite similar but there are a number of points of difference to look for. The racemes are longer (4–5 in.) and the flowers more numerous (25–30). The wood is purplish and the leaves narrower and more tapered. There is a variegated variety **'Magpie'** with cream-edged and rose-tinged grey-green leaves.

SITE & SOIL: Requires humus-rich, non-chalky soil — thrives in sun or partial shade.

PRUNING: With a mature bush about one-third of the old wood should be cut down to ground level after flowering.

PROPAGATION: Plant semi-ripe cuttings in a cold frame in summer.

Stachyurus praecox

STAPHYLEA Bladder Nut

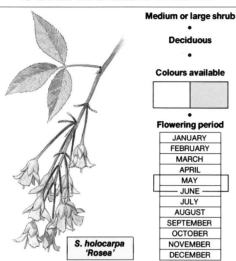

Medium or large shrub
•
Deciduous
•
Colours available
•
Flowering period

JANUARY
FEBRUARY
MARCH
APRIL
MAY
JUNE
JULY
AUGUST
SEPTEMBER
OCTOBER
NOVEMBER
DECEMBER

S. holocarpa 'Rosea'

The Bladder Nut is a rarity — it is not often seen in gardens and it is listed in few catalogues. The eye-catching feature of this plant is the presence of 4 in. long bladder-like fruits in late summer and autumn. These can be cut and used in flower arrangements. Staphylea is hardy and not difficult to grow but it does need space as the shrub will reach 8–15 ft when mature. The flowers appear in late spring or early summer, and are borne on panicles which may be upright or pendent, depending on the species.

VARIETIES: S. colchica is an erect shrub which grows about 8–10 ft high. The flower-heads are about 5 in. long — upright and bearing a cluster of fragrant white blooms in May. These are followed by the large thin-walled fruits in late summer. Each leaf is composed of up to five oval leaflets. **S. holocarpa 'Rosea'** differs in a number of ways. It has a spreading growth habit and the panicles of pale pink flowers in May are drooping rather than erect. The three-leaflet leaves are bronze-coloured when young. **S. pinnata** is the tallest species (12–15 ft) and has the longest flower-heads — pendent with white flowers in May–June. The pinnate leaves bear five to seven leaflets.

SITE & SOIL: Well-drained, reasonably fertile soil is required. Thrives in sun or light shade.

PRUNING: Not necessary — cut back unwanted or damaged branches in spring.

PROPAGATION: Layer branches or plant semi-ripe cuttings in a cold frame in summer.

Staphylea colchica

STEPHANANDRA Stephanandra

Dwarf, small or medium shrub
•
Deciduous
•
Colour available
•
Flowering period

JANUARY
FEBRUARY
MARCH
APRIL
MAY
JUNE
JULY
AUGUST
SEPTEMBER
OCTOBER
NOVEMBER
DECEMBER

S. incisa 'Crispa'

Stephanandra only just qualifies for inclusion in this book. Each white or greenish-white starry flower is tiny and the flower clusters are small, but they are often present in such large numbers that a pleasing but not showy floral display is produced in early summer. The main purpose of Stephanandra, however, is to provide dense attractive foliage with bright autumn colours for growing between showy-flowered trees and shrubs. If your soil is moist then this easy-to-grow shrub can be a good choice to provide autumn leaf colour, winter stem colour or ground cover, depending on the species or variety chosen.

VARIETIES: S. incisa has zig-zagging stems which reach 3–4 ft high and when mature the shrub reaches a width of 5–7 ft. The leaves are deeply lobed and toothed, turning yellow in winter. The flower-heads open in June. The variety **'Crispa'** is a good ground cover — a 2 ft mound of small, deeply cut and crinkled leaves. For something different there is **S. tanakae**. This is a taller shrub, reaching 6 ft x 6 ft when mature. The leaves are Maple-like and turn deep gold in autumn. Small flowers appear in June–July, but this species is grown mainly for its showy reddish stems in winter.

SITE & SOIL: A damp site is preferred — water in dry weather. Thrives best in partial shade.

PRUNING: Cut back some of the old stems to ground level after flowering.

PROPAGATION: Divide clumps in autumn or plant semi-ripe cuttings in a cold frame in summer.

Stephanandra incisa

STEWARTIA Stewartia

Large shrub
•
Deciduous
•
Colour available

Flowering period

JANUARY	
FEBRUARY	
MARCH	
APRIL	
MAY	
JUNE	
JULY	
AUGUST	
SEPTEMBER	
OCTOBER	
NOVEMBER	
DECEMBER	

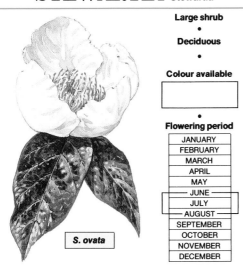

S. ovata

You will find this plant named as 'Stewartia' or 'Stuartia' on the label. It may be in the Shrub or the Tree section of the garden centre or catalogue, as some have a bushy growth habit and others have a single trunk. All bear lovely white flowers with showy stamens — solitary and measuring up to 4 in. in diameter. There is a continuous succession of these short-lived blooms for several weeks in summer, which makes Stewartia a beautiful specimen plant. Before you rush out and buy one it must be remembered that both shrub and tree forms need mild and sheltered conditions and it is quite fussy about soil type. But if you have a woodland garden in the southern counties, do buy one.

VARIETIES: S. malacodendron (15 ft) is a tall bush which bears 3 in. white blooms with showy purple anthers in June and July. Another shrubby Stewartia is **S. ovata** (15 ft) which has even larger blooms — 3–4 in. across, cup-shaped with a central boss of bright orange stamens. The flowering period is July–August and the leaves turn yellow in autumn. **S. sinensis** is a bush when young, with attractive flaking bark and bright red leaves in autumn.

SITE & SOIL: Requires moist, lime-free soil — thrives in sun or light shade.

PRUNING: Not necessary — remove dead or unwanted branches in winter.

PROPAGATION: It is difficult to propagate from cuttings — buy a container-grown plant.

Stewartia malacodendron

STRANVAESIA Stranvaesia

Dwarf, medium or large shrub
•
Evergreen
•
Colours available

Berrying period

JANUARY	
FEBRUARY	
MARCH	
APRIL	
MAY	
JUNE	
JULY	
AUGUST	
SEPTEMBER	
OCTOBER	
NOVEMBER	
DECEMBER	

S. davidiana 'Salicifolia'

Stranvaesia davidiana and its varieties are berry-forming plants which look like Cotoneaster but are occasionally listed as Photinia in the garden centre. It is generally a tall and spreading plant which will grow almost anywhere and is useful for screening or informal hedging, but there is a dwarf form which can be used for ground cover. In May or June the 3 in. wide heads of white Hawthorn-like flowers appear, and these are followed by bunches of bright berries. Branches bearing these pendent berry clusters can be cut and used for indoor decoration.

VARIETIES: The variety which is most commonly available is **S. davidiana 'Salicifolia'**. It is a vigorous and upright plant which reaches 10–15 ft and bears narrow leathery leaves. The older foliage turns red in autumn, when the stems are clothed with bunches of bright red berries. Birds find these fruits unattractive and so the display persists all winter. For a more compact growth habit and yellow berries which are ignored by birds, grow the variety **'Fructuluteo'** (6–9 ft) — the leaves have a wavy margin. For ground cover there is the near-prostrate variety **'Prostrata'** — 1–2 ft high and 2–4 ft wide after 10 years.

SITE & SOIL: Any well-drained garden soil will do — thrives in sun or partial shade.

PRUNING: Not necessary — cut back unwanted or damaged stems in spring.

PROPAGATION: Layer branches in spring or plant semi-ripe cuttings in a cold frame in summer.

Stranvaesia davidiana 'Fructuluteo'

STYRAX Snowbell

Medium or large shrub

•

Deciduous

•

Colours available

Flowering period

JANUARY	
FEBRUARY	
MARCH	
APRIL	
MAY	
JUNE	
JULY	
AUGUST	
SEPTEMBER	
OCTOBER	
NOVEMBER	
DECEMBER	

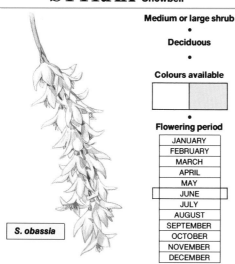

S. obassia

A splendid specimen plant which is not often seen. It needs space — with time it develops into a large bush or small tree 20 ft high and 15–20 ft wide. It is reasonably hardy but it is best to grow this shrub in a sheltered spot where it has some protection from the morning sun. The flowers look like 1 in. Snowdrops with open mouths (hence the common name) and prominent yellow anthers. White is the usual colour, but there is an attractive pink variety.

VARIETIES: Only a few types are available — the one you are most likely to find is **S. japonica** (Japanese Snowbell), which is generally regarded as the most reliable and attractive of the hardy species. It is an elegant plant with spreading branches which droop at the tips. The oval leaves are glossy and in the flowering season the white, open bells hang in clusters along the branches. The variety **'Pink Chimes'** is similar, but the flowers are pale pink. **S. obassia** (Fragrant Snowbell) differs from S. japonica by having a narrow growth habit, almost round leaves and with white flowers which are fragrant and borne on 8 in. long pendent racemes. The smallest species is the rare 6 ft high **S. americana** (American Snowbell).

SITE & SOIL: Requires well-drained, humus-rich and lime-free soil — thrives in sun or light shade.

PRUNING: Not necessary — cut back damaged or unwanted branches in spring.

PROPAGATION: Layer branches in spring or plant semi-ripe cuttings in a cold frame in summer.

Styrax japonica

SYMPHORICARPOS Snowberry

Dwarf, small or medium shrub

•

Deciduous

•

Colours available

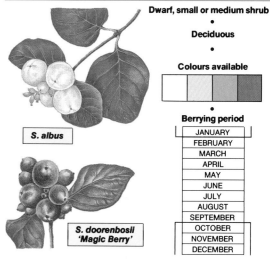

S. albus

S. doorenbosii 'Magic Berry'

Berrying period

JANUARY	
FEBRUARY	
MARCH	
APRIL	
MAY	
JUNE	
JULY	
AUGUST	
SEPTEMBER	
OCTOBER	
NOVEMBER	
DECEMBER	

Few plants are easier to grow than Symphoricarpos — this rampant shrub will flourish in any soil, in full sun and in the dense shade under trees and it will cover large areas in the wilder part of the garden. The small white or pink flowers are followed by a mass of marble-like berries in autumn which persist for months. Good for indoor decoration and for hedging, but take care to keep the freely-suckering types in check.

VARIETIES: S. albus produces 6 ft high slender shoots — white berries appear in early autumn. **S. rivularis** is really a variety of S. albus — it suckers freely and soon forms a thicket of tall bluish stems which bear white berries. **S. chenaultii 'Hancock'** is quite different — it is a ground cover plant growing 2 ft high and spreading 8 ft or more with purplish-pink berries. **S. orbiculatus** (Coral Berry) bears white flowers which are followed by pale purple berries. There is a variegated form (**'Variegatus'**) which has yellow-edged leaves but rarely fruits. The varieties of **S. doorenbosii** are generally compact and do not sucker. There are **'Magic Berry'** (3 ft, rose-pink berries), **'Mother of Pearl'** (4 ft, pink-flushed white) and **'White Hedge'** (2 ft, white).

SITE & SOIL: Any garden soil will do — thrives in full sun or shade. Variegated types need full sun.

PRUNING: Remove about one-third of the old stems in early spring. Trim hedges in summer.

PROPAGATION: Remove and plant up rooted suckers or plant hardwood cuttings in the open in late autumn.

Symphoricarpos doorenbosii 'Mother of Pearl'

SYRINGA Lilac

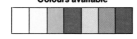

Small, medium or large shrub

•

Deciduous

•

Colours available

•

Flowering period

JANUARY
FEBRUARY
MARCH
APRIL
MAY
JUNE
JULY
AUGUST
SEPTEMBER
OCTOBER
NOVEMBER
DECEMBER

S. vulgaris 'Souvenir de Louis Spaeth'

S. vulgaris 'Madame Lemoine'

S. vulgaris 'Michel Buchner'

S. microphylla 'Superba'

'Go down to Kew in Lilac time' advises the Victorian poem — if you do then there will certainly be an impressive display of blooms in colours ranging from white to deep purple. There is no need to go to Kew to be impressed by this shrub — a walk down any suburban street in late May is likely to offer the sight of numerous varieties in full bloom. The types which brighten up gardens in May or early June are nearly always varieties of S. vulgaris, the Common Lilac. They will grow in nearly all soils but they are not happy in acid, peaty ground. The small, tubular flowers are borne in crowded conical spires. They need feeding and mulching annually and both suckers and dead blooms should be removed.

VARIETIES: S. vulgaris bears oval or heart-shaped leaves and will reach 10–15 ft when mature. The flowering season is short, about three weeks, but the fragrance and the size of the flower-heads compensate for this. You will find a wide choice of varieties at the garden centre. Some bear single blooms — examples include **'Charles X'** (purplish-red), **'Firmament'** (lilac-blue), **'Marechal Foch'** (carmine-rose), **'Maud Notcutt'** (white), **'Primrose'** (pale yellow), **'Sensation'** (white-edged purplish-red), **'Souvenir de Louis Spaeth'** (wine-red) and **'Vestale'** (white). There are also numerous double-flowering varieties, including **'Charles Joly'** (deep purplish-red), **'Katherine Havemeyer'** (lavender), **'Madame Antoine Buchner'** (pink), **'Madame Lemoine'** (white), **'Michel Buchner'** (rosy-lilac), **'Mrs Edward Harding'** (red) and **'Paul Thirion'** (claret-rose). Syringa species with their looser flower-heads are much less popular than these large-flowered named varieties and hybrids of S. vulgaris, but many are well worth growing. Best known is **S. microphylla 'Superba'** (5 ft) which bears masses of small pink flower-heads in May and again in September. Another small Lilac is **S. persica** which bears small loose heads of mauve flower-heads in May — **'Alba'** is a white variety. **S. prestoniae** (8 ft) is a vigorous shrub which produces large flower-heads in June — varieties include **'Elinor'** (lavender) and **'Desdemona'** (pink). Other species Syringas include **S. chinensis** (8 ft, drooping sprays of lavender flowers), **S. josiflexa 'Bellicent'** (10 ft, large plume-like heads of pink flowers), **S. reflexa** (12 ft, purplish-pink outside, white within) and one for a tub or rockery — **S. meyeri 'Palibin'** (3 ft, small heads of lilac-pink flowers).

SITE & SOIL: Any reasonable garden soil will do, but chalky ones are best. Full sun is preferred but tolerates some shade.

PRUNING: Cut out thin and unproductive branches immediately after flowering.

PROPAGATION: Named varieties of S. vulgaris are generally grafted, but species can be propagated by planting semi-ripe cuttings in a cold frame in summer.

Syringa vulgaris 'Maud Notcutt'

Syringa persica

Syringa josiflexa 'Bellicent'

TAMARIX Tamarisk

Large shrub
•
Deciduous
•
Colours available

Flowering period

| JANUARY |
| FEBRUARY |
| MARCH |
| APRIL |
| MAY |
| JUNE |
| JULY |
| AUGUST |
| SEPTEMBER |
| OCTOBER |
| NOVEMBER |
| DECEMBER |

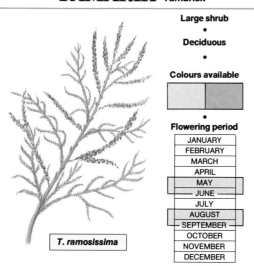

T. ramosissima

When in bloom the tiny leaves and the tall plumes of small pink flowers combine to give a feathery effect. It is an easy plant to recognise, and apart from the flowering period there is not much difference between the various species and varieties. Some experts say you should leave Tamarisk unpruned, but it will become a gaunt bush over 10 ft high in time and is best pruned annually. Despite its appearance it is not a delicate plant — it is a favourite subject for exposed coastal sites.

VARIETIES: T. tetrandra is the spring-flowering form — an open bush which bears 2 ft high plumes of pale pink flowers at the top of the dark branches before the scale-like foliage appears. The most popular summer-flowering Tamarisk is **T. ramosissima (T. pentandra)** which has pink flower-heads above reddish-brown branches. For a darker shade of pink choose the variety **'Pink Cascade'** or the red-budded **'Rubra'**. Other Tamarisks are not easy to find in the catalogues. **T. gallica** (Common Tamarisk) is not often listed despite its English name, and you will have to search for the purple-stemmed **T. parviflora**.

SITE & SOIL: Most well-drained soils will do — heavy clays are not suitable. Choose a sunny site.

PRUNING: With T. tetrandra cut back shoots with faded blooms immediately flowering is over. With T. ramosissima cut back some of last year's growth in March.

PROPAGATION: Plant hardwood cuttings in the open in late autumn.

Tamarix tetrandra

TEUCRIUM Germander

Dwarf or small shrub
•
Evergreen
•
Colours available

Flowering period

| JANUARY |
| FEBRUARY |
| MARCH |
| APRIL |
| MAY |
| JUNE |
| JULY |
| AUGUST |
| SEPTEMBER |
| OCTOBER |
| NOVEMBER |
| DECEMBER |

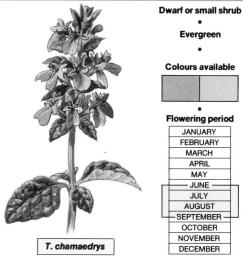

T. chamaedrys

The two popular varieties of the other shrub on this page are quite similar apart from the time of flowering. With Teucrium the two popular varieties differ in size, flower colour, cultural needs and form of the flower-head. There are some similarities — both have a long flowering period throughout the summer and there is a need for a sunny, well-drained site. The stems of all the Germanders are square in cross-section and the flowers are two-lipped.

VARIETIES: T. chamaedrys (T. lucidrys) is the Wall Germander — a low-growing and aromatic sub-shrub which has long been grown as a medicinal herb. It grows about 9 in. high and spreads to 1½ ft, with oval toothed leaves and spikes of pink flowers from July to September. The Wall Germander is a tough and hardy plant for the rockery or the front of a mixed border — which cannot be said for the other popular Teucrium **T. fruticans** (Shrubby Germander). This species grows about 5 ft high and both the stems and underside of the leaves are silvery grey. The pale blue flowers look like tiny Orchids and are borne in terminal racemes between June and September. It is a tender plant, needing wall protection and a mild locality.

SITE & SOIL: Requires a free-draining site — do not grow in heavy or rich soil. Thrives in full sun.

PRUNING: Cut back about half of last year's growth in April.

PROPAGATION: Plant semi-ripe cuttings in a cold frame in summer.

Teucrium fruticans

TRACHELOSPERMUM Star Jasmine

Climbing shrub

•

Evergreen

•

Colours available

•

Flowering period

JANUARY
FEBRUARY
MARCH
APRIL
MAY
JUNE
JULY
AUGUST
SEPTEMBER
OCTOBER
NOVEMBER
DECEMBER

T. asiaticum

There is no doubt that this beautiful self-clinging climber would be much more popular if it was hardier. It is a vigorous grower reaching 20 ft x 20 ft when mature, and the Jasmine-like flowers are sweetly scented. These blooms are borne in loose clusters amongst the glossy dark green leaves in summer, but it does require a south- or west-facing wall which is sheltered from the icy winds of winter.

VARIETIES: T. asiaticum is the hardiest and most reliable species. The flat-faced tubular flowers measure about ¾ in. across — cream in colour with a yellow centre. The flower colour deepens with age. **T. jasminoides** is the Confederate Jasmine found in so many gardens of the Southern States of the U.S. Its leaves and flowers are larger than those of T. asiaticum — the 1 in. blooms are white at first, later changing to cream. Unfortunately it is not easy to grow in Britain as it is a tender plant which is killed by severe frosts. If you live in a mild area in the South or West it is worth a try — varieties include **'Variegatum'** (leaves edged and splashed with cream) and **'W776' ('Wilsonii')** with prominently veined leaves which redden in winter.

SITE & SOIL: Requires well-drained acid soil. Full sun is essential.

PRUNING: If practical dead-head faded blooms. Remove damaged and weak stems in March.

PROPAGATION: Plant semi-ripe cuttings in a propagator in summer.

Trachelospermum jasminoides

ULEX Gorse

Dwarf, small or medium shrub

•

Evergreen

•

Colour available

•

Flowering period

JANUARY
FEBRUARY
MARCH
APRIL
MAY
JUNE
JULY
AUGUST
SEPTEMBER
OCTOBER
NOVEMBER
DECEMBER

U. europaeus 'Plenus'

Furze, Gorse or Whin — these names all refer to Ulex europaeus, a native shrub which is such a common sight in many areas of the country. It is not often grown as a border plant, but it is extremely useful for hedging or large-scale ground cover. The location will have to be right — it needs sandy or stony soil and there must be little or no shade. All species of Gorse are spiny and bear yellow, Pea-like flowers. It does not like transplanting — choose a small, container-grown specimen.

VARIETIES: The Common Gorse **U. europaeus** grows about 6 ft high — a densely spined plant which bears masses of flowers between March and May and then on and off throughout the year. Although it is a native shrub it may be severely damaged in an abnormally hard winter. You will have to buy a plant if you want one — do not dig up a wild shrub. A better and more popular choice is the variety **'Plenus' ('Flore Pleno')** — it is more compact (4 ft) and bears an abundant display of semi-double flowers in spring. Much less popular are the autumn-flowering dwarfs. There are **U. gallii 'Mizzen'** which grows about 2 ft high and the 1½ ft **U. minor (U. nanus)**.

SITE & SOIL: Avoid fertile and humus-rich soils. Thrives best in full sun.

PRUNING: To keep the plant bushy trim back the stems after flowering.

PROPAGATION: Sow seed or plant semi-ripe cuttings in a cold frame in summer.

Ulex europaeus 'Plenus'

VIBURNUM Viburnum

Winter-flowering Group

V. tinus

V. bodnantense

Spring-flowering Group

V. opulus 'Sterile'

Dwarf, small or medium shrub
•
Deciduous
or
Evergreen

Colours available

Flowering period

JANUARY
FEBRUARY
MARCH
APRIL
MAY
JUNE
JULY
AUGUST
SEPTEMBER
OCTOBER
NOVEMBER
DECEMBER

Autumn-berrying Group

V. davidii

There is an assortment of Viburnums at the average garden centre and a bewildering array listed in the specialist catalogue. They come in a range of shapes and sizes. There is no standard leaf form nor flower-head pattern and there are both evergreen and deciduous varieties. All this makes the genus a confusing one for the gardener, but it is also an invaluable one with year-round interest and plants for ground cover, hedging or as specimens in the border. The simplest but certainly not the only way of separating the various species is to divide them into just three groups — the winter-flowering Viburnums, the spring-flowering ones and the autumn-berrying types. As a general rule all are easy to grow and will succeed in chalky soil. There is no need for regular pruning and all are hardy. They are usually pink in bud and white in flower.

VARIETIES: The *Winter-flowering Group* prefer full sun and are deciduous unless indicated below. The popular **V. tinus** belongs here — a useful 10 ft high evergreen with large, oval leaves and clusters of pink buds which open into small white flowers in December–April. The best known varieties are **'Eve Price'**, **'Gwenllian'** and **'Variegatum'**. For earlier flowers choose **V. farreri (V. fragrans)** — an 8 ft shrub with clusters of fragrant white flowers in November–February. This old favourite is being overtaken these days by the pink-flowered **V. bodnantense** and its variety **'Dawn'**. The *Spring-flowering Group* usually have their blooms in large flat heads or globular 'snowballs', and thrive best in light shade. One of the basic species is **V. carlesii** (5 ft) with very fragrant white flowers and its variety **'Aurora'** with pink flowers, but its hybrids are now taking over — examples include **V. burkwoodii** (6 ft, white flowers April–May, evergreen) and **V. 'Anne Russell'** (5 ft, white flowers March–April). Taller Viburnums include the evergreen **V. rhytidophyllum** (10 ft, huge foliage, June flowers and red berries) and **V. opulus 'Sterile'** (8 ft, white, ball-like flower-heads). For flat flower-heads ('lace-caps') choose **V. plicatum 'Mariesii'**, **'Lanarth'** or **'Pink Beauty'**. The *Autumn-berrying Group* is dominated by **V. opulus** and some of its varieties. June 'lace-cap' flowers are followed by berries — look for **'Compactum'** (3 ft, red berries), **'Xanthocarpum'** (yellow) and the large **'Notcutt's Variety'** (10 ft, red). For blue berries grow the evergreen **V. davidii** (2 ft) — a nearby male plant is needed.

SITE & SOIL: Requires well-cultivated soil which is rich in humus. Thrives best in sun or light shade, depending on the species.

PRUNING: Not necessary — cut back damaged or unwanted branches after flowering (deciduous types) or in May (evergreen types).

PROPAGATION: Layer branches in autumn or plant semi-ripe cuttings in a cold frame in summer.

Viburnum farreri

Viburnum plicatum 'Lanarth'

Viburnum opulus 'Compactum'

VACCINIUM Vaccinium

Prostrate, dwarf, small or medium shrub

•

Deciduous, Semi-evergreen
or
Evergreen

•

Colours available

•

Flowering period

| JANUARY |
| FEBRUARY |
| MARCH |
| APRIL |
| MAY |
| JUNE |
| JULY |
| AUGUST |
| SEPTEMBER |
| OCTOBER |
| NOVEMBER |
| DECEMBER |

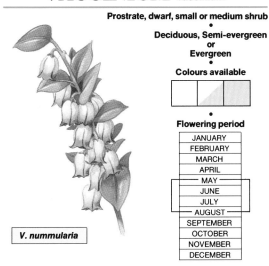

V. nummularia

The Vacciniums are all lime-hating shrubs — acid soil is essential. If your soil is peaty and Rhododendrons flourish it is worth trying this plant as it bears attractive clusters of urn-like flowers followed by berries and leaves with autumn hues. Some species are bushy and upright — others are low and spreading. Depending on the type chosen, the leaves may fall in autumn or be retained in winter, the flowers may open in spring or summer and the berries may be red or black.

VARIETIES: V. corymbosum (Swamp Blueberry) is a 4 ft high thicket-forming shrub, bearing white or pale pink flowers in May followed by edible black fruits. In autumn the leaves turn bright red. The giant is the semi-evergreen **V. cylindraceum** (10 ft). At the other end of the scale is the prostrate and evergreen **V. vitis-idaea** (Cowberry) — 6 in. high with a spread of 1½ ft. **'Koralle'** is the popular variety — pink pendent bells in June–August followed by red edible fruits. Other species include the 1 ft high evergreen **V. nummularia** for the rockery and the 4 ft high **V. ovatum** (Cranberry).

SITE & SOIL: Well-drained, acid and moist soil is essential — thrives best in light shade.

PRUNING: Not required — remove dead or unwanted branches in late winter.

PROPAGATION: Sow seed in spring or plant semi-ripe cuttings in a cold frame in summer.

Vaccinium nummularia

VINCA Periwinkle

Prostrate shrub

•

Evergreen

•

Colours available

•

V. minor

Flowering period

| JANUARY |
| FEBRUARY |
| MARCH |
| APRIL |
| MAY |
| JUNE |
| JULY |
| AUGUST |
| SEPTEMBER |
| OCTOBER |
| NOVEMBER |
| DECEMBER |

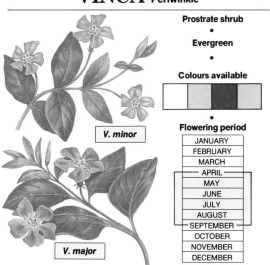

V. major

The lowly Periwinkle is a sub-shrub which you will find in the Shrub or Hardy Perennial section of the garden centre. It is a trailing plant with green stems and oval leaves which form a tangled mat. An excellent choice if you want a ground cover for under trees or on a steep bank — it thrives in sun or shade and its stems root into the soil as they spread.

VARIETIES: The popular large Periwinkle is **V. major**, growing about 8–10 in. high and producing a succession of 1 in. wide blue flowers from May to September. It can be very invasive — so keep away from small and delicate plants. There are variegated forms with leaves edged or splashed with yellow (**'Maculata'**) or creamy-white (**'Variegata'**). The uncommon **V. difformis** is similar in size to V. major, but its lilac-blue flowers appear from October to December and the stems are not fully frost-hardy. **V. minor** (2–4 in.) is a smaller and less invasive plant. The flowers are mauve — variety colours include rich blue (**'Bowles Variety'**), white (**'Gertrude Jekyll'**) or purple (**'Atropurpurea'**). April–May is the main flowering period, but blooms continue to appear until September. There are variegated forms with leaves edged or splashed with yellow (**'Aureovariegata'**) or creamy-white (**'Variegata'**).

SITE & SOIL: Any reasonable well-drained soil will do — thrives in sun or shade.

PRUNING: Cut back the shoots in spring.

PROPAGATION: Divide plant or remove rooted side-shoots in late autumn or winter.

Vinca minor 'Gertrude Jekyll'

WEIGELA Weigela

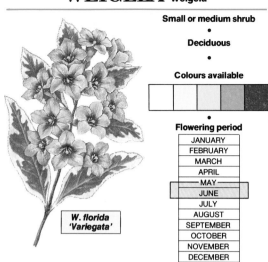

Small or medium shrub

•

Deciduous

•

Colours available

•

Flowering period

JANUARY
FEBRUARY
MARCH
APRIL
MAY
JUNE
JULY
AUGUST
SEPTEMBER
OCTOBER
NOVEMBER
DECEMBER

W. florida 'Variegata'

Weigela is in all the lists of basic bushes for use in shrub or mixed borders. The reason is that it produces a colourful floral display in late spring and early summer, and is completely reliable. It grows in all soils and flowers quite merrily in partial shade. Weigela will withstand neglect, but for best results it needs rich soil and annual pruning. It does not grow very tall, 6 or 7 ft at the most, but it does need space to show off its arching stems.

VARIETIES: The most popular species is **W. florida** (6 ft, pale pink tubular flowers). The usual choice is a variety rather than the species — look for **'Variegata'** (4 ft, pale pink flowers, cream-edged leaves), **'Foliis Purpureis'** (2½ ft, deep pink flowers, purple-flushed leaves) and **'Versicolor'** (6 ft, cream flowers ageing to red). **W. middendorffiana** is an unusual species with orange-marked yellow flowers which are bell-shaped. Another unusual one is **W. praecox 'Variegata'** (6 ft, yellow-edged leaves, yellow-marked pink flowers). There are a number of hybrids, including **W. 'Bristol Ruby'** (free-flowering red, popular), **W. 'Looymansii Aurea'** (pink flowers, yellow leaves in spring) and **W. 'Candida'** (white flowers).

SITE & SOIL: Any reasonable soil will do, including chalky ones. Thrives in sun or partial shade.

PRUNING: Cut back shoots which bear faded blooms immediately after flowering.

PROPAGATION: Plant hardwood cuttings in the open in late autumn.

Weigela florida 'Foliis Purpureis'

WISTERIA Wistaria

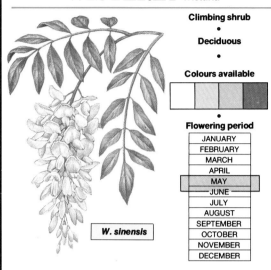

Climbing shrub

•

Deciduous

•

Colours available

•

Flowering period

JANUARY
FEBRUARY
MARCH
APRIL
MAY
JUNE
JULY
AUGUST
SEPTEMBER
OCTOBER
NOVEMBER
DECEMBER

W. sinensis

There is no more spectacular flowering climber for the front of the house than a mature Wisteria in full bloom — its twining stems are covered with hanging chains of Pea-like flowers in May and June. To ensure this eye-catching effect you must take care over selection, planting and pruning. Buy a container-grown plant and choose a sunny site such as a house wall, old tree or pergola. You will also need patience — Wisteria may remain dormant for months after planting and the first season's display may be disappointing, but it will grow quickly once established.

VARIETIES: W. sinensis (Chinese Wistaria) is a popular species with 1 ft long flower-heads with sweetly-scented lilac-blue blooms. It is a rampant grower which can reach 50 ft or more, and is not recommended for a house wall as it often gets into gutters. Varieties include **'Alba'** (white), **'Black Dragon'** (double, purple) and **'Plena'** (double, lilac). The Japanese Wistaria (**W. floribunda**) is less vigorous — the flower-heads are about 9 in. long and stems grow about 20–30 ft high. **'Alba'** has white flowers, **'Rosea'** has pink blooms and **'Macrobotrys'** (**'Multijuga'**) has lilac-blue flower-heads up to 2½ ft long.

SITE & SOIL: Any reasonable soil will do — dig in compost before planting. Requires full sun.

PRUNING: Cut back current year's side growths to about 6 in. in July.

PROPAGATION: Layer stems in spring or plant semi-ripe cuttings in a cold frame in summer.

Wisteria floribunda 'Macrobotrys'

YUCCA Yucca

Small or medium shrub

•

Evergreen

•

Colours available

•

Flowering period

JANUARY	
FEBRUARY	
MARCH	
APRIL	
MAY	
JUNE	
JULY	
AUGUST	
SEPTEMBER	
OCTOBER	
NOVEMBER	
DECEMBER	

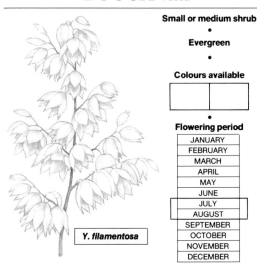

Y. filamentosa

Yucca is the shrub to grow if you want to give an exotic touch to a border or patio tub — there are large sword-like leaves and immense flower-heads made up of masses of 2–3 in. long bell-like blooms. Despite its tropical origin and liking for hot and dry conditions the popular types are quite hardy in Britain. It is a slow starter — a newly-planted Yucca may hardly grow at all for the first year or two and it takes about three years for the first flowers to appear. Once it starts, however, you can expect to see the impressive flower-heads every year.

VARIETIES: The stemless species are the ones usually grown. The favourite one is **Y. filamentosa**, which has a basal rosette of 2 ft long stiff leaves which bear twisted white threads along the edges. The 4–6 ft flower stalk crowded with creamy-white flowers appears in summer. The variety **'Bright Edge'** has leaves edged with yellow — **'Variegata'** has leaves edged and striped with yellow. **Y. flaccida** has foliage which droops at the tip and 2–4 ft high flower stalks — **'Golden Sword'** has yellow-striped leaves. Take care with **Y. gloriosa** — the leaves are bayonet-tipped. The giant is **Y. whipplei** — the purple-edged flowers are borne on 7–10 ft high stalks.

SITE & SOIL: Needs good drainage and the absence of heavy clay. Thrives best in full sun.

PRUNING: Not necessary or practical, so plant it where space will not be a problem. Cut off dead leaves.

PROPAGATION: Remove rooted offsets growing at the base of the shrub and plant in spring.

Yucca gloriosa

ZENOBIA Zenobia

Small shrub

•

Semi-evergreen

•

Colour available

•

Flowering period

JANUARY	
FEBRUARY	
MARCH	
APRIL	
MAY	
JUNE	
JULY	
AUGUST	
SEPTEMBER	
OCTOBER	
NOVEMBER	
DECEMBER	

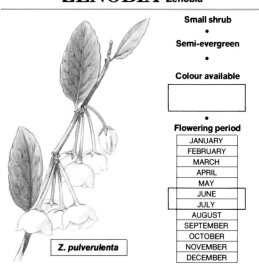

Z. pulverulenta

This plant is one of a number which can be used to accompany the classic lime-haters such as Rhododendron, Camellia, Calluna and Pieris. Some experts have expressed surprise that it is such a rarity — its mature size of 3 ft x 3 ft can be used to add height to a Heather border or an unusual edging to a Rhododendron one. The open, arching growth habit is an attractive feature and both leaves and stems change their colour as the season progresses. The bell-like blooms are borne in drooping clusters in midsummer, following on when the rather similar blooms of Pieris have faded.

VARIETY: There is just one species — **Z. pulverulenta** (**Z. speciosa**). In spring the young stems and leaves have a distinct silvery bloom. This disappears as the 2 in. long oval leaves mature, and in autumn both the stems and some of the foliage turn orange or red, and partial leaf-fall occurs. An interesting succession of colour changes for stem and leaf, but it is the floral display which is the main feature. The pendent white flowers are about ½ in. across and look like a group of large Lily-of-the-Valley blooms with an aniseed-like fragrance.

SITE & SOIL: Acid soil is necessary — add peat at planting time. Requires partial shade.

PRUNING: Not necessary — remove flower stems when the blooms have faded.

PROPAGATION: Layer shoots in spring or plant semi-ripe cuttings in a cold frame in summer.

Zenobia pulverulenta

CHAPTER 3

PLANTING

The purchase of shrubs often represents a sizeable outlay and you don't want to waste your money. Poor planting rather than poor stock is the usual cause of failure, so read this chapter before you begin. You will discover that there is more to it than just digging a hole and dropping in the plant. There are four basic types of planting material and each one has its own advantages and disadvantages, so choose wisely and plant properly.

TYPES OF PLANTING MATERIAL

CONTAINER-GROWN

The most convenient way to buy both deciduous and evergreen shrubs. Suitable for planting all year round.

A container-grown plant may be expensive but it has one great advantage — it can be planted at any time of the year as long as the soil is suitable and the weather is reasonable. It is not, however, a fool-proof method of planting shrubs — you have to choose and plant with care. Look for danger signs before you buy — these include wilted or diseased leaves, split container, dry soil and a thick root growing through the base. Don't buy the biggest size you can afford — large and old specimens take a long time to establish and are often overtaken by younger and less expensive ones. A rooted cutting in a pot is an even cheaper way of buying a container-grown plant, but you will often have to wait some time for it to reach flowering size. At planting time make sure that the earth around the soil ball is enriched with organic matter — roots hate to move from a peat compost into a mineral soil.

BARE-ROOTED

The traditional way to buy deciduous shrubs. Suitable for planting between October and March.

A bare-rooted plant is dug up at the nursery and the soil is removed from the roots. Damp material such as peat is packed around the roots to prevent them from drying out and at no stage should the roots be allowed to become dry. Once all deciduous shrubs were sold this way, but they have been largely replaced by container-grown specimens. However, bare-rooted plants are worth considering as they are less expensive than their container-grown counterparts and it is not true that they are always more difficult to establish — some shrubs root more readily when planted as bare-rooted stock. The correct time for planting is during the dormant season. Examine the plant carefully if you are buying from a shop, nursery or market stall. Reject it if the leaf buds are beginning to open, if the stems are shrivelled or diseased or if there are small white roots growing into the peat.

BALLED

The traditional way to buy evergreen shrubs. Suitable for planting in September, October or April.

Evergreen shrubs are occasionally sold as balled plants. The specimen is dug up at the nursery and the soil around the roots is left intact, the soil ball being tightly wrapped in hessian sacking, nylon netting or polythene sheeting. When moving a balled plant make sure you hold it under the sacking or netting — never use the stems as a handle which can dislodge soil from around the roots. Look at the plant carefully before purchase. Feel for strong girdling roots through the sacking — they run horizontally near the top of the soil ball and are a bad sign. The soil should be firm and moist and the leaves and stems should be healthy. Do not buy a plant with wilted leaves.

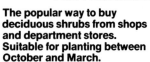

PRE-PACKAGED

The popular way to buy deciduous shrubs from shops and department stores. Suitable for planting between October and March.

Pre-packaged shrubs are the standard planting material sold by hardware shops, department stores and supermarkets. The pre-packaged plant is a bare-rooted specimen with its roots surrounded by moist peat and the whole plant packed into a plastic bag. Labels are descriptive and colourful, and such plants are cheaper than their container-grown counterparts, but there are drawbacks. It may be hard to see what you are buying and premature growth may occur in the warm conditions in the shop. So look for the standard bare-rooted danger signs — leaf buds beginning to open, shrivelled or diseased stems and small white roots growing into the peat.

TIMING

CONTAINER-GROWN PLANTS

JULY	AUG	SEPT	OCT	NOV	DEC	JAN	FEB	MARCH	APRIL	MAY	JUNE

BALLED EVERGREENS   BARE-ROOTED PLANTS &   BALLED EVERGREENS
PRE-PACKAGED PLANTS

Container-grown plants can be planted at any time of the year, but it is advisable to avoid the depths of winter and midsummer if you can. The time for planting bare-rooted and pre-packaged plants is much more restricted. For most gardens the best time is between October and late November, but if the weather is abnormally wet or if the soil is heavy clay then it is better to wait until March. With balled evergreens the best time is early autumn (early September–mid October) — plant in April if you miss the autumn planting date. Soil conditions are as important as the calendar. The ground should be neither frozen nor waterlogged. Squeeze a handful of soil — it should be wet enough to form a ball and yet dry enough to shatter when dropped on to a hard surface.

SPACING

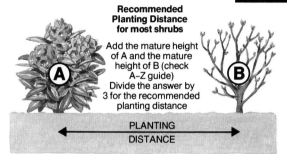

Recommended Planting Distance for most shrubs

Add the mature height of A and the mature height of B (check A–Z guide) Divide the answer by 3 for the recommended planting distance

PLANTING DISTANCE

Planting too closely is a common problem. It is easy to see why people do this — the plants from the garden centre are usually small, and it is hard to imagine at this stage what they will look like when they are mature. When you plant at the recommended distances the border will look bare and unattractive. You can plant a little closer, but that is not really the answer. One solution is to plant a number of 'fill-in' shrubs between the choice shrubs you have planted. These 'fill-in' shrubs should be inexpensive old favourites (Forsythia, Spiraea, Ribes etc) and are progressively removed as the choice shrubs develop. A second alternative is to fill the space between the planted shrubs with bulbs, bedding plants or herbaceous perennials.

GETTING READY FOR PLANTING

BALLED PLANT

Balled plants can be left unplanted for several weeks provided the soil ball is kept moist

CONTAINER-GROWN PLANT

Container-grown plants can be left unplanted for several weeks provided the soil is kept moist

BARE-ROOTED and PRE-PACKAGED PLANT

Bare-rooted plants can be left unplanted for 3–4 days provided the peat is kept moist

To prevent the plant from toppling over, secure the stem to a firm support if planting is to be delayed

Keep the soil ball moist until you are ready to plant

Do *not* remove the covering at this stage

If the shrub is tall, secure the stem to a firm support if planting is to be delayed

Keep the roots moist by watering the soil until you are ready to plant

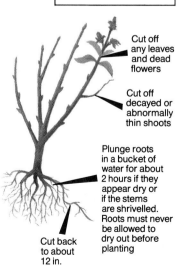

Cut off any leaves and dead flowers

Cut off decayed or abnormally thin shoots

Plunge roots in a bucket of water for about 2 hours if they appear dry or if the stems are shrivelled. Roots must never be allowed to dry out before planting

Cut back to about 12 in.

PLANTING

CONTAINER-GROWN and BALLED PLANTS

One of the common complaints raised by gardeners is the failure of the roots of a container-grown plant to move into the surrounding soil. The reason is generally poor planting technique — if your soil is low in organic matter you must use a planting mixture to fill the hole, and you must make sure that this mixture is firmly pressed up against the soil ball of the plant.

Planting Mixture

Make up the planting mixture in a wheelbarrow on a day when the soil is reasonably dry and friable — 1 part topsoil, 1 part moist peat and 3 handfuls of Bone Meal per barrow load. Keep this mixture in a shed or garage until you are ready to start planting.

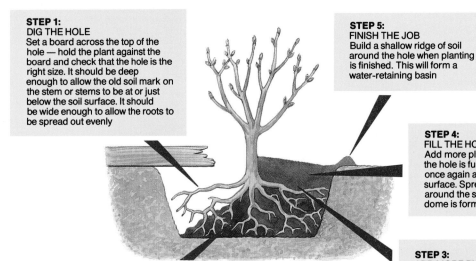

STEP 1:
DIG THE HOLE
Make it large enough to hold a 3–4 in. layer of planting mixture all round. It should be deep enough to ensure that the soil ball will be 1 in. below the surface after planting

STEP 2:
ADD LAYER OF PLANTING MIXTURE
Spread a 3–4 in. layer at the bottom of the hole

STEP 5:
FINISH THE JOB
After planting a shallow water-retaining basin should remain

STEP 4:
ADD MORE PLANTING MIXTURE TO THE HOLE
Fill the space between the soil ball and the side of the hole with planting mixture. Firm down the planting mixture at intervals with your finger tips. Stop when the top of the soil ball is reached

STEP 3:
PUT THE PLANT IN POSITION
Container-grown plant: Cut down the side of the container and remove it very carefully. Cut away any thick circling roots and gently tease out some of the roots on the side of the soil ball
Balled plant: Untie and loosen top of the sacking — do not remove. If the covering is netting or sheeting, carefully remove but do not break up the soil ball

BARE-ROOTED and PRE-PACKAGED PLANTS

STEP 1:
DIG THE HOLE
Set a board across the top of the hole — hold the plant against the board and check that the hole is the right size. It should be deep enough to allow the old soil mark on the stem or stems to be at or just below the soil surface. It should be wide enough to allow the roots to be spread out evenly

STEP 2:
ADD PLANTING MIXTURE AROUND THE ROOTS
Work a couple of trowelfuls around the roots. Shake the plant gently up and down — add a little more planting mixture and firm around the roots with your fists

STEP 5:
FINISH THE JOB
Build a shallow ridge of soil around the hole when planting is finished. This will form a water-retaining basin

STEP 4:
FILL THE HOLE
Add more planting mixture until the hole is full. Tread down once again and then loosen the surface. Spread a little soil around the stem so that a low dome is formed

STEP 3:
ADD MORE PLANTING MIXTURE
Half-fill the hole with more planting mixture and firm it down by gentle treading. On no account should you stamp heavily. Start treading at the outer edge of the hole and work gradually inwards

CHAPTER 4
PLANT CARE

TRAINING & SUPPORTING

Supporting and training are not quite the same thing. Supporting involves the provision of a post, stake or framework to which weak stems can be attached. Training involves the fixing of branches into desired positions so that an unnatural but desirable growth habit is produced.

Some shrubs with lax spreading stems may require some means of support after a few years. Use 3 or 4 stakes with a band joining the top of each stake — never rely on a single pole and twine.

Climbers must be grown against a support from the outset to ensure that they remain attached to it and grow in the desired direction. Use trellis work, posts, pillars, pergolas, fences etc. Make sure that all fence posts are well-anchored. For covering walls use plastic-covered straining wire stretched horizontally at 1½ ft intervals — there should be at least 3 in. between the  wire and the wall. Many plants can be grown against walls in this way, including weak-stemmed non-climbers such as Winter Jasmine and Forsythia suspensa. The wire ties used to attach the main stems to the supports should not be tied too tightly. Plant the climber about 1–1½ ft away from the base of the wall. When growing climbers up a pillar, wind the stems in an ascending spiral (see illustration) rather than attaching to one side of the support.

The main stems need not all be trained vertically — spreading them horizontally to form an espalier or at an angle to form a fan can dramatically increase the display.

CARE AFTER PLANTING

Once the new shrub is in place it should be watered in thoroughly. Cut back the branches of bare-rooted plants to about two-thirds of their length — container-grown and balled plants should not need trimming. Evergreens may need extra care. Winter browning of the foliage can take place when they are planted in autumn and so it is a wise precaution to protect choice specimens with a polythene screen (see below). When spring arrives, spray the leaves with water on warm days and mulch around the stems.

HOEING

The main purpose of hoeing is to keep down weeds, such as couch grass, which are not smothered by mulching. For this purpose hoeing must be carried out at regular intervals so that the underground parts of the weeds will be eventually starved. Hoeing should not go deeper than an inch below the surface, or shallow roots may be damaged. Do not bother to hoe as a way of conserving moisture — the old idea of creating a 'dust mulch' is of little value.

CUTTING & DEAD-HEADING

Cutting blooms and attractive foliage from shrubs for arranging indoors is, of course, a basic part of the gardening scene. This form of spring and summer pruning generally does no harm, but take care during the first year after planting. A newly-planted shrub needs all the stems and green leaves it can produce, so only cut a few of the flowers and do not remove many leaves.

The removal of dead flowers has several advantages — it keeps the bush tidy, it may prolong the flowering season by preventing seed formation and in a few cases it may induce a second flush later in the season. Make sure that the stalk is cut cleanly and do not remove too much stem. It is impractical to dead-head most shrubs, but it is necessary with large-flowered varieties such as Lilac and Buddleia. Do not remove the faded flower-heads of Hydrangea until March. The dead flowers of Rhododendron should be carefully broken off with finger and thumb.

WINTER PROTECTION

The snow and frost of an average winter usually do little or no harm to the shrubs in the garden, but an abnormally severe winter can cause losses. With types which are not fully hardy, the base of the shrub should be covered with a blanket of straw or peat. Newly-planted stock will benefit from some form of frost protection, especially if it is evergreen and known to be rather tender. Build a plastic screen — make sure that the bottom of the plastic sheeting is pinned down to prevent draughts. Established plants are more resistant than newly-planted ones to frost, but they are more liable to damage by the other winter enemy — snow. The weight on large branches can cause them to break. If heavy snow is forecast it may be worth tying the branches of a choice evergreen with twine, but it is usually not necessary — just gently shake the branches to remove most of the snow.

PRUNING

Pruning has a very simple meaning — the cutting away of unwanted growth from woody plants. But the purpose of pruning is less easy to understand, as there is nearly always more than one reason for carrying out this work:

- To remove poor quality wood, such as weak twigs, dead or diseased branches and damaged shoots.
- To shape the shrub to your needs. This calls for the removal of healthy but unwanted wood — examples include the removal of a minor branch which is rubbing against a major one and the cutting back of branches which are blocking a pathway.
- To regulate both the quality and quantity of blossom and/or fruit production.

The craft of pruning is perhaps the most difficult lesson the gardener has to learn. Both the timing and the technique depend on the age and type of shrub. If you are a novice you must check carefully the rules for the particular plant you wish to tackle. The table on the right is only a general guide and you should consult the A–Z section for instructions relating to individual shrubs.

PRUNING RULES

- Use good quality tools and make sure they are sharp.
- Cut out all diseased, dead and weak growth. Always prune back to healthy wood, free from the tell-tale staining of infected tissue.
- When pruning any woody plant, realise the difference between light and hard pruning. Light pruning results in **heading back** — the tips of the branches are removed and this stimulates the buds below to burst into growth. The long-term effect is to produce a plant which is smaller but denser than one left unpruned. This technique is used for formal shaping. Hard pruning results in **thinning** — entire branches are removed back to the main stem and energy is diverted to the remaining branches. The long-term effect is to produce a plant which is larger but more open than one left unpruned. This technique is used for informal shaping.
- If you are a beginner in the craft of pruning do not attempt any drastic treatment. Too little pruning of healthy wood is safer than too much.
- Collect up all prunings. Compost them if they are soft and healthy — burn them if they are woody or diseased.
- All cuts must be clean. Pare off ragged parts left on sawn surfaces.
- Cut hedges so that the top is narrower than the base. In this way the base will remain clothed with leaves.

BASIC TOOLS

TWO-BLADED ▶ SECATEURS will cut cleanly for many years with proper care. The cut must be made at the centre of the blades — maximum diameter ½–¾ in.

◀ LONG-HANDLED PRUNER for stems ½–1½ in. across — many gardeners prefer them to a pruning saw for dealing with thick stems. Essential for tall shrubs

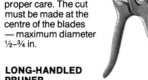

TYPES OF PRUNING

STANDARD PRUNING The partial removal of the woody structure of the plant, each cut being made individually. In some cases hardly any wood is removed (light pruning) but in others a significant proportion of the stems and branches are cut away (hard pruning).

SHEARING The partial removal of the woody structure of the plant, the cuts being made in wholesale fashion with garden shears or an electric hedge trimmer. This is the method of producing topiary (a decorative-shaped shrub) or a formal hedge.

STOOLING The complete removal of the woody structure of the plant. Some shrubs can be pruned back each spring to almost ground level — examples include Romneya, Fuchsia, Caryopteris and Spiraea japonica. This type of pruning is known as coppicing in forestry.

LOPPING The removal of a large branch from a main stem — only applies to large shrubs which have become tree-like with age. Make a shallow saw-cut on the under-side of the branch before sawing downwards.

THE PRUNING CUT

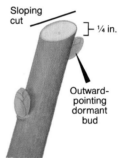

Sloping cut

¼ in.

Outward-pointing dormant bud

When dealing with a few large branches it is worth while taking the trouble to use the classic pruning cut. It is not possible to avoid making some wrong cuts — as a result snags of dead wood will form above new shoots. Cut off these dead bits. With smaller multi-stemmed shrubs it may not be practical to attempt the recommended pruning cut as each branch is shortened.

TIMING

The correct time for pruning each shrub is given in the A–Z section. There are no watertight rules — a general guide is set out below, but there are a number of exceptions.

DECIDUOUS SHRUBS WHICH BLOOM BEFORE THE END OF MAY
Cut out weak, dead and awkwardly-placed shoots. Remove overcrowded branches. Finally, cut back all the branches which have borne blooms. Time to prune: As soon as flowering has finished — do not delay

DECIDUOUS SHRUBS WHICH BLOOM AFTER THE END OF MAY
Cut out weak, dead and awkwardly-placed shoots. Remove overcrowded branches. Finally, cut back hard all old wood. Time to prune: January–March — do not wait until growth starts

EVERGREEN SHRUBS
Cut out weak, dead and awkwardly-placed shoots. Remove overcrowded branches. Time to prune: May

HEDGES
Trim after the flowers have faded

MULCHING

The benefits of using an organic mulch in the spring are numerous and remarkable, but most gardeners still do not bother to mulch their shrubs. There are five basic reasons for using this underrated technique:

● The soil below is kept moist during the dry days of summer.

● The soil surface is kept cool during the hot days of summer. This moist and cool root zone promotes more active growth than in unmulched areas.

● Annual weeds are kept in check — the ones that do appear can be easily pulled out.

● Some mulches provide plant foods.

● Soil structure is improved by the addition of humus.

Many materials are suitable for mulching — you can use moist peat, pulverised bark, leaf mould, well-rotted manure, mushroom compost and garden compost. Grass clippings are sometimes recommended and are often used, but a word of caution is necessary. Add a thin layer and stir occasionally — do not use them if they are weedy nor if the lawn has been treated with a weedkiller.

The standard time for mulching is May. Success depends on preparing the soil surface properly before adding the organic blanket. Remove debris, dead leaves and weeds, and then water the surface if it is dry. Apply a spring feed if this has not been done, hoe in lightly and you are now ready to apply the mulch. Spread a 2–3 in. layer over the area which is under the branches and leaves. Do not take the mulch right up to the stems — a build-up of moist organic matter around the crown may lead to rotting. In October lightly fork this dressing into the top inch of soil — replace in spring. Autumn mulching is sometimes recommended as a way of preventing frost getting down to the roots, but it will increase the risk of dangerous air frosts around the plants in spring.

Azaleas, Magnolias and Camellias respond particularly well to mulching.

FIRMING

Some of the techniques in this chapter are practised by all gardeners — watering, pruning etc, but firming is generally the sign of an experienced gardener. During the winter months strong winds can disturb newly-planted shrubs and shallow-rooted ones such as Escallonia. This windrock causes a gap to appear in the soil around the roots, and water collects here when the heavy spring rains fall. The situation can be made worse by the soil heave caused by frost. To combat the effect of these root-disturbing agents you should firm the soil in spring — gently tread down the soil above the root zone of shrubs which have worked loose during the winter. Wait until the soil is fairly dry before doing this job.

FEEDING

The production of stems, leaves and flowers is a drain on the soil's reserves of nitrogen, phosphates, potash and other nutrients. However the extensive root system of an established shrub can effectively tap the resources in the soil, which means that regular feeding is not always necessary. There are exceptions:

● A newly-planted shrub has not had time to develop a wide-ranging root system. It is necessary therefore to incorporate a slow-acting fertilizer in the soil which surrounds the limited root system. The best plan is to add Bone Meal to the planting mixture — see page 108.

● A balanced fertilizer such as Growmore is applied by many gardeners to the soil around their shrubs in spring. This is a useful technique, but there are times when root feeding is not effective, as in shallow soils and during prolonged periods of drought. In these cases use the foliar feeding technique — dilute fertilizer sprayed on to the leaves. Follow the manufacturer's instructions.

● Shrubs with large flower-heads and/or a prolonged flowering season do need feeding at least once a year. Use a potash-rich fertilizer, such as a proprietary Rose food. Remember that shrubs should not be fed after the end of July.

WATERING

The battle against water shortage should begin before the dry days of summer. Add organic matter to the soil before planting, water in thoroughly after planting and mulch the plant in spring every year.

For the first couple of years of a shrub's life in your garden, copious watering will be necessary during a prolonged dry spell in late spring or summer. Once established the plant will need watering much less often.

The need to water, however, cannot be ignored. If the weather is dry, look at the trouble spots. Climbers growing next to the house, shrubs in tubs and all plants growing in very sandy soil will probably need watering. Then there are the shallow-rooted plants which can quite quickly suffer even in good soil once the dry spells of summer arrive. Rhododendron is a well-known example of a shrub which quickly suffers in drought, but there are others.

Once you decide to water, then water thoroughly — a light sprinkling can do more harm than good. As a rough guide use 1 gallon for each small shrub and 4 gallons for each large one. A watering can is often used, but a hose-pipe is a much better idea unless your garden is very small. Remember to water slowly close to the base of the plant.

Trickle irrigation through a perforated hose laid close to the bushes is perhaps the best method of watering. A quick and easy technique popular in America is to build a ridge of soil around each bush and then fill the basin with a hose.

CHAPTER 5

PRONOUNCING DICTIONARY

Several different shrubs can have the same common or English name, and so it is generally preferable to use the more precise Latin name when ordering plants or talking about them. The first word is the genus — equivalent to a surname, and this is followed by the species which can be likened to a Christian or given name. The species may have several varieties — a variety which has originated in cultivation rather than in the wild is properly called a cultivar. The cultivar name is usually not in Latin — examples are Camellia japonica 'Apollo' and Euonymus europaeus 'Red Cascade'.

One problem is that learned botanists sometimes decide to change the genus name, as happened when all the shrubby Veronicas were reclassified as Hebes. Such changes are generally not popular with gardeners and the old Latin name may be retained as a common one — Cotinus coggygria is still frequently referred to as Rhus cotinus. Another difficulty with Latin names is that there are no rules for correct pronunciation. The generally agreed genus pronunciations for the shrubs in this book are given below — each name is divided into phonetic syllables, and the stressed syllable is printed in bold type.

ABELIA	a-**bee**-lee-ya	CERCIS	**ser**-sis
ABELIOPHYLLUM	a-bee-lee-oh-**fil**-um	CHAENOMELES	kee-**no**-may-lees
ABUTILON	a-**bew**-ti-lon	CHIMONANTHUS	ky-mo-**nanth**-us
ACACIA	a-**kay**-she-ya	CHOISYA	**shwah**-zee-ya
ACTINIDIA	ak-tin-**id**-ee-ya	CISTUS	**sis**-tus
AESCULUS	es-**cue**-lus	CLEMATIS	**klem**-a-tis
AKEBIA	a-**kee**-bee-ya	CLERODENDRUM	clair-oh-**den**-drum
AMELANCHIER	a-me-**lang**-kee-er	CLETHRA	**kleth**-ra
ANDROMEDA	an-**drom**-e-da	COLUTEA	koh-**loo**-tee-ya
ARALIA	a-**ray**-lee-ya	CONVOLVULUS	kon-**vol**-view-lus
ARBUTUS	ah-**bew**-tus	CORNUS	**kor**-nus
ARCTOSTAPHYLOS	ark-toe-**sta**-fil-os	CORONILLA	kor-oh-**nil**-a
ARISTOLOCHIA	a-ris-toe-**lok**-ee-ya	CORYLOPSIS	kor-ill-**op**-sis
AUCUBA	ow-**cue**-ba	CORYLUS	**kor**-ill-us
AZALEA	a-**zay-lee**-ya	COTINUS	koh-**tie**-nus
AZARA	a-**zah**-ra	COTONEASTER	koh-ton-ee-**as**-ter
BERBERIDOPSIS	bear-bear-ee-**dop**-sis	CRATAEGUS	kra-**tee**-gus
BERBERIS	**bear**-bear-is	CRINODENDRON	cry-no-**den**-dron
BUDDLEIA	bud-**lee**-ya	CYTISUS	**sigh**-ti-sus
BUPLEURUM	boo-**plur**-um	DABOECIA	dab-**ee**-she-ya
CAESALPINIA	see-sal-**pee**-nee-ya	DAPHNE	**daf**-nee
CALLICARPA	ka-lee-**kar**-pa	DECAISNEA	dee-**kayz**-nee-ya
CALLISTEMON	ka-lee-**stay**-mon	DESFONTAINIA	des-fon-**tay**-nee-ya
CALLUNA	ka-**loo**-na	DEUTZIA	**doytz**-ee-ya
CALYCANTHUS	ka-lee-**kanth**-us	DIPELTA	di-**pel**-ta
CAMELLIA	ka-**mee**-lee-ya	DORYCNIUM	doh-**rik**-nee-um
CAMPSIS	**kamp**-sis	ELSHOLTZIA	ell-**sholtz**-ee-ya
CARAGANA	ka-ra-**gah**-na	EMBOTHRIUM	em-**both**-ree-um
CARPENTERIA	kar-pen-**tea**-ree-ya	ENKIANTHUS	en-kee-**anth**-us
CARYOPTERIS	ka-ree-**op**-te-ris	ERICA	e-**rik**-a
CASSINIA	ka-**sin**-ee-ya	ESCALLONIA	e-skah-**lon**-ee-ya
CASSIOPE	ka-**see**-oh-pay	EUCRYPHIA	ew-**krif**-ee-ya
CEANOTHUS	see-a-**no**-thus	EUONYMUS	ew-**on**-ee-mus
CELASTRUS	see-**la**-strus	EXOCHORDA	eks-oh-**kor**-da
CERATOSTIGMA	ser-at-oh-**stig**-ma	FABIANA	fab-ee-**ah**-na

FATSIA	**fats**-ee-ya
FORSYTHIA	for-**syth**-ee-ya
FOTHERGILLA	foth-er-**gil**-a
FREMONTODENDRON	free-mont-oh-**den**-dron
FUCHSIA	**few**-sha
GARRYA	**ga**-ree-ya
GAULTHERIA	gawl-**thair**-ee-ya
GENISTA	jeh-**nis**-ta
GREVILLEA	gre-**vil**-ee-ya
HALESIA	**haylz**-ee-ya
HAMAMELIS	ham-a-**may**-lis
HEBE	**hee**-bee
HEDYSARUM	hed-ee-**sar**-um
HELIANTHEMUM	hel-ee-**anth**-e-mum
HELICHRYSUM	hel-ee-**kry**-sum
HIBISCUS	hi-**bis**-kus
HIPPOPHAE	hip-oh-**fee**
HOHERIA	ho-**her**-ee-ya
HYDRANGEA	hy-**drayn**-gee-ya
HYPERICUM	hy-**per**-ee-cum
ILEX	**eye**-lex
INDIGOFERA	in-di-**goh**-fe-ra
ITEA	**eye**-tee-ya
JASMINUM	jaz-**meen**-um
KALMIA	**kal**-mee-ya
KERRIA	**ke**-ree-ya
KOLKWITZIA	kol-**kwitz**-ee-ya
LAVANDULA	la-**van**-dew-la
LAVATERA	la-va-**tee**-ra
LEPTOSPERMUM	lep-toh-**sperm**-um
LESPEDEZA	les-pe-**dee**-za
LEUCOTHOE	loo-ko-**thoh**-ee
LEYCESTERIA	ly-ses-**teer**-ee-ya
LIGUSTRUM	lig-**us**-trum
LONICERA	lon-**i**-sir-a
LUPINUS	loo-**pee**-nus
LYCIUM	**li**-see-um
MAGNOLIA	mag-**noh**-lee-ya
MAHONIA	ma-**hoh**-nee-ya
MENZIESIA	men-**zee**-zee-ya
MYRICA	**mir**-i-ka
MYRTUS	**mir**-tus
NANDINA	nan-**dee**-na
NEILLIA	**nee**-lee-ya
OLEARIA	oh-**ler**-ee-ya
OSMANTHUS	oz-**manth**-us
OZOTHAMNUS	oh-zoh-**tham**-nus
PAEONIA	pee-**oh**-nee-ya
PARAHEBE	pa-ra-**hee**-bee
PASSIFLORA	pa-see-**flor**-a
PERNETTYA	per-**net**-ee-ya
PEROVSKIA	per-**off**-skee-ya
PHILADELPHUS	fil-a-**del**-fus
PHLOMIS	**flo**-mis
PHYGELIUS	fy-**gee**-lee-us
PHYSOCARPUS	fi-soh-**kar**-pus
PIERIS	**pee**-e-ris
PIPTANTHUS	pip-**tanth**-us
PITTOSPORUM	pit-toh-**spor**-um
POLYGONUM	po-**li**-goh-num
PONCIRUS	pon-**si**-rus
POTENTILLA	poh-ten-**til**-a
PRUNUS	**proo**-nus
PYRACANTHA	py-ra-**kanth**-a
RHAPHIOLEPIS	raf-ee-oh-**lee**-pis
RHODODENDRON	roh-doh-**den**-dron
RIBES	**ry**-beez
ROMNEYA	rom-**nay**-a
ROSA	**roh**-za
ROSMARINUS	ros-ma-**ry**-nus
RUBUS	**roo**-bus
SALIX	**say**-liks
SAMBUCUS	sam-**bew**-kus
SANTOLINA	san-toh-**lee**-na
SARCOCOCCA	sar-koh-**ko**-ka
SENECIO	se-**nee**-kee-oh
SKIMMIA	**skim**-ee-ya
SOLANUM	soh-**lay**-num
SOPHORA	**soh**-fo-ra
SORBARIA	sor-**bay**-ree-ya
SORBUS	**sor**-bus
SPARTIUM	**spar**-tee-um
SPIRAEA	**spy**-ree-ya
STACHYURUS	sta-kee-**ew**-rus
STAPHYLEA	sta-fil-**ee**-ya
STEPHANANDRA	ste-fan-**and**-ra
STEWARTIA	stew-**art**-ee-ya
STRANVAESIA	stran-**veez**-ee-ya
STYRAX	**sty**-raks
SYMPHORICARPOS	sim-for-i-**kar**-pos
SYRINGA	si-**ring**-a
TAMARIX	**tam**-a-riks
TEUCRIUM	**too**-kree-um
TRACHELOSPERMUM	trak-el-oh-**sperm**-um
ULEX	**ew**-leks
VACCINIUM	vak-**sin**-ee-um
VIBURNUM	**vy**-bur-num
VINCA	**vin**-ka
WEIGELA	wy-**gee**-la
WISTERIA	wis-**tea**-ree-ya
YUCCA	**yuk**-ah
ZENOBIA	zen-**oh**-bee-ya

CHAPTER 6

SHRUB SELECTOR

Hundreds of flowering shrubs are described in this book and the display in a large garden centre can be extensive. This makes selection difficult, and the golden rule is that you should never buy on impulse. Buying a plant solely on the basis of a colour photograph or the beauty of the floral display at the nursery is a recipe for disappointment. There are two safe routes when selecting shrubs. You can look up a particular feature in this chapter and then check the recommended list to find a plant which fits the situation, or check in the A–Z guide to see if a plant which has caught your fancy is suitable — do this before you buy.

Flowers for every Season

By careful selection it is quite easy to ensure that even a modest shrub border will be in bloom during every month of the year. For each month there is a list of shrubs which can be expected to be at the start of their flowering season or in full flower — remember that some of these plants may come into bloom earlier and can continue to bloom for many weeks afterwards.

JANUARY

Chimonanthus praecox
Erica carnea
Erica darleyensis
Garrya elliptica
Hamamelis mollis
Jasminum nudiflorum
Lonicera fragrantissima
Viburnum bodnantense
Viburnum farreri
Viburnum tinus

FEBRUARY

Abeliophyllum distichum
Acacia species
Corylus avellana
Daphne mezereum
Daphne odora
Erica carnea
Erica darleyensis
Hamamelis japonica
Mahonia japonica
Mahonia media 'Charity'
Sarcococca species
Stachyurus species

MARCH

Azara microphylla
Camellia japonica
Chaenomeles speciosa
Cornus mas
Corylopsis species
Daphne tangutica
Erica mediterranea
Forsythia species
Magnolia stellata
Mahonia aquifolium
Prunus incisa
Ribes sanguineum
Salix species
Spiraea thunbergii

APRIL

Amelanchier canadensis
Arctostaphylos species
Berberis darwinii
Berberis stenophylla
Camellia japonica
Cassiope species
Clematis alpina
Daphne cneorum
Erica arborea
Fothergilla species
Grevillea alpina
Kalmia polifolia
Kerria japonica
Magnolia soulangiana
Osmanthus delavayi
Pieris japonica
Prunus species
Rosmarinus officinalis
Skimmia species
Spiraea — spring-flowering
Ulex europaeus
Viburnum — spring-flowering

MAY

Abutilon suntense
Aesculus neglecta
Akebia species
Andromeda polifolia
Caragana arborescens
Ceanothus impressus
Choisya ternata
Clematis species
Cornus florida
Coronilla species
Cotoneaster species
Crinodendron hookerianum
Cytisus species
Daphne burkwoodii
Daphne retusa
Dipelta species
Embothrium coccineum
Enkianthus species
Exochorda racemosa
Genista species
Grevillea juniperina
Halesia species
Helianthemum nummularium
Kalmia angustifolia
Kolkwitzia amabilis
Leptospermum species
Leucothoe species
Menziesia ciliicalyx
Neillia species
Paeonia species
Pernettya species
Piptanthus laburnifolius
Pittosporum tobira
Pyracantha species
Rhododendron species
Rubus tridel
Sambucus racemosa
Sophora species
Sorbus reducta
Staphylea species
Stranvaesia davidiana
Tamarix tetrandra
Wisteria species

Flowers for every Season contd.

JUNE

Abelia schumannii
Actinidia kolomikta
Aesculus pavia
Aristolochia species
Azara dentata
Buddleia alternifolia
Buddleia globosa
Caesalpinia japonica
Callistemon species
Calycanthus species
Cercis siliquastrum
Cistus species
Clematis species
Colutea species
Convolvulus cneorum
Cotinus coggygria
Crataegus species
Deutzia species
Erica tetralix
Escallonia species
Fabiana imbricata
Fremontodendron species
Gaultheria miqueliana
Genista species
Grevillea rosmarinifolia
Hebe species
Helichrysum species
Hoheria glabrata
Hydrangea petiolaris
Kalmia latifolia
Lonicera tatarica
Nandina domestica
Philadelphus species
Phlomis species
Physocarpus opulifolius
Rhaphiolepis species
Sambucus nigra
Senecio greyi
Stephanandra species
Styrax species
Syringa species
Vaccinium species
Weigela species
Zenobia pulverulenta

JULY

Actinidia chinensis
Aesculus parviflora
Aralia spinosa
Azara serrata
Buddleia davidii
Bupleurum fruticosum
Caesalpinia gilliesii
Calluna vulgaris
Carpenteria californica
Cassinia species
Clematis species
Clethra species
Daboecia cantabrica
Dorycnium hirsutum
Erica cinerea
Erica terminalis
Erica vagans
Eucryphia species
Gaultheria procumbens
Hedysarum species
Hoheria lyallii
Hoheria sexstylosa
Hypericum species

Indigofera species
Itea virginica
Lavandula species
Lavatera species
Ligustrum japonicum
Lupinus arboreus
Olearia species
Ozothamnus species
Parahebe lyallii
Passiflora caerulea
Polygonum baldschuanicum
Potentilla species
Sambucus canadensis
Santolina species
Sorbaria species
Spiraea — summer-flowering
Stewartia species
Symphoricarpos species
Teucrium species
Trachelospermum species

AUGUST

Berberidopsis corallina
Callicarpa species
Campis species
Ceanothus 'Autumnal Blue'
Ceanothus 'Burkwoodii'
Ceanothus 'Gloire de Versailles'
Ceratostigma willmottianum
Clematis tangutica
Clerodendrum trichotomum
Crinodendron patagua
Desfontainia spinosa
Elsholtzia stauntonii
Fuchsia species
Hibiscus syriacus
Hoheria populnea
Hydrangea species
Itea ilicifolia
Leycesteria formosa
Ligustrum chenaultii
Ligustrum quihoui
Magnolia grandiflora
Myrtus communis
Parahebe catarractae
Perovskia atriplicifolia
Phygelius species
Rhus typhina
Romneya species
Solanum species
Sophora japonica
Spartium junceum
Tamarix ramosissima
Vinca species
Yucca filamentosa

SEPTEMBER

Abelia grandiflora
Aralia elata
Calluna species
Caryopteris clandonensis
Erica species
Fuchsia species
Hebe species
Hibiscus species
Hydrangea species
Hypericum species
Lespedeza species
Osmanthus heterophyllus

OCTOBER

Abelia species
Arbutus unedo
Calluna species
Erica species
Fatsia japonica
Fuchsia species
Hebe 'Autumn Glory'
Hebe 'Midsummer Beauty'
Hibiscus species
Hypericum 'Hidcote'
Myrica species

NOVEMBER

Erica darleyensis
Hebe 'Autumn Glory'
Jasminum nudiflorum
Viburnum bodnantense
Viburnum farreri

DECEMBER

Camellia williamsii
Erica darleyensis
Hamamelis mollis
Jasminum nudiflorum
Mahonia 'Bealei'
Mahonia japonica
Viburnum bodnantense
Viburnum farreri
Viburnum tinus

Shrubs suitable for Shade

Aucuba japonica
Camellia species
Fatsia japonica
Hypericum calycinum
Ligustrum species
Lonicera nitida
Mahonia aquifolium
Osmanthus heterophyllus
Prunus laurocerasus
Prunus lusitanica
Rubus species
Skimmia japonica
Symphoricarpos species
Viburnum davidii
Vinca species

Shrubs suitable for Clay Soils

Aucuba japonica
Berberis species
Chaenomeles species
Choisya ternata
Cornus species
Corylus species
Cotoneaster species
Forsythia species
Hypericum species
Mahonia species
Philadelphus species
Potentilla species
Pyracantha species
Ribes sanguineum
Skimmia japonica
Spiraea species
Symphoricarpos species
Viburnum species
Vinca species
Weigela species

Shrubs suitable for Chalky Soils

Arbutus species
Aucuba species
Berberis species
Buddleia species
Callicarpa species
Ceanothus species
Chaenomeles species
Chimonanthus species
Choisya species
Cistus species
Colutea species
Cornus mas
Cotoneaster species
Deutzia species
Escallonia species
Forsythia species
Fremontodendron species
Fuchsia species
Garrya species
Hebe species
Hypericum species
Ilex species
Kerria species
Kolkwitzia species
Lavandula species
Ligustrum species
Mahonia species
Myrtus species
Olearia species
Paeonia species
Philadelphus species
Pittosporum species
Potentilla species
Prunus lusitanica
Pyracantha species
Ribes species
Romneya species
Rosmarinus species
Sambucus species
Santolina species
Senecio species
Spartium species
Symphoricarpos species
Syringa species
Tamarix species
Vinca species
Weigela species
Yucca species

Shrubs for Industrial Areas

Aucuba species
Berberis species
Buddleia davidii
Camellia species
Chaenomeles species
Cistus species
Colutea species
Cotinus species
Cotoneaster species
Crataegus species
Cytisus species
Deutzia species
Escallonia species
Euonymus species
Fatsia japonica
Forsythia species
Garrya elliptica
Genista species
Hebe species
Hibiscus syriacus
Hydrangea species
Hypericum species
Ilex species
Kerria japonica
Ligustrum species
Lonicera pileata
Magnolia species
Mahonia species
Pernettya mucronata
Philadelphus species
Potentilla species
Prunus laurocerasus
Pyracantha species
Rhododendron species
Ribes sanguineum
Rubus tridel 'Benenden'
Salix species
Skimmia japonica
Spartium species
Spiraea species
Symphoricarpos species
Syringa species
Tamarix tetrandra
Ulex species
Viburnum species
Vinca species
Weigela species

Shrubs suitable for Sandy Soils

Aralia species
Berberis species
Bupleurum species
Caragana species
Ceratostigma species
Cistus species
Clerodendrum species
Convolvulus species
Coronilla species
Corylus species
Cotinus species
Cotoneaster species
Cytisus species
Dorycnium species

Genista species
Hedysarum species
Helianthemum species
Helichrysum species
Hibiscus species
Hippophae species
Hypericum species
Indigofera species
Kerria species
Lavatera species
Leptospermum species
Lespedeza species
Lupinus species
Lycium species

Ozothamnus species
Perovskia species
Phlomis species
Physocarpus species
Potentilla species
Romneya species
Rosmarinus species
Sambucus species
Senecio species
Spartium species
Spiraea species
Symphoricarpos species
Tamarix species
Ulex species

Fragrant Shrubs

Many shrubs bear sweet-smelling flowers — Honeysuckle, Mock Orange, Daphne, Viburnum and Witch Hazel are all well known for their perfume. Fragrance is not restricted to the flowers — some shrubs have aromatic foliage.

✿ *Fragrant flowers*

🍃 *Aromatic leaves*

Abelia chinensis ✿
Abeliophyllum distichum ✿
Acacia dealbata ✿
Akebia species ✿
Azara species ✿
Berberis stenophylla ✿
Buddleia alternifolia ✿
Buddleia davidii ✿
Buddleia globosa ✿
Callistemon species 🍃
Calycanthus species ✿ 🍃
Caragana arborescens ✿
Carpenteria californica ✿
Caryopteris clandonensis 🍃
Celastrus species ✿
Chimonanthus praecox ✿
Choisya ternata ✿ 🍃
Clematis montana ✿
Clerodendrum trichotomum ✿
Clethra alnifolia ✿

Coronilla glauca ✿
Corylopsis species ✿
Crataegus species ✿
Cytisus battandieri ✿
Daphne species ✿
Elsholtzia species 🍃
Escallonia macrantha 🍃
Eucryphia lucida ✿
Hamamelis species ✿
Hoheria species ✿
Itea species ✿
Jasminum species ✿
Lavandula species ✿ 🍃
Lonicera fragrantissima ✿
Lonicera periclymenum ✿
Lupinus arboreus ✿
Magnolia grandiflora ✿
Magnolia stellata ✿
Mahonia species ✿
Myrica species 🍃
Myrtus communis ✿ 🍃
Osmanthus species ✿
Passiflora caerulea ✿

Perovskia atriplicifolia 🍃
Philadelphus species ✿
Phlomis fruticosa 🍃
Pittosporum tobira ✿
Poncirus species ✿
Prunus lusitanica ✿
Rhododendron — deciduous Azaleas ✿
Ribes odoratum ✿
Romneya hybrida ✿
Rosa species ✿
Rosmarinus officinalis 🍃
Rubus tridel 'Benenden' ✿
Santolina species 🍃
Sarcococca species ✿
Skimmia japonica 🍃
Staphylea species ✿
Styrax species ✿
Syringa species ✿
Trachelospermum species ✿
Viburnum bodnantense ✿
Viburnum farreri ✿
Wisteria species ✿
Zenobia species ✿

Shrubs to encourage Wildlife

🐝 Bees   🐦 Birds   🦋 Butterflies

Aucuba
Berberis
Buddleia
Callicarpa
Ceanothus
Chaenomeles
Cistus
Clerodendrum
Cotinus
Cotoneaster
Cytisus
Daphne
Escallonia
Euonymus europaeus
Fuchsia
Hebe
Hippophae
Hypericum

Ilex
Lavandula
Ligustrum
Mahonia
Olearia
Pernettya
Perovskia
Potentilla
Pyracantha
Ribes odoratum
Sambucus
Skimmia
Spiraea
Symphoricarpos
Syringa
Ulex
Viburnum
Weigela

Shrubs for Flower Arranging

Acacia species
Aucuba japonica
Berberis species
Buddleia species
Callicarpa species
Camellia species
Ceanothus species
Chaenomeles species
Chimonanthus species
Choisya ternata
Clematis species
Convolvulus cneorum
Cornus species
Corylus species
Cotinus coggygria
Cotoneaster species
Daphne species
Deutzia species
Escallonia species
Euonymus europaeus
Fatsia japonica

Forsythia species
Fuchsia species
Garrya elliptica
Genista species
Hamamelis species
Hebe species
Hedysarum species
Hydrangea species
Ilex species
Jasminum species
Kerria japonica
Kolkwitzia amabilis
Lavandula species
Lavatera species
Ligustrum species
Lonicera species
Magnolia species
Mahonia species
Neillia species
Philadelphus species
Phlomis species

Physocarpus opulifolius
Pieris species
Pittosporum species
Pyracantha species
Rhododendron species
Ribes species
Rosa species
Sarcococca species
Senecio species
Skimmia species
Sophora species
Spartium species
Spiraea species
Stachyurus species
Staphylea species
Stranvaesia species
Symphoricarpos species
Syringa species
Viburnum species
Vinca species
Weigela species

Shrubs for the Rockery

Berberis thunbergii 'Atropurpurea Nana'
Calluna species
Caragana arborescens 'Nana'
Cassiope species
Cistus lusitanicus 'Decumbens'
Convolvulus cneorum
Cotoneaster congestus
Daboecia cantabrica
Daphne cneorum
Daphne retusa
Erica species
Fabiana imbricata 'Prostrata'
Gaultheria procumbens
Hebe 'Carl Teschner'
Hebe pinguifolia 'Pagei'
Helianthemum species
Hypericum coris

Hypericum polyphyllum
Leptospermum 'Kiwi'
Parahebe species
Philadelphus 'Manteau d'Hermine'
Philadelphus microphyllus
Rhododendron 'Blue Tit'
Rhododendron 'Bow Bells'
Rhododendron 'Elizabeth'
Rosmarinus 'Prostratus'
Salix lanata
Santolina 'Nana'
Sorbus reducta
Spiraea japonica 'Alpina'
Spiraea japonica 'Bullata'
Syringa meyeri 'Palibin'
Teucrium chamaedrys
Vaccinium nummularia

Fruit-bearing Shrubs

Akebia species
Amelanchier species
Arbutus species
Arctostaphylos species
Aucuba species
Callicarpa species
Chaenomeles species
Clerodendrum species
Cornus species
Corylus species
Cotoneaster species
Crataegus species
Daphne species
Decaisnea species
Euonymus species
Fatsia species
Gaultheria species
Hippophae species
Hypericum species
Ilex species
Jasminum beesianum
Leycesteria species
Lonicera species
Mahonia species
Myrica species
Myrtus species
Pernettya species
Prunus species
Pyracantha species
Ribes species
Rosa species
Rubus species
Sambucus species
Sarcococca species
Skimmia species
Solanum species
Sorbus species
Stranvaesia species
Symphoricarpos species
Vaccinium species
Viburnum species

Shrubs for the Seaside

Arbutus unedo
Buddleia species
Bupleurum species
Choisya ternata
Cistus species
Colutea species
Corylus species
Cotoneaster species
Crataegus species
Cytisus species
Escallonia species
Fatsia species
Fuchsia species
Garrya elliptica
Genista species
Hebe species
Helianthemum species
Hippophae rhamnoides
Hydrangea macrophylla
Hypericum species
Ilex aquifolium
Lavandula species

Lupinus species
Lycium species
Olearia species
Philadelphus species
Phlomis species
Pittosporum species
Potentilla species
Pyracantha species
Ribes species
Rosmarinus species
Salix species
Sambucus species
Santolina species
Senecio species
Skimmia species
Spartium species
Spiraea species
Symphoricarpos species
Tamarix species
Ulex species
Viburnum tinus
Yucca species

CHAPTER 7
INCREASING YOUR STOCK

There are three basic reasons for raising new shrubs in your own garden. First of all, there is the satisfaction of having plants which are actually home-grown and not raised by somebody else. Next, it is the only way to reproduce a much-admired variety which is not available from a nursery and lastly, but certainly not least, there is the purely practical reason of saving money.

Not all shrubs can be raised at home and the ease with which new plants can be produced varies from child's play to near impossible. There are several techniques — the one most likely to succeed for each plant is given in the A–Z guide. Every gardener should try his or her hand at layering, division or taking cuttings — there is nothing to lose and much to gain.

DIVISION

Some small shrubs form clumps which can be lifted and then split up like herbaceous perennials into several rooted sections. Each section should be planted firmly and then watered in thoroughly.

Best time:	Early winter
Examples:	Ceratostigma Lavender
	Daboecia Vinca

Many shrubs spread by means of suckers, which are shoots arising from an underground shoot or root. Removing and planting suckers is one of the easiest of all methods of propagation.

Best time:	Early winter for deciduous plants;
	April or September for evergreens
Examples:	Cotinus Mahonia
	Hazel Pernettya
	Kerria Snowberry

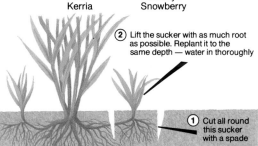

② Lift the sucker with as much root as possible. Replant it to the same depth — water in thoroughly

① Cut all round this sucker with a spade

LAYERING

Shrubs with flexible stems can be raised very easily by layering — some plants (e.g Rhododendron, Magnolia) produce new plants naturally by this method. To layer a shrub or climber, a stem is pegged into the ground and left attached to the parent plant until roots have formed at the base of the layered shoot. This takes about 6 to 12 months.

Best time:	Spring or autumn	
Examples:	Berberis	Honeysuckle
	Camellia	Japonica
	Clematis	Lilac
	Forsythia	Magnolia
	Heather	Rhododendron

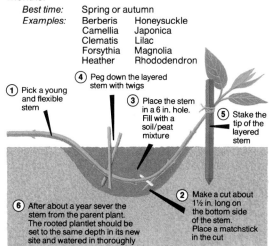

① Pick a young and flexible stem

④ Peg down the layered stem with twigs

③ Place the stem in a 6 in. hole. Fill with a soil/peat mixture

⑤ Stake the tip of the layered stem

② Make a cut about 1½ in. long on the bottom side of the stem. Place a matchstick in the cut

⑥ After about a year sever the stem from the parent plant. The rooted plantlet should be set to the same depth in its new site and watered in thoroughly

SEED SOWING

Seed sowing is the standard method of raising flowers and vegetables, but it is not widely used for propagating shrubs at home. Germination is not always straightforward — some seeds take many months to germinate and others need exposure to months of cold weather before they start to grow. It may be several years before the seedling is large enough to be decorative and many varieties will not breed true. Despite the drawbacks, there are several shrubs which can be readily raised from seed:

Examples:	Cistus	Genista	Leycesteria
	Clerodendrum	Hippophae	Potentilla

Spring is the best time. Fill a pot with seed & cutting compost; firm lightly with the finger tips and water gently. Sow seed thinly — space out each seed if they are large enough to handle. Cover large seeds with a layer of compost; small seeds not at all. Place a polythene bag over the container and secure with a rubber band.

Stand the pot in a shady place, a temperature of 65°–70°F is ideal. As soon as the seeds have germinated move them to a bright spot, away from direct sunlight. Remove the cover, keep the surface moist and turn the pot regularly to avoid lop-sided growth. As soon as the seedlings are large enough to handle they should be pricked out into small pots filled with potting compost.

TAKING CUTTINGS

A cutting is a small piece removed from a plant which with proper treatment can be induced to form roots and then grow into a specimen which is identical to the parent plant. You cannot guess the best type of cutting to take nor the best time to propagate it — consult the A–Z guide. There are, however, a few general rules. Plant the cutting as soon as possible after severing it from the parent plant and make sure that the compost is in close contact with the inserted part. Do not keep pulling at the cutting to see if it has rooted — the appearance of new growth is the best guide.

SOFTWOOD and SEMI-RIPE CUTTINGS

Softwood cuttings are green at the tip and base, and are taken from early spring to midsummer. Some small shrubs are propagated in this way. Basal cuttings are shoots formed at the base of the plant and pulled away for use as softwood cuttings in spring. **Semi-ripe cuttings** are green at the top and partly woody at the base — they are usually heel cuttings (see below). Midsummer to early autumn is the usual time and most shrubs are propagated by this method.

Stem-tip cutting

Cut off leaves from lower half of the cutting

1–6 in. depending on the size of the parent plant

Leaf joint

Straight cut

Dip bottom ½ in. of the cutting into a rooting hormone

or
Heel cutting

Cut off leaves from lower half of the cutting

Pull off side shoot with a heel attached. Dip bottom 1 in. of the cutting into a rooting hormone

④ Insert cutting; firm around the base with the pencil. Label if necessary

② Trim foliage of large-leaved plants by half

③ Make a hole in the compost with a pencil

① Fill a 5 in. pot with seed & cutting compost

⑤ Water in cutting very gently

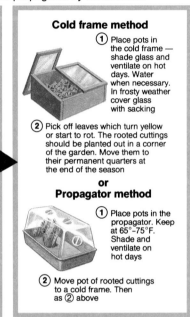

Cold frame method

① Place pots in the cold frame — shade glass and ventilate on hot days. Water when necessary. In frosty weather cover glass with sacking

② Pick off leaves which turn yellow or start to rot. The rooted cuttings should be planted out in a corner of the garden. Move them to their permanent quarters at the end of the season

or
Propagator method

① Place pots in the propagator. Keep at 65°–75°F. Shade and ventilate on hot days

② Move pot of rooted cuttings to a cold frame. Then as ② above

HARDWOOD CUTTINGS

Can be used for a number of shrubs. The usual time is late autumn. Choose a well-ripened shoot of this year's growth.

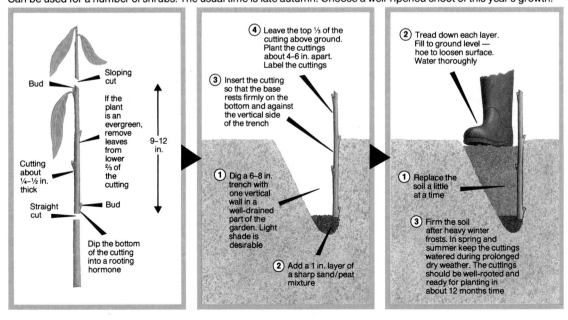

Bud

Sloping cut

If the plant is an evergreen, remove leaves from lower ⅔ of the cutting

9–12 in.

Cutting about ¼–½ in. thick

Straight cut

Bud

Dip the bottom of the cutting into a rooting hormone

④ Leave the top ⅓ of the cutting above ground. Plant the cuttings about 4–6 in. apart. Label the cuttings

③ Insert the cutting so that the base rests firmly on the bottom and against the vertical side of the trench

① Dig a 6–8 in. trench with one vertical wall in a well-drained part of the garden. Light shade is desirable

② Add a 1 in. layer of a sharp sand/peat mixture

② Tread down each layer. Fill to ground level — hoe to loosen surface. Water thoroughly

① Replace the soil a little at a time

③ Firm the soil after heavy winter frosts. In spring and summer keep the cuttings watered during prolonged dry weather. The cuttings should be well-rooted and ready for planting in about 12 months time

CHAPTER 8

TROUBLES

You are never likely to see more than a few shrub troubles in your garden. When things go wrong it is usually due to a fault in the environment rather than a specific pest or disease, so don't reach for the sprayer every time you see a few insects on the leaves. The danger time is the first season after planting — thorough watering is necessary during prolonged dry weather and evergreens may suffer if exposed to cold drying winds.

PESTS are animals, varying in size from tiny eelworms to majestic deer, which attack plants. The general term 'insect' covers small pests — mites, slugs, woodlice and true insects.

DISEASES are plant troubles caused by living organisms which are transmitted from one plant to another. Fungal diseases are the most common. Others are caused by bacteria and viruses.

DISORDERS are plant troubles which have disease-like symptoms but which are not due to a living organism — they are caused, not caught. Common causes are waterlogging and frost.

How to reduce the risk of troubles in your garden

● **Choose wisely.** Make sure that the plants you have picked are not too tender for the climatic conditions in your area, and check that the soil and light requirements can be satisfied.

● **Buy good plants.** Abundant roots and sound stems are essential. Don't buy evergreens with large, brown patches — reject container-grown plants which easily lift out of the pot.

● **Prepare the ground thoroughly.** A shrub in poorly-drained soil is likely to succumb to root-rotting diseases.

● **Plant in the proper place and in the proper way.** This will reduce the risk of problems due to drought, poor root development, waterlogging, windrock, frost damage and light deficiency. Stake if necessary. Remember that it is difficult or impossible to cure the problems caused by poor planting once the plant is established.

● **Avoid overcrowding.** Do not plant too closely as this can encourage mildew and other diseases.

● **Inspect plants regularly.** Catch problems early, when an occasional caterpillar can be picked off and the first spots of disease can be kept under control by spraying with a fungicide.

● **Provide frost protection if necessary.** Both snow and frost can cause a great deal of damage in a severe winter. Read the section on Winter Protection (page 109).

● **Spray if necessary.** Unlike Roses and vegetables, shrubs do not often require spraying. In general, spraying only takes place at the start of a serious problem, such as a sudden and heavy invasion by aphids or caterpillars.

Why shrubs fail to survive

A shrub planted in the manner described in this book should grow and flourish for many years. Failure to survive will almost certainly be due to one of the following causes:

Poor-quality planting material

Poor site preparation

Loose planting of bare-rooted plants

Break-up of the soil ball of container-grown or balled plants

Windrock especially in exposed sites. Staking of tall specimens in such locations is essential

Waterlogged soil around the roots due to poor drainage

Winter damage and spring scorch — see pages 109 and 124

Dry roots at planting time or during the first season in the garden

One of the fatal pests or diseases — die-back, silver leaf, fire blight, clematis wilt, honey fungus, canker or butt rot can kill a susceptible plant

Weedkiller damage is a rare cause of death, but a few general herbicides, such as sodium chlorate, can be fatal if allowed to creep into the soil around the roots

PESTS

CAPSID BUG

¼ in.
active bugs

The first signs of capsid damage are reddish-brown spots. As the leaf expands these tear to produce ragged brown-edged holes. Damaged foliage is usually puckered and distorted. Spray with a systemic insecticide.

VINE WEEVIL

½ in.
beetles

Small U-shaped notches are cut out of the leaf edges of several shrubs by these small weevils. Rhododendron is the most common host, but Camellia, Clematis and Azalea may also be attacked. If serious spray plants and the soil with a systemic insecticide.

CHAFER BEETLE

The cockchafer (1¼ in. long) and the garden chafer (½ in. long) feed on the leaves of many shrubs in May and June. If the pests are numerous spray the foliage with a systemic insecticide. The soil-living grubs of these beetles are serious root pests.

APHID

Greenfly can attack many shrubs — blackfly tend to be more selective but Viburnum and Honeysuckle can be badly infested. Aphids may be a serious pest — leaves are discoloured and blistered, shoots distorted and the whole plant covered with sticky honey-dew. Spray with a systemic insecticide before aphid colonies are large enough to be damaging.

CATERPILLAR

Leaf-eating caterpillars are more serious on shrubs than in the flower garden. Defoliation can take place, so early spraying may be a wise precaution when caterpillars and their damage are seen on choice shrubs. Use a persistent insecticide such as Fenitrothion.

RED SPIDER MITE

If leaves develop an unhealthy bronze colour, look for tiny spider-like mites on the underside. The presence of fine silky webbing is a tell-tale sign. On broad-leaved shrubs the culprits are the **fruit tree red spider mite** and the **bryobia mite**. These sap-sucking pests can be crippling in hot, settled weather and spraying is necessary. Apply Derris — repeat 3 weeks later.

BIRDS

The stripping of flower buds from ornamental shrubs in winter and early spring is a particularly difficult problem, as protective netting is not practical. Forsythia and flowering Prunus are the main victims, and bullfinches the chief offenders. Note that tits devour insects, not buds. Try a bird deterrent spray.

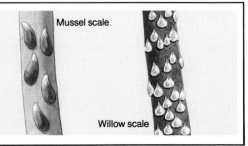

WOOLLY APHID

Aphid colonies live on branches, secreting white waxy 'wool' which protects them. Their presence does little direct harm, but the corky galls they cause are a common entry point for canker spores. Brush off 'wool' with an old toothbrush and methylated spirits.

SCALE

Several types of scale are found on branches, but their lifestyle is generally the same. The adults spend their lives in one place on the stem, protected by a hard shell. Their feeding on the sap causes leaf yellowing and a loss of vigour. Some attack a wide range of woody plants — **brown scale, mussel scale** and **oyster-shell scale** are examples. Others attack only those trees which bear their name. **Willow scale** gives a white-washed effect. Scale is difficult to control as spraying is not really effective. Brush affected area with methylated spirits or rub off with soapy water. Cut out badly affected shoots.

Mussel scale

Willow scale

DISEASES

HONEY FUNGUS

Honey fungus (root rot, armillaria disease) is a common cause of the death of shrubs. A white fan of fungal growth occurs below the bark near ground level. On roots, black 'bootlaces' are found. Toadstools appear in autumn at the base. Burn stems and roots of diseased shrubs — treat soil with Armillatox.

SILVER LEAF

A serious disease of Laburnum, Willow, Hawthorn and many other shrubs. The spores enter through a wound and the first sign is silvering of the leaves. Die-back of shoots occurs — wood is stained. Cut out dead branches 6 in. below level of infection. Dig out the shrub if purple-coloured bracket-like toadstools have appeared on the trunk.

CLEMATIS WILT

A destructive disease — most suscep-tible are young plants of large-flowered varieties. Shoots wilt and then collapse and die. Cut out affected shoots — new shoots often develop from the base. Spray new growth with a systemic fungicide and remove old stems. When planting make sure that 1–2 in. of stem is below the surface.

VIRUS

Viruses are carried by insects, tools or fingers. There are many symptoms — yellow-blotched or crinkled leaves, stunted growth, streaked flowers etc. There is no cure, so it is fortunate that very few shrubs are susceptible to serious virus attack. Buy healthy stock — keep aphids under control.

FIREBLIGHT

A devastating disease of shrubs belonging to the Rose family. Affected shoots wilt and die. Tell-tale sign is the presence of brown withered leaves which do not fall. If the disease spreads to the stems the plant is killed. Old cankers ooze in spring. Cut out infected branches back to clean wood.

CANKER

A diseased infectious area on the bark. The canker is usually cracked and sunken, and will kill the branch if it is encircled. Many different fungi and bacteria are involved — some attack a range of shrubs, others are specific. Cut out large cankers back to clean wood.

CORAL SPOT

Raised pink spots appear on the surface of affected branches. Dead wood is the breeding ground for the fungus, and the air-borne spores infect living shrubs through cuts and wounds. Never leave dead wood lying about. Cut out all dead and diseased branches.

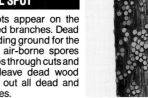

BUD BLAST

Infected flower buds of Rhododendron turn brown and are covered with black fungal bristles. They do not rot and remain firmly attached to the bush and flowering in future seasons may be affected. Remove and burn diseased buds. Do not confuse with frost-damaged buds, which are soft and easily pulled away. To prevent attack spray with a systemic insecticide in August to kill the disease-carrying leafhopper.

LEAF SPOT

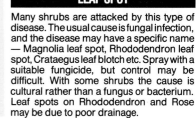

Many shrubs are attacked by this type of disease. The usual cause is fungal infection, and the disease may have a specific name — Magnolia leaf spot, Rhododendron leaf spot, Crataegus leaf blotch etc. Spray with a suitable fungicide, but control may be difficult. With some shrubs the cause is cultural rather than a fungus or bacterium. Leaf spots on Rhododendron and Rose may be due to poor drainage.

POWDERY MILDEW

White, powdery patches appear on the leaves of many shrubs, particu-larly if they are overcrowded and the soil is dry. Powdery mildew is common on Mahonia, Clematis, Hawthorn and Willow. Spray with a systemic fungicide at the first sign of disease. Repeat one week later. If not sprayed, cut off badly diseased shoots in autumn.

RUST

Yellow or brown raised spots appear on the leaves of many shrubs. Rust is sometimes trouble-some on Berberis, Willow and Mahonia. Pick off and burn the diseased leaves. Avoid over-crowding. Spraying is rarely necessary — a fungicide can be used at fortnightly intervals. Apply a potash-rich foliar feed.

DISORDERS

NUTRIENT DEFICIENCY

An abnormal change in leaf colour often indicates a shortage of an essential element. Spray the plants with a foliar feed. If the symptoms of iron or magnesium deficiency are severe, water a sequestered compound on the soil around the base of the stems. In spring apply Growmore to the soil and rake in.

NITROGEN SHORTAGE
Red & yellow tints

POTASH SHORTAGE
Leaf edge scorch

MAGNESIUM SHORTAGE
Brown between veins

IRON SHORTAGE
Yellow between veins

DROUGHT

In prolonged dry weather the soil reserves of moisture are seriously reduced. The first sign is wilting of the foliage and in the early stages the effect is reversible. The next stage is browning of the foliage and leaf drop which is extremely serious or fatal, especially with evergreens. Water before symptoms appear, and improve the water-holding capacity of the soil *before* planting.

WINTER DAMAGE

Many shrubs are at risk in a severe winter, especially if they are slightly tender or newly planted. They can be damaged in several ways — water-logging in an abnormally wet season can lead to root rot, temperatures well below freezing point can cause frost damage (brown blotches on leaves, usually at the tips) and heavy snow can break the branches of evergreens.

SPRING SCORCH

Bright sunny weather after a cold spell surprisingly leads to browning or death of evergreens instead of active growth. The cause is cold-induced drought — sunshine and drying winds stimulate water loss from the leaves, but the roots are not active and cannot replace the loss. Spray newly-planted evergreens with water in spring — provide protection from frosts and east winds.

NO FLOWERS

There are a number of possible causes. **Too much shade** — many flowering shrubs are sun lovers and will produce few or no flowers if the light intensity is too low. **Impatience** — it is quite normal for some shrubs (Yucca, Wisteria etc) to take several years after planting before coming to flower. **Dryness at the roots** — drought will delay the onset of flowering and it may also cause bud and flower drop. Drought in summer can cause poor flowering in the following year. **Poor pruning** — drastic pruning at the wrong time of the year is an all-too-common cause of failure to flower. **Frost damage** — buds of many shrubs can be killed by late spring frosts.

LOSS OF VARIEGATION

Some shrubs bear yellow and green leaves ('variegata') or green, yellow and red leaves ('tricolor'). In dense shade the green areas spread and variegation is diminished. Even in good light there is often a tendency for the shrub to revert to the all-green form. Cut out such shoots immediately.

CHLOROSIS

Many shrubs, such as Rhododendron, Azalea, Camellia, Ceanothus and Hydrangea, develop pale green or yellow leaves if grown in chalky soil. This is lime-induced chlorosis, and is prevented by incorporating peat into the soil and by applying a sequestered compound. Chlorosis of the lower leaves is often due to poor drainage.

DIE-BACK

A serious problem — begins at the tips and progresses slowly downwards. There are several possible causes, including diseases such as canker, coral spot or silver leaf. If no disease is present, waterlogging or drought is the likely cause. Cut out dead wood, feed with a foliar feed and improve the soil by mulching regularly each spring.

SPLIT BARK

A crack may appear in the bark at any time of the year. The cause can be a severe frost, and it is not uncommon for the base of Rhododendron bushes to split in this way. Another cause is poor growing conditions. Cut away any dead wood and paint with a sealing compound. Feed and mulch to restore good health.

CHAPTER 9

PLANT INDEX

Acknowledgements

The author wishes to acknowledge the painstaking work of John Woodbridge, Gill Jackson, Paul Norris, Linda Fensom, Angelina Gibbs and Constance Barry. Grateful acknowledgement is also made for the help or photographs received from Gill McGregor, Capel Manor Horticultural & Environmental Centre, Carleton Photographic, Joan Hessayon, Norman Barber, Harry Smith Horticultural Photographic Collection, Pat Brindley, Hillier Nurseries Ltd, Heather Angel, Tania Midgley, Brian Carter/The Garden Picture Library, Didier Willery/The Garden Picture Library, Elizabeth Whiting & Associates, Jerry Harper/Elizabeth Whiting & Associates, Marie O'Hara/Elizabeth Whiting & Associates, Karl-Dietrich Buhler/Elizabeth Whiting & Associates, Hans Reinhard/Bruce Coleman Ltd, Syndication International and Robert Harding Picture Library/Rainbird.

John Dye provided both artistry and design work for this book.